Scripting Media

Bringing together professional standards, practices, and jargon from across the industry, *Scripting Media* provides a complete overview of writing for divergent forms of media.

While some forms of media writing have been honed and standardized over generations, others demand new ways of thinking and collaborating. Covering traditional forms of scriptwriting, such as news, advertising, and film scripting, as well as newer and more emerging areas of social media and virtual reality, this book is designed to prepare readers for the varying formats, styles, and techniques specific to each medium. Each chapter contains a list of key terms, an historical overview of the area, and technical specifications for students to be aware of. Exercises, essay prompts, and online links help reinforce students' knowledge and provide avenues for private study.

Written in an accessible and engaging style by two renowned media practitioners, authors, and teachers, *Scripting Media* is essential reading for students approaching media writing for the first time.

Frank and Marie Barnas work in the award-winning College of Media and Entertainment at Middle Tennessee State University. He designs and teaches courses in media writing and production while she serves as the Chair for the Department of Media Arts. Their professional scripts span the media fields of film, television, theatre, podcasts, news, radio, and documentary.

Scripting Media

Frank Barnas and Marie Barnas

NEW YORK AND LONDON

Designed cover image: aee_werawan/iStock/Getty Images Plus via Getty Images

First published 2024
by Routledge
605 Third Avenue, New York, NY 10158

and by Routledge
4 Park Square, Milton Park, Abingdon, Oxon, OX14 4RN

Routledge is an imprint of the Taylor & Francis Group, an informa business

© 2024 Frank Barnas and Marie Barnas

The right of Frank Barnas and Marie Barnas to be identified as authors of this work has been asserted in accordance with sections 77 and 78 of the Copyright, Designs and Patents Act 1988.

All rights reserved. No part of this book may be reprinted or reproduced or utilised in any form or by any electronic, mechanical, or other means, now known or hereafter invented, including photocopying and recording, or in any information storage or retrieval system, without permission in writing from the publishers.

Trademark notice: Product or corporate names may be trademarks or registered trademarks, and are used only for identification and explanation without intent to infringe.

Library of Congress Cataloging-in-Publication Data
Names: Barnas, Frank, author. | Barnas, Marie, author.
Title: Scripting media / Frank Barnas and Marie Barnas.
Description: New York, NY : Routledge, 2023. | Includes bibliographical references and index.
Identifiers: LCCN 2023002069 (print) | LCCN 2023002070 (ebook) |
  ISBN 9781032229232 (hardback) | ISBN 9781032229225 (paperback) |
  ISBN 9781003274766 (ebook)
Subjects: LCSH: Mass media—Authorship.
Classification: LCC P96.A86 B37 2023 (print) | LCC P96.A86 (ebook) |
  DDC 808.066302—dc23/eng/20230420
LC record available at https://lccn.loc.gov/2023002069
LC ebook record available at https://lccn.loc.gov/2023002070

ISBN: 978-1-032-22923-2 (hbk)
ISBN: 978-1-032-22922-5 (pbk)
ISBN: 978-1-003-27476-6 (ebk)

DOI: 10.4324/9781003274766

Typeset in Sabon LT Pro
by Apex CoVantage, LLC

Contents

Acknowledgements   *vii*

Introduction   1

1 Language Foundations   3

2 Theatrical Plays   15

3 Newspaper and Magazine   27

4 Graphic Novels   36

5 Advertising   46

6 Public Relations   56

7 Corporate, Training, and Educational Videos   68

8 Documentary   77

9 Television News   88

10 Radio   100

11 Interview Shows   112

12 Reality and Live Television   122

13 Episodic and Serialized Television   135

14	Feature Film	149
15	Social Media and Podcasts	164
16	Virtual Reality	175
	References	*185*
	Index	*186*

Acknowledgements

The written word spans countless languages, multiple media platforms, and millennia of time as people strive to inform and entertain their audiences. Some scripting formats date back centuries, others just a few decades, and still others are evolving in an embryonic stage.

While writing may be perceived as an individual endeavor, the creation of media is a collaborative process, and we are thankful to have worked with so many talented people. In support of the development of this text, our deep appreciation goes out to the media professionals who have collaborated with us during our careers.

The town of Wheatland, Missouri, is used in many writing examples throughout this text. While that town is real, the scenarios are fictitious. Slurp Cola, SteveRabbit, Sparky, Janine Nougat, and the other scripting examples are similarly fictional and for instructional examples only.

We are grateful to Curt Casassa, Camille Cowin, Ed Pitts, Walter Rollenhagen, Jason Usry, and Chad Whittle for their contributions to this textbook. We count each of them as our friends and colleagues across the various realms of media. Also, thanks to Nick Cominos, John Jenkins, and Stacey Woelfel for their work in helping to shape us in these writing techniques.

Very special thanks go out to David Lynch, Rick Miller, Dave Hartman, and Mary Huff. As always, we appreciate Casey Grillo, Eddie Jackson, Todd La Torre, Mike Stone, and Michael Wilton for their continued inspiration.

Finally, we are indebted to Church and Aloura for their unwavering support as cheerleaders and motivators. This is for them.

Frank and Marie Barnas

Introduction

Scripting Media is designed to provide students with a working knowledge of the many types of media formats that they may encounter in their careers. Each chapter begins with Key Words, which is a list of the primary terms that students should learn for that section. Next, the students are provided with an Historical Overview. This segment informs the student of how the formatting evolved over time for that specific type of media.

Students are then introduced to Technical Specifications. These professional standards illuminate the best practices that are used in the media industries today. Once students learn these techniques, they will be prepared to deliver professional scripts in whatever format is demanded of them. The next section, Looking Forward, provides a quick insight as to what changes may be coming with that specific scripting format in the near future.

Each chapter then concludes with a trio of summative sections: Exercises, Chapter Essentials, and Online Links. The section of Exercises provides hands-on challenges for students to better learn the contents of the chapter. The next section, Chapter Essentials, features a bullet-point list of important information that can be used for discussion boards or learning reinforcement. The final section, Online Links, provides several professional websites for students to independently explore for up-to-date information about that scripting format.

For ease of use, the textbook is divided into the following broad areas:

Part I – Script Formats for Writing, Reading and Speaking. These chapters focus on the forms of communication that rely on non-electronic media skills: Language Foundations, Theatrical Plays, Newspaper and Magazine, Graphic Novels.

Part II – Script Formats for Media Messaging. These chapters address the forms of media that send primarily informational messages: Advertising, Public Relations, Corporate, Training and Educational Videos, Documentary, Television News.

Part III – Script Formats for Entertainment. These chapters delve into the areas of communication that are designed primarily to entertain: Radio, Interview Shows, Reality and Live Television, Episodic Television, Feature Film.

Part IV – Script Formats for Interactive Media. These chapters focus on the newest forms of media scripting that include evolving scripting formats: Social Media and Podcasts, Virtual Reality.

DOI: 10.4324/9781003274766-1

There is some overlap in these areas, as a medium like Radio offers entertainment, but it also promotes media messaging. The beauty of media is that so many platforms, such as Documentary, Interview Shows, and Social Media can both entertain and inform.

Although this text is designed to be used linearly, the chapters may be effectively used in whatever order best suits the individual courses.

1 Language Foundations

Key Words

Active Structure
Adjective
Adverb
Article
Complex Sentences
Compound Sentences
Conjunction
Coordinating Conjunction
Demonstrative
Determiner

Interjection
Noun
Passive Structure
Possessive
Preposition
Pronoun
Quantifier
Simple Sentences
Subordinating Conjunction
Verb

Historical Overview

Sumerian is the oldest written language in the world. Researchers have found clay tablets dating back to 3,200 BC in cuneiform script. The word cuneiform means "wedge-shaped", since the images in the clay were made by pressing a reed stylus into the surface, giving them a slight wedge appearance. But Sumerian died off as a spoken language, leaving only the written images behind. The only classical language that has survived into the modern era is Tamil. Spoken by about 78 million people, Tamil is an official language in Sri Lanka and Singapore while it is also spoken in parts of India. It dates to the 3rd century BC.

Languages are broadly grouped into 94 families, such as Indo-European, Sino-Tibetan, Niger-Congo, Afro-Asiatic, and Austronesian. About 7,000 languages are currently spoken worldwide within these families, but nearly 2,800 are endangered, meaning fewer than 1,000 people speak them. On the other hand, a few languages account for billions of speakers. If you combine everyone who speaks English, Mandarin Chinese, Hindi, Spanish, French, and Arabic as either a primary or secondary language, you will have more than four billion speakers. That means half of the world's population can communicate in just six languages.

There are countless opinions about which language is the most difficult for a non-speaker to learn. Of course, it depends on your native language. English is a Germanic language that uses a Latin alphabet, so languages with the same parameters, like German and Dutch, are the most accessible. Romance languages, like French, Italian, and Spanish, are also comparatively easy to learn, given their use of the Latin alphabet.

The U.S. Foreign Services Institute ranks Japanese as the hardest language for native English speakers to learn because of the complex writing systems that comprise three different alphabets. Other difficult languages for native English speakers are Arabic, Cantonese, and Korean. However, the difficult Japanese language (for Americans) is much easier for native Koreans to learn.

One commonality of all languages is that they each have a system of organizing words into sentences. These sentences convey information, spark emotion, and sustain the culture and history of those speakers and writers. Before we delve into the different types of scripts that are crafted throughout this textbook, it is vital to first examine the foundations of the written language itself.

Technical Specifications

We will build the language foundations from the basic elements, starting with the proper usage of punctuation marks. We will then move into the different types of words, then we will expand into sentence structure and, finally, paragraph structure. Each of these elements is crucial to crafting scripts in the various formats in this text.

Punctuation Marks

The English language uses 14 different punctuation marks. Some of them are common while others appear with less frequency in typical writing. The marks are the period, comma, question mark, exclamation point, quotation marks, colon, semicolon, dash, hyphen, apostrophe, ellipsis, parentheses, brackets, and braces.

There are other symbols that are found on your keyboard. Some of these, like the percentage sign " % " and equals sign " = " are used only in mathematical functions. Others, like the pound sign " # ", have found their way into social media postings. We will explore these lesser symbols as they arise in script formats throughout this text.

Period – This mark is used to show the end of a sentence, like:
The man is watching television.

Comma – This mark shows a reader when to pause, combines two clauses, or allows the writer to make a short list of items within a sentence, such as:
The man is watching television, although he should be going to bed.

Question mark – This mark is used at the end of a sentence to indicate that someone is asking a question (or interrogative), like:
Is the man watching television?

Exclamation mark – This mark adds emotion, like surprise or fear, to the end of a sentence. When used on even a straightforward sentence, this mark changes the tone to indicate excitement, such as:
The man is watching television!

Quotation Marks – These marks, which are used in pairs, show when someone is speaking on the page, like:
The man said, "I am watching television".
The above is an example of double quotation marks. Their counterparts, single quotation marks, are more specialized and are used when the person talking is quoting something else – literally, the single marks denote a quote within a quote. This is called a nested quote. An example would be:
The man said, "I hate when that television actor uses the phrase 'I'm all about culture' when he is trying to make a cute point."

Apostrophe – These marks can be used two different ways. First, an apostrophe can show a contraction when letters are removed from a word:
The man can't watch television.
Second, an apostrophe can be used to show possession, like this:
The man is watching Clark's television.
When someone's name ends in an "s" or "z", the apostrophe is placed at the end of the name, such as:
The man is watching Lois' television.

Colon – This mark serves two different purposes. First, it can be used to introduce a list of three or more items:
The man watched several shows on television: *Judge Judy*, *Family Guy*, and *The Office*.
The other use for a colon is to connect two independent sentences, especially when the second sentence clarifies the first sentence, such as:
The man watched television: he was exhausted after working all day.

Semicolon – This mark joins two related clauses without using a conjunction, like the word "and" or "because". It also serves as a smooth connection between the two related thoughts:
The man watched television; it always seemed to put him in a better mood.

Dash – This mark shows a range, break, or combines words. There are actually two types of dashes, the en dash and the em dash. They are named this because of their approximate length. The en dash is shorter and about the length of the letter "N" on the keyboard, while the em dash is longer and spans the length of the letter "M".

The en dash indicates a range of numbers and dates, such as:
The man watched the Red Sox win 4–2.
The en dash also clears up compound adjectives, like:
The man saw a pro-United States political commercial on the television.
This demonstrates a compound adjective, since the "pro-" modifies "United States", not just the word "United".

The em dash is handy for providing extra information in a sentence and can be used in place of parentheses.

The man watched television — he seldom listened to the radio — every night until bedtime.

Hyphen – This mark has two purposes. First, it is used to form compound words, such as:
The man watched singer-songwriter Dolly Parton perform on the television show.
The second use is for when you are spelling out numbers, like:
The twenty-five-year-old man watched television when he could not fall asleep.

Parentheses – These marks are always used in pairs, known as open paren " (" and close paren ") ". When used in a basic sentence, they indicate an aside or an afterthought to the main thrust of the sentence. They clarify the information but are usually seen as providing lesser information to the sentence's main idea.
The man watched television (after taking ten minutes to pick a program) until he went to bed.

Brackets – Like parentheses, these marks are used exclusively in pairs. But brackets have two special conditions. First, they are used only within quoted material and second, they are an interruption that indicates someone has edited the piece. For example:
The man watching television, saying "I would rather be sitting on my couch and watching TV then [sic] be pestered repeatedly about being in a textbook."

The [sic] indicates that the word "then" was used in error; it should be a "than". The brackets are in a direct quote and clearly were placed by an editor after the quote was printed. For these reasons, brackets are very seldom used in media scripts.

Braces – Also used in pairs, braces are reserved for special uses that do not occur frequently. They are handy for listing various options when all the choices are the same. For example:
The man wanted to watch an animated comedy on television {*Bob's Burgers, South Park, Family Guy, The Simpsons*} because he was tired of crime dramas.

Braces are also found in specific academic fields, such as in math equations or computer programming commands.

Ellipsis – This mark is made up of three sequential dots (or periods) that indicate the omission of words in a sentence. They are handy in writing dialogue in scripts when actors interrupt one another or their thoughts trail off, like:
The man said, "I think I'll watch some television. . ."

Types of Words

The cornerstones of any language are four basic elements: nouns, verbs, adjectives, and adverbs. If you want to learn a foreign language, picking up just 500 basic words in that new language can allow you to function as a beginner in many tourist situations. If you know a thousand words, you should be able to carry on a basic conversation. Many of the first words you will encounter belong in the following four categories.

Noun

A noun is a person, place, or thing that is used in a sentence, such as:
Baker, circus, computer, dog, gold, moon, pharmacist, shoeshine, waterfall, wife
A proper noun refers to a specific person, place, or thing, like:
Alice Cooper, Ukrainian President Volodymyr Zelenskyy, the Solomon Islands, Idaho, the Hope Diamond, *SpongeBob SquarePants*

Verb

Verbs are action words that indicate something is happening:
Leap, shout, sleep, fly, dance, vibrate, call, go, say, juggle, stand
There are also auxiliary verbs. These alter the tense or mood of other verbs in the same sentence, such as:

Is (The dog is running quickly.)
Can (Can you study for the test?)
Do (Do you like the lunch?)
Must (They must arrive on Monday.)

Adjective

Adjectives modify the noun, meaning that they give an attribute to the noun, such as:
Angelic, awkward, cruel, good, mighty, slow, tall, unique
When used correctly, an adjective will strongly impact an entire sentence:

The lonely man is watching television.
The wicked man is watching television.
The cheerful man is watching television.

Adverb

Adverbs modify the verb, showing manner, place, time or degree:
Annually, calmly, far, madly, more, mysteriously, only, painfully, quicker, very
Like an adjective, the correct adverb can alter a sentence's tone dramatically:

The man is quietly watching television.
The man is happily watching television.
The man is angrily watching television.

Those four types of words (nouns, verbs, adjectives, and adverbs) will allow you to convey a meaning to someone. The drawback is that limiting yourself to using only them results in a clipped, unusual form of communication. Although you could get your point across, it would end up looking something like this:

Big train go quickly. Fat bakers jump excitedly. Bright shoes gleam unexpectedly.

You are conveying information, but it comes across in a stilted, robotic fashion. This is why the remaining five elements of language are so important, as they allow your words to flow

8   Language Foundations

more naturally to the readers. The five secondary elements of language are pronouns, prepositions, conjunctions, interjections, and determiners. Coupling these with the four elements listed above can lead to advanced proficiency in writing and developing your language skills.

Pronoun

A pronoun is a word that takes the place of a noun, including:

I, we, she, they, he, him, it

These are generally used on second reference, meaning a pronoun is effective only after the noun has been established as the subject. For example, this sentence by itself makes no sense:

He says the charges are false and he will plead not guilty.

But adding a sentence or two before that with a noun establishes the subject and gives it context, thus the pronoun can be used effectively:

Mayor Jeffrey Brown faces two new charges that he accepted bribes before he approved construction of the city's new landfill. But Brown says the allegations are a politically motivated smear campaign. He says the charges are false and he will plead not guilty.

It is crucial to establish what a pronoun is referring to, as multiple subjects in the introductory sentence can lead to confusion:

The President of the Kiwanis Club, Gordon Mulligan, was happy to present a medal to Darian Conway for being such a good assistant. But during the presentation, he found out the medal also came with a fifty-dollar gift certificate to a local restaurant.

This brief passage is already confusing since Gordon or Darian could be the "he" in the second sentence. While the pronoun is appropriate in the second sentence, it should be rewritten to avoid confusion.

Preposition

Prepositions are words that are placed *before* nouns or pronouns to form a prepositional phrase. Examples of prepositions and how they are used are:

With, until, from, by
The engineer shared the reward with his friend.
The student received the high grade from the professor.
The deadline for the contest stated applications must arrive by noon.

Conjunction

Conjunctions join words, phrases, and clauses. The two types of conjunctions are coordinating and subordinating. Coordinating conjunctions connect elements that are considered equal, such as:

And, but, or, so, for, yet

The woman ordered the fish for dinner and the man ordered the chicken.
You have the choice of taking either algebra or geometry for college credit.

Subordinating conjunctions connect clauses that are not equal, like:

Although, because, since, while

Although the couple broke up during Homecoming weekend, they still plan to spend the Thanksgiving holiday together.
Since the travel restrictions have been lifted, the number of passengers flying to Europe has increased dramatically.

Interjection

Interjections are words that express emotion in a language. They are usually followed by exclamation points, making them easy to spot in dialogue:

Oops! Wow! Jeepers! Dang! Oh!

While interjections may be used in any of the script formats in this textbook, they are especially handy in the chapter about writing for Graphic Novels. Unlike other forms of speech, interjections can be used as "voices" for animals, robots, or any other object that may yelp, growl, or beep a message to the audience.

These words should also be used with caution if there is a broad audience. Mild expletives from a century ago, like "Zounds!" or "Golly!", have been replaced by modern words that test the limits of governing bodies like the Federal Communications Commission, the Motion Picture Association of America, and a bevy of advertisers, editors, readers, and viewers.

Determiner

Determiners are used in sentences before nouns. There are four broad types of determiners: articles, demonstratives, possessives, and quantifiers. The basic determiners, called *articles*, are:

A (a hat), an (an orange), the (the nachos)

Other determiners are *demonstratives*, that indicate specific nouns, like:

This (this hat), that (that orange), these (these nachos), those (those couches)

Possessive determiners are like demonstratives, but they indicate ownership, such as:

My (my hat), her (her dog), their (their nachos), our (our couches)

The final type of determiner is the *quantifier*. These can appear as broad amounts, like:

Each, few, many, some
Or they can be specific numbers, such as:

One, five, seventy, ten million

Or they can be ordinals, which are specific like numbers but indicate ranking:

First, second, third, 1st, 2nd, 3rd, last, next

Finally, there are words that can easily hop from one category to the next. One excellent example is the word "what", which spans five different types of words with ease.

As an adverb	– "What a pity"	– meaning this is or that is
As a pronoun	– "What is your number?"	– asks specification of identity
As an interjection	– "What! That's crazy!"	– expression of surprise
As a conjunction	– "I know what I want"	– connecting different thoughts
As a determiner	– "What car will you drive?"	– determines which choice

Types of Sentences

Writing these different types of words into a logical progression is the basis of creating scripts in every format described throughout this book. Some sentences can be just one word long, like "Wow!" (an interjection), "Run!" (a verb), or "Car!" (a noun). But the basic types of sentence structures are simple, compound, and complex sentences.

Simple Sentence Structure

There are five types of simple sentence structures, which are:

Subject – Verb	The dog eats.
Subject – Verb – Object	The man knitted the socks.
Subject – Verb – Adjective	Donna is happy.
Subject – Verb – Adverb	The cat purred loudly.
Subject – Verb – Noun	Sheila is a dancer.

Each of these sentences can be subsequently lengthened by adding different elements, such as adjectives or adverbs.

Subject – Verb	The dog eats.
Adding an adverb	The dog hungrily eats.
Adding an adjective	The happy dog hungrily eats.
Adding an object	The happy dog hungrily eats steak.
Subject – Verb – Object	The man knitted the socks.
Adding an adjective	The old man knitted the socks.
Adding an adverb	The old man knitted the socks quickly.
Adding a determiner	The old man knitted the ten socks quickly.
Subject – Verb – Adjective	Donna is happy.
Subject – Verb – Adverb	The cat purred loudly.
Subject – Verb – Noun	Sheila is a dancer.

Compound Sentence Structure

Although it sounds intimidating, compound sentence structure is straightforward. Essentially, a compound sentence is made up of at least two simple sentences that are joined together. These sentences are called independent clauses. The trick is that each independent clause must be able to stand on its own. As an example:

Jesse got on his bicycle and he rode to his job.

The two independent clauses "Jesse got on his bicycle" and "he rode to his job" each stand alone as individual sentences. The sentences are joined by the conjunction word "and" to form a compound sentence.

Complex Sentence Structure

A complex sentence is like a compound sentence but with one important difference; there is only one independent clause but there are one or more dependent clauses. A dependent clause is not a sentence that can stand on its own. To slightly alter the previous example:

Jesse got on his bicycle and then rode to his job.

The first clause "Jesse got on his bicycle" can be read as a simple sentence, thus it is an independent clause. We again have the conjunction "and". After that, the next clause is "then rode to his job". That part does not stand on its own, so it is a dependent clause. Joining the first part of the sentence (independent clause) with a conjunction and then the second part of the sentence (dependent clause) results in a complex sentence.

Active Voice, Phrasing, and Tone

There are endless voices that use unique scripting in plays, films, news, advertising, and every other form of media to convey their messages. Each voice is different, so there is no "right" way to tell a story. William Shakespeare dialogue sounds like William Shakespeare while Quentin Tarantino dialogue sounds like Quentin Tarantino. Trying to make your words mirror someone else's is a disservice to your own voice in any medium.

However, there are a few techniques that can universally help with scripting across the media. These are knowing the difference between the active and passive voices, alliterative phrasing, and tone. We will briefly step through each of these.

Active Versus Passive Structure

Many of the formats we will examine in this textbook require brevity because of time and space constraints. For this reason, it is important to put the subject of the sentence as prominently as possible. This is the active voice, which looks like this:

Gordon ate a dozen hotdogs.

This is a simple sentence in which the subject (Gordon) acts upon the object (a dozen hotdogs). However, the passive structure flips the order of the sentence, such as:

A dozen hotdogs were eaten by Gordon.

This example makes the hotdogs into the subject of the sentence. However, it doesn't read as smoothly as the active sentence; passive structure should always be eliminated in favor of active structure whenever possible. One strategy to identify a passive sentence is to look for the word "by" that doesn't imply a spatial relationship.

If you see the word "by", check if the subject and object can be flipped to create a more dynamic phrase.

Alliterative Phrase

Alliteration is when two or more words that begin with the same sound are placed sequentially in a sentence or phrase. They can be used to create a catchy brand name that is easily memorable, like Coca-Cola, Dunkin' Donuts, or Krispy Kreme. Even names can have alliteration in them, such as Mickey Mouse, Peter Parker, or Lex Luthor.

One advantage of alliterative phrasing is that it can be recognized easily and pops off the page when written into a script. Of course, alliteration is not limited to brand names and fictional characters. Alliterative sentences can be written like "Peter Piper picked a peck of pickled peppers."

Alliteration is most useful in advertising and public relations. However, expect to see it appear occasionally in films, plays, episodic television, and graphic novels.

Tone

The tone of the written word conveys how the mood impacts the reader. A written page by Stephen King will be creepy while a passage from Dr. Seuss will be amusing. The choice of words and how they are placed within a sentence dramatically alters the feeling of the script.

As an example, we will take a very simple idea of a student walking down a hallway. In its most basic form, the sentence reads like this:

The student walked down the hallway.

Let's modify that sentence by changing the word "walked" into something more descriptive. Watch for how the tone changes with each different verb.

The student stomped down the hallway.
The student waddled down the hallway.
The student tiptoed down the hallway.

There are countless other examples, like stroll, saunter, hop, bolt, etc. Each verb modifies the feeling of the sentence; thus, they should be inserted carefully into your writing. The emotional impact of any given word should not be taken lightly. Some forms of media, like graphic novels and narrative film scripts, embrace more marked tones in their writing. Other scripting formats, notably news reporting, beg for more neutrality in their tone.

Paragraphs

A paragraph is a section of writing that covers a topic in a larger body of work. The three elements of a successful paragraph are:

- A strong topic sentence that introduces the paragraph and sets the tone
- Supporting sentences that build upon the topic sentence
- A narrative flow that ties the sentences together

There are no minimum or maximum number of lines in a paragraph, but most paragraphs have at least one topic sentence and two supporting sentences. In a narrative essay, a single paragraph should never extend more than a single page. Paragraph length is flexible beyond these two broad guidelines.

There are different limits for the various types of media scripts. Newspaper and magazine articles often have one-sentence paragraphs, especially with direct quotes. But a long soliloquy in a feature film will have an overly long dialogue section, resulting in a paragraph that may indeed consume more than one page. Regardless of length, each paragraph should convey information, be self-contained, and contribute to the overall theme of the script.

Specialized Formats

Punctuation marks, types of words, sentence structure, and paragraph formatting are all necessary when writing a standard narrative essay. However, some of these elements are altered or even ignored when scripting some of the media forms in this textbook.

For example, dialogue drives feature film scripts as the characters speak to one another. But there are no quotation marks used in these scripts, nor do they appear in television news copy, plays, or episodic comedy shows. However, quotation marks do make an appearance in other formats, such as newspapers and magazines.

Social media relies on certain punctuation marks to serve as shortcuts, such as the ampersand "&". It is notable that the pound sign "#" has also come to be known as a hashtag due to its use on social media platforms. Aside from those instances, these marks rarely appear in any other types of media scripts.

Even some types of words are used differently depending on which media format is needed. Interjections are great for some formats (graphic novels, narrative film) but awful in others (news, public relations). By examining the different formats and practicing your scripting in various media styles, you can readily obtain a working knowledge of the best ways to deliver your message.

Looking Forward

New words enter languages on a daily basis. Twenty years ago, the word "deplatform" did not exist, a "google" was just a very large number, and no one knew what an "emoji" looked like. Each of these words came into the English language as parts of new technology. Other words enter the lexicon when immigrants bring in new words, new generations coin new phrases, and slang words become commonplace.

As languages evolve, nouns, verbs, and other types of words will still have their place in basic sentence structures. Communication is based on a common language for people to exchange their ideas. Keeping up with the dynamic changes in any language will produce skilled writers in all of the types of media discussed in this text.

Exercises

1. Read a story from a newspaper website. Which punctuation mark appears first in the story? How many of the 14 punctuation marks appear in that entire story? Which punctuation marks do not appear in the story at all?
2. Write a one-page story about two friends getting together to watch a baseball game. Correctly use all 14 punctuation marks in the text of that story. Note how many of

those punctuation marks you use frequently and how many you may have never used in an assignment before.
3. Explain the difference among a simple, complex, and compound sentence.
4. Write a one-page story by just using nouns, verbs, adjectives, and adverbs; you may not use pronouns, determiners, conjunctions, or any other types of speech. Read the story aloud once you have finished. Does the story make sense?
5. Think of your favorite "short" piece of dialogue from a movie. It can be one sentence, a few words, or just a single word. Then think of your favorite monologue from a movie where a character talks for an extended period of time. How do these two different parts of dialogue violate the normal minimum and maximum sentences in a standard narrative paragraph?

Chapter Essentials

- The basic elements of any language, such as punctuation and types of words, are essential to all writers.
- There are 14 standard punctuation marks in the English language. These are the period, comma, question mark, exclamation point, quotation marks, colon, semicolon, dash, hyphen, apostrophe, ellipsis, parentheses, brackets, and braces.
- The four basic types of words are the noun, verb, adjective and adverb.
- Other types of words are commonly used to tie the basic types of words together in sentence format, to convey more meaning, and to make the basic words flow more naturally. These five secondary elements of language are pronouns, prepositions, conjunctions, interjections, and determiners.
- Sentences may be structured in simple, compound, or complex structures.
- Paragraphs are comprised of a strong topic sentence, supporting sentences, and a narrative flow that holds those elements together.

Online Links

Blurb.com. This gateway site provides links to other sites to motivate you to start writing in a variety of formats. These resources are ideal for kickstarting your writing project by dividing the process into five sections: Get Started; Improve Your Writing; Develop Your Characters; Edit, Review, Repeat; and Promote Your Writing.

Dictionary.com. This site provides definitions, synonyms, usages, and examples of how to use any word desired. There are also games, flashcards, SAT test prep resources, and aids to help solve daily crossword and wordle puzzles.

Grammarly.com. This site suggests changes for writing documents in various formats, including text, emails, and social media.

2 Theatrical Plays

Key Words

Act
At Rise
Blackout
Character
Center Stage
Curtain
Parenthetical
Scene
Setting

Dialogue
Downstage
Dramaturgy
End of Scene
External Format
Internal Format
Stage Left
Stage Right
Upstage

Historical Overview

The first scripted media delivered to a general audience is arguably the birth of tragedies, comedies, and histories in the form of the theatrical play. While no one can accurately pinpoint the first time someone stood in front of others as a form of entertainment, stage plays are the oldest forms of media communication. Early performers were interacting with audiences more than 8,000 years ago.

Thespis, who lived in Greece in the 6th century BC, is regarded as the first person to appear on a stage as a character; that is, he was portraying someone else, not speaking to the audience as himself. He would also change masks and costumes during his performances. This allowed him to create more dynamic stories, giving birth to the tragedy as a form of stage play. Thespis was so successful that he invented theatrical touring. This involved him driving a horse-drawn carriage from town to town with a collection of props, masks, and costumes. Another enduring acknowledgement is that modern stage actors are called thespians, a direct homage to his name.

Early Greek plays also included a chorus, which was an ensemble that spoke directly to the audience. The chorus usually opened the play by providing a contextual history before anyone else would take the stage. Eventually, other Greek dramatists began to embrace this entertainment form, introducing new innovations in how stories were presented. Aeschylus (525 to 455 BC) expanded many stories from a single actor to two. Sophocles (497 to 406 BC) increased the number of actors to three and sometimes four.

Finally, Euripides (480 to 406 BC) expanded the cast to more actors while also limiting and sometimes eliminating the chorus.

Playwriting grew exponentially in the ensuing centuries, as theatrical plays appealed to all audiences equally. Books were reserved for the literate upper classes and media like radio and films had not yet been invented. Plays were the primary source of entertainment for thousands of years with countless writers like Terence, William Shakespeare, Henrik Ibsen, and Eugene O'Neill bringing their works to the stage. Today, Broadway shows like *Hamilton*, *The Phantom of the Opera*, *Wicked*, and *The Lion King* enjoy long-running performances in front of packed houses. Off-Broadway, community theater and school productions add many more options for aspiring playwrights and performers.

As theatrical plays and the number of playwrights multiplied, the need for a standard script template became obvious for several reasons. First, a common format would make it easy for actors, directors, and producers to read and comprehend the different elements (like dialogue and stage directions). Second, a producer could easily estimate the running time of the script, as one page of the standard template equals one minute of performance time. Finally, the format indicates to the producer whether the playwright understands the process of scripting; after all, if the writer does not know how to format a simple page, how could they know the intricacies of plot, dialogue, and characterization?

Plays are divided into acts. The term "three-act structure" originated in theater and was eventually incorporated into film vernacular; we will discuss the acts in more detail later in this chapter. As an overview, act one serves as the introduction (beginning), act two has confrontation between the protagonist and antagonist with more action taking place (middle), then the third act has climactic scenes that resolve the story (end). *Who's Afraid of Virginia Woolf?* by acclaimed playwright Edward Albee is an example of a successful stage play that follows this structure.

However, not all plays have three acts. William Shakespeare relied on a five-act structure for plays such as *Macbeth*, *Romeo and Juliet*, and *As You Like It*. Other plays including *Death of a Salesman* and *Hamilton* utilized a two-act structure. One-act plays are also popular, especially among those who want to write a production that lasts between 20 and 40 minutes. Most plays performed in elementary and middle schools tend to have a shorter performance time.

Irrespective of the number of acts in a play, the writing formatting is the same. You will notice strong similarities if you compare the writing templates of playscripts with those used in episodic television and feature films, but the subtle differences used in theatrical plays are quite rigid. Let's set the stage by looking at how a sample play is written. It all begins with two mandatory pages that appear before the playscript is even seen.

Technical Specifications

One interesting quirk about playscripts is that they should be written in 12-point Courier font. This typeface was developed for IBM typewriters and has since been adapted as a computer font. It is a core font on all versions of Windows, so changing your font from a standard like Times New Roman or Helvetica is simple. Once you are in a Word document, go to the Home ribbon (it's a button near the top left corner) and locate the font dropdown box. Click the down carrot and scroll to Courier. The box to the immediate right of the font dropdown box allows you to change the size of the font. Make sure it is set at 12.

The two required pages before the playscript appears are the Title Page and the Cast of Characters Page, which is also called the Dramatis Personae Page. These pages are not numbered but they do require specific formatting.

Title Page

The Title Page contains the name of the play, the writer's name, and the number of acts within the play. The writer's contact information and copyright number (if the play has already been copyrighted) are here as well.

To format this page, let's start with the title, writer's name, and number of acts. We'll use the title *Slumber Party*, a two-act play written by Gerard Key Hutcheson. The title should appear in ALL CAPS, 3.5 inches down from the top of the page and indented 4 inches from the left margin. An underscore line then appears two spaces below the title; this is an underline that runs the same length as the title. Two spaces below that line is a brief sentence noting the number of acts (which is two in this example). Another two blank lines and we insert the word "by" in all lowercase type. Another two lines and we put in the playwright's name. This part of the title page will be formatted like this, but remember the title will be 3.5 inches down from the top of the page:

>   SLUMBER PARTY
>   _____
>
>   A Play in Two Acts
>
>   by
>
>   Gerard Key Hutcheson

Next, let's assume the writer copyrighted the playscript in 2023. This information will be noted in the bottom left-hand corner of the page. The writer's contact information will appear in the bottom right-hand corner of the page, except for the writer's name, which is already on the page. Adding this to the Title Page results in the following:

>   SLUMBER PARTY
>   _____
>
>   A Play in Two Acts
>
>   by
>
>   Gerard Key Hutcheson

Copyright © 2023,
By Gerard Key Hutcheson

2879 Bayliner Drive
Wheatland, MO 65779
Phone: (417) 555–5555
Email: hutchesonscripts94@hotmail.com

Cast of Characters Page

The Cast of Characters page, also called the Dramatis Personae page, follows directly after the Title Page. The words "Cast of Characters" are centered and underlined at the top of the page. Two columns appear two spaces beneath that heading. The left column contains the character names, which are underlined and followed by a colon. The right-hand column provides a very brief outline of the characters. These columns are double spaced.

If there is enough room on the Cast of Characters page, the Scene and Time descriptions are added below the cast list. The word "Scene" is centered and underlined, then a brief description of the location follows beneath that. Similarly, the word "Time" is centered and underlined with a brief description underneath that heading. The final product is:

<u>Cast of Characters</u>

<u>Charley:</u>   Ten-year-old boy, Ally's brother.

<u>Tommy:</u>   Ten-year-old boy, Charley's best friend.

<u>Ally:</u>   Eleven-year-old girl, Charley's sister.

<u>Samantha:</u>   Eleven-year-old girl, Ally's best friend.

<u>Mr. Stone:</u>   Middle aged man, Charley and Ally's dad.

<u>Scene</u>

Two side-by-side bedrooms, one belongs to Charley, the other to Ally.

<u>Time</u>

The present.

The main script immediately follows the Title Page and Cast of Characters page. Eight different elements are used to make up a properly formatting playscript. These are Page Numbers, Act/Scene Names, Setting/At Rise, Characters, Dialogue, Parentheticals, Stage Directions, and Blackout/Curtain/End Designations. We will step through each of these, as they all have very specific formatting requirements.

Page Numbers

Numbering of the pages starts with the first page of the playscript; remember the Title Page and Cast of Characters Page are not numbered. The page numbers will appear in the top right-hand corner of the page. If it is a one act play, simply use the Arabic numerals, like 1, 2, and 3. But if there is more than one act, the formatting includes Roman numerals as well. *Slumber Party* is a two-act play, so the first act will start on page I-1, then go to I-2, I-3, etc. Once we start the second act, the Roman numeral will change to a II.

However, the Arabic numbers do NOT restart, as that running tally continues throughout the script. If Act I of *Slumber Party* ends on page 30, that will be shown as I-30. The second act will begin on page II-31.

Act/Scene Names

When you start a new act or scene, it must start at the top of a new page. These designations are indented four inches from the left edge of the page and are underlined, but there are two significant differences. First, the act should appear in all caps, while the scene designation is written in traditional upper and lower case. Second, the numbering system mirrors the Arabic and Roman differences used in the page number. For example, if we are starting the second scene in the first act, the correct formatting would be:

<u>ACT I</u>
<u>Scene 2</u>

We then double space and describe what the audience sees before them on the stage. This is called the setting.

Setting/At Rise

This part of the script is in two columns, but only the single word "Setting" appears in the left column. It is written in all caps, flush to the left margin, and followed by a colon, like this:

SETTING:

The right column is set four inches from the left-hand margin. It shows the scene, the furniture, and the props, but it does NOT mention what the actors are doing when the curtain comes up. We reserve that for the At Rise section. For now, our *Slumber Party* scene shows two bedrooms with a short divider between them. The setting section would be as follows:

SETTING:	Two very different bedrooms are before us with a short wall between them (the action will take place as if there is a full wall dividing them but it is short for audience sight lines). The stage left bedroom is Charley's messy bedroom, filled with toys and everything a ten-year-old boy would want. The stage right tidy bedroom belongs to eleven-year-old Ally. It's clean, neat, and very feminine. Both rooms have a window facing upstage that shows tree branches. They are on a second floor of the house.

Notice the words "stage right", "stage left" and "upstage" in the above Setting description. These words explain where the action is taking place in the different parts of the stage. We will go more in depth about locations on the stage later in this chapter.

The At Rise segment directly follows the Setting. This introduces the characters and describes what is happening when the curtain goes up. Remember, the setting is the physical space, while the action happening in that space goes into At Rise. The formatting for this section is identical to the Setting. The only nuance is that the characters names are in all caps, resulting in this example:

AT RISE: CHARLEY untangles a mess of video cables, expertly setting up a video game console in his bedroom. A dirty sock is nested in the cords. He regards it like an alien life form and chucks it to the corner. ALLY rearranges the many pillows on her bed, plumping them just so.

At this point, the curtain has risen to the waiting audience. The setting has been established and the characters that appear on stage have been identified in the playscript. The next elements of Character, Dialogue, Parentheticals, and Stage Direction will appear in rapid succession.

Characters

Character names are not centered on the page, but they are indented four inches from the page's left side. They appear in all caps, like this:

SAMANTHA

If the character has a name, use it. Do not write "Girl", "Boy", or anything of that nature unless that character is literally nameless throughout the production. The producer and talent want specific names for the characters. A generic label of a background character, like "Chef" or "Landscaper", is fine.

Dialogue

The dialogue sections in plays are much different from those in film and episodic television. Those templates indent the dialogue 2.5 inches from the left edge of the page, plus there is a similar indentation from the right side. The dialogue thus appears as rectangular vertical blocks near the center of the page. In playscripts, the dialogue simply appears as regular text that starts from the left side of the page without quotation marks. There is no blank space between the character name and their dialogue, such as:

SAMANTHA
I am so excited to go to the slumber party tonight!

One unique quality of dialogue in a play is that it is the only element that can literally span across the entire page. Every other part, like settings and stage directions, are more tightly regimented as to where they appear on the left- or right-hand sides of the page. Dialogue does not have these restrictions.

Parentheticals

A parenthetical is a description of how a character is delivering a line of dialogue and can be described as a verb (shouting, whispering) or as an adverb (sadly, happily). This is inserted, single space, on the line following the Character and before Dialogue. It is tabbed 2.75 inches from the left edge of the page. Continuing with our idea of Samantha being excited about the slumber party, she could say something like this:

SAMANTHA
(happily)
I am so excited to go to the slumber party tonight!

A parenthetical is more powerful than its small size indicates. Just changing the word can powerfully impact how a line is delivered, thus altering the entire tone of the scene and the dynamic of the characters involved. For example:

SAMANTHA
(whispering)
I am so excited to go to the slumber party tonight!

Like their use in feature films, parentheticals should be used only if the writer has a specific goal in mind. Otherwise, the director and the actors should be able to bring their own creative input into the scene. The parentheticals are formatted like the stage directions below.

Stage Directions

One telling difference between a stage play and a feature film is how the stage directions are presented. While these are referred to as stage directions in plays, these lines that indicate action are simply called action lines in feature films. In stage plays, they are contained in parentheses and indented 2.75 inches from the left edge of the page. Each line should not go past 2.5 inches before continuing to the next line. They look like this:

(CHARLEY finishes hooking up the video
game and toggles it to life. It works! He
punches the air in glee. In the other bedroom,
ALLY smooths a final pillowcase. Perfect!
She also punches the air in glee.)

Another difference between stage plays and film or episodic television is how character names are formatted when describing action. In plays, the character names are always capitalized. In the other media, those names are only capitalized the first time you introduce the character. After that, they are written in standard upper and lowercases, so you'll have SAMANTHA on first reference, then Samantha after that.

There is one final note about stage directions for plays, which can be split between "internal" and "external" to dialogue formatting. If a stage direction takes place within a single character's dialogue, that needs an *internal format*. You write the first bit of dialogue, then the stage direction is single spaced below that, then the dialogue resumes, also after a single space. For example:

CHARLEY
No doubt, this is going to be the best slumber party ever! All I have to do now is ask my parents for permission and we're good to go!
(CHARLEY grabs a pair of dirty socks off the
floor and smells them dramatically. He shudders
involuntarily.)
You know, that's not so bad! I think I can wear these!

But let's say the stage direction happens between two different characters speaking, so one character says something, there is a stage direction, then a different character speaks. This is an *external format*. In this case, the stage direction should be double spaced in its own section between those bits of dialogue, like this:

CHARLEY
Mom and Dad are cool with getting us pizza, and I know the guys will want some pepperoni. Is Caleb still being weird about only eating pizza that has pineapple on it?

(TOMMY rifles through his backpack and brings
out a pineapple.)

TOMMY
I brought along this bad boy just in case. Just get the pepperoni.

The difference between internal and external formatting is subtle, but it is one way in which beginning playwrights are quickly weeded out of the professional ranks. Now that all the main elements have been covered to write the bulk of the play, all that remains is to end it with a curtain.

Blackout/Curtain/End Designations

These are a two-step process at the end of a scene. First, the word "Blackout" or "Curtain" is typed in all caps, in parentheses, double spaced below the last line of the scene, and indented four inches from the left edge of the page; the placement is similar to the act and scene lines, which were shown above. A blackout or curtain designation is:

(BLACKOUT)
or
(CURTAIN)

The second step is to determine if it is the end of the act or the end of the scene. Double space below the blackout or curtain designation and write the information in the same style, such as:

(CURTAIN)
(END OF ACT)

Once the formatting is understood, there are other elements that are important for a quality playscript. These include dramaturgy, stage directions that indicate physical locations on the stage, three-act structure, and audience interaction. We will step through each of these in turn.

Dramaturgy

Plays set in a historical time, called period pieces, have certain demands. The settings must be authentic, the costumes should be appropriate to the time, and the dialogue must be accurate to that era. Having actors in Greek times utter "Hey, how's it going, dude?" shatters the illusion that is being created for the audience.

Such attention to detail is known as dramaturgy; those literary experts who work in the theatrical world are known as dramaturges. Professional theatrical groups will have a dramaturge available, but smaller houses and student productions must rely on the writer to get the historic information right. These include nuances like making sure the set pieces are carefully researched to checking that an actor doesn't wear a wristwatch during a production set in Medieval times. If you are ever given the opportunity to work with a dramaturge, listen to their input and take careful notes. It is disappointing to produce an historical piece only to mar it with a glaring inaccuracy.

Stage Directions

The terminology here is admittedly confusing, as stage directions in a play's script refer to the lines denoting action. Once the play is written, stage directions describe the basic positions and directions for stage movement. The writer must convey instructions so the actors know from which side to enter, where to stand and deliver the lines, and which way they should leave the scene. This is akin to blocking, which dictates onstage movement and positioning.

Some of the stage positions are rooted in history. During the Renaissance, people flocked to theaters for entertainment. Common people who couldn't afford a seat were allowed to stand for the duration of the play right in front of the stage. This sounds like a great vantage point, but the stages were elevated, so the stage could be level with the viewer's head. This meant the commoner could see the actor as they performed near the front of the stage but if the actor went to the back of the stage, they would disappear from view.

The solution was to slightly tilt the stage so the back was higher than the front. This allowed the audience to always see the performers. Of course, when the actor was moving away from the audience, he was literally walking up an incline, or upstage. Moving toward the front of the stage meant walking slightly downhill, or downstage. One result of this is when one actor "upstages" another by having the audience focus on them. Imagine an actor, Brad, downstage (near the audience) when a second actor, George, enters the rear of the stage, or the upstage. This means Brad must turn his back to the audience to see George, putting Brad in a poor position from the audience's point of view. Literally, George is stealing the scene by upstaging Brad, even though George is physically further away from the audience.

Other stage directions are from the viewpoint of the actor as he faces the audience. Let's spin Brad back around so he's facing the audience. If he is standing in the middle of the stage, he is simply located at center stage. When Brad steps to his right, he is moving stage right. The audience will perceive him moving to their left, but again, the stage direction is

24   Theatrical Plays

given from the actor's perspective. Breaking the stage into a small grid can be helpful, plus we will use common abbreviations that are used for the stage locations.

	Upstage (U)	
Upstage Right (UR)	Upstage Center (UC)	Upstage Left (UL)
Stage Right (R)	Center Stage (C)	Stage Left (L)
Downstage Right (DR)	Downstage Center (DC)	Downstage Left (DL)
	Downstage (D)	
	Audience	

Mastering the terminology is essential for playwrights as they visual the performances as they write the playscripts. Of course, following the basic three-act structure below is also important for narrative storytelling.

Three-Act Structure

The classic structure of a stage play is based on Aristotle's dramatic theory that he outlined in *Poetics*. The idea is simply that each story has a beginning, middle and end. In the theater, this is defined as the setup, the confrontation, and the resolution. This basic template is used in other forms of media as well, such as narrative films and episodic television.

Act One introduces the main character as the protagonist while also starting with exposition; this is one or more introductory scenes that establish the ground rules of the story. If the piece is set in the 1300s, if the world they are in is supposedly underwater, or if the characters have supernatural powers, these parameters are laid out here. Before the act ends, an inciting incident or plot twist occurs to prompt the protagonist into action. For this example, let's suppose the lead actor learned a jewelry heist took place and he was the main suspect.

Act Two, which tends to be the longest of the three acts, consists of raising the dramatic stakes. Subplots are fleshed out as the tension rises for the protagonist. He could learn his fingerprints were found at the crime scene, a stolen necklace was planted at his apartment, and the police are closing in. The second act should end with another incident that shows the lead actor will surely fail.

Act Three serves as the climax where the hero must either succeed or lose. This is where the subplots are wrapped up, the protagonist finally confronts the antagonist, and the main plot comes to a dramatic conclusion. In our example, the lead actor shows a sympathetic detective that an off-duty policeman was the actual thief all along. An arrest is made, handshakes are delivered, and life returns to normal for our hero.

As noted before, not all stage plays are told in three acts. However, the underlying premise of introducing the characters early, giving them obstacles to overcome throughout the play, and then wrapping up the conflict in the final minutes is the basis of narrative storytelling. This can be accomplished in a short 20-minute one act or a lengthy Shakespearean five act performance. Each play will have a three-act structure even if they are physically delivered in fewer or more sections.

Audience Interaction

Most theatrical performances are limited to a stage with the action performed in front of a viewing audience. The audience members are passive and simply watch the play unfold. However, some plays break the "fourth wall" and allow the performers to directly address the audience. This is nothing new; if you recall the history of theater, the original Greek chorus was used to describe the backstory to the audience thousands of years ago. This type of interactive play can extend to popular shows like *Hair* (performers walk down the aisles), *Tony and Tina's Wedding* (the audience members are wedding guests that experience the play as active participants) and *The Mystery of Edwin Drood* (during a break, the audience members vote on one of seven possible endings).

Scripting for this interaction is surprisingly simple. For the stage direction, the playwright expands the acting space, so the performers leave the stage and interact with the audience. In dialogue, after the character line, a parenthetical is inserted that directs the performer to speak to the audience. Using Samantha as our example, she can deliver her line like this:

SAMANTHA
(to the audience)
I am so excited to go to the slumber party tonight! Who thinks I should go?

An audience reaction should be expected whenever a performer breaks the fourth wall. Although it isn't necessarily scripted, the actor should take a pause while the audience responds. After all, it's counterproductive to ask the spectators to take part in the production, only to prematurely shut them down.

Looking Forward

Theatrical plays have a long and colorful history, which has led to a commonly accepted template that is used in both professional and amateur settings. Thousands of years of live performances have brought the theatrical script into what is the most standardized media script format around the world.

Given this track record, there is little reason to expect this form of media scripting will dramatically change in the coming years. Anyone seeking to write a play should be confident that the scripting template will stay essentially the same for years to come.

Exercises

1. Research the different plays that are produced in your university theater program during the semester. Is it easy to figure out the genre of each play from the title and description? How many are listed for targeted audiences (family, students, seniors, etc.)? How many productions are advertised as one-act plays?
2. Track down the plays that are currently on Broadway in New York City; playbill.com and broadway.com are excellent sources. How many of these plays have you already heard about? Discuss which of these plays you might be interested in seeing in person.

3. Write a short (one to three page) theater scene using correct formatting. The scene should have at least two actors and be set in a college dining hall. The plot should focus on a student who cannot decide if he should go home for Spring Break or if he should join his friends on a road trip to Florida.
4. Examine a playscript next to a feature film script. What differences do you spot, particularly with the scene descriptions and the action lines/stage directions? What similarities do you see between the two media forms?
5. Write the Title Page and Cast of Characters Page for a theatrical play about your life. How many characters would you list? What would you title your play?

Chapter Essentials

- Thespis, who lived in Greece in the 6th century BC, is credited with numerous advances in early theater. Modern stage actors are called thespians in honor of his work.
- The two pages that appear before the main text of the play are the Title Page and the Cast of Characters (or Dramatis Personae) Page.
- The eight formatting elements of a stage play consist of Page Numbers, Act/Scene Names, Setting/At Rise, Characters, Dialogue, Parentheticals, Stage Directions, and Blackout/Curtain/End Designations.
- The three-act structure is considered standard, but there are many deviations from it. Shakespeare wrote in five acts, many plays are in two acts, and one act plays are used for shorter productions.
- Stage directions can be formatted as internal (within a single character's dialogue) or external (taking place between two characters speaking).
- Some theatrical formatting is like film and episodic television, but there are subtle differences with tabs and margins.
- The stage is physically divided into upstage (furthest from the audience), center stage, and downstage (closest to the audience). All other directions, like stage right and stage left, are from the performers' point of view.
- Dramaturgy is the practice of immersing the story in the proper historical or cultural context through accurate dialogue, scene descriptions, and settings.

Online Links

Broadway.com. In addition to providing details and ticket information about the current shows on Broadway, this site gives behind-the-scenes news of the theatrical industry.

Dramatistsguild.com. Home to the Dramatists Guild of America, this site delves into the business of writing plays, negotiating contracts, copyrights, contests, and much more for the serious playwright.

Playbill.com. Theater news fills this website, but it also has job postings, reviews, and details about shows in the following categories: Broadway, off Broadway, touring, regional, and London.

Playscripts.com. Thousands of plays are available for schools and theater companies on this website. These stage plays can be purchased for productions, but they can also be previewed on the website to show professional writing technique.

3 Newspaper and Magazine

Key Words

Associated Press Style
Attribution
Byline
Column Inches
Copy
Cut

Cutline
Delayed Attribution
Inverted Pyramid
Lead
News Hole
Quote

Historical Overview

September 25, 1690, witnessed the publication of the first newspaper in America. *Publick Occurrences, Both Foreign and Domestick*, consisted of four pages that were 6x10 inches. It was printed in Boston by Richard Pierce and was originally planned as a monthly publication. However, British authorities were infuriated by the paper's account of the French and Indian War, as well as gossip about the King of France's immoralities. The government quickly ordered that the newspaper be suppressed and that no future editions could be published without prior approval. Ironically, the first newspaper published in America was also the first one to be shut down by the government.

Other periodicals sprang up throughout the colonies, usually filled with satire, political editorials, and community news. In 1729, Ben Franklin became the editor and printer of the *Philadelphia Gazette*, which was in one of the most important colonial cities at the time; it is notable that he was only 23 years old. In the subsequent years, he developed a loose network of newspapers that ranged from New York to the South Carolina. Of the 15 English-language newspapers in the colonies in 1753, eight were published by Franklin or one of his network's partners.

Over the coming years, newspapers would continue to flourish in the new country for several reasons: the Penny Press in the 1800s offered the day's news and gossip for a mere penny, immigrants entering the country used newspapers to learn English, and a sense of community developed around newspapers that bonded people together.

The use of the telegraph during the 1860s Civil War influenced how newspapers presented their news. War reporters would use the telegraph to "wire" their stories back to their editors instantly. But these messages cost money, so reporters were trained to stack the most important information into the lead paragraphs. This created the inverted pyramid style of writing, in which the main components were placed at the start of the story.

Stories became tighter, leaner, and had the salient facts (who, what, where, when, why, and how) near the top of the message.

Newspaper and magazine circulations continued to increase during the 1900s. Some large cities had more than one local newspaper, and foreign language papers (usually Spanish) began publication. Readership skyrocketed across all income brackets as literacy became the norm. Magazines evolved to become more specialized with their subject matter, targeting smaller subsets of readers with more focused content.

Once radio and television became widespread, the days of soaring readership began to dim. Newspaper readership then plunged dramatically with Internet news websites, as readers could receive information instantly in their homes with little or no money spent. Magazines also suffered a hit in circulation, with more readers turning to online offerings. Still, the printed periodical is vital despite having fewer readers. Local news remains the hallmark of the city newspaper while magazines continue to target their readers according to their own specific interests. While printed periodicals may not have the same robust readership as before, they still play a crucial role in delivering messages to an audience.

Technical Specifications

Although newspapers, magazines, and related periodicals are one of the oldest forms of media, there is no technical standard for writing those stories, which is also called *copy*. Stories are written as narrative prose, generally in a standard font such as Times New Roman or Cambria in a 12- or 14-point size. The greatest technical concern is the desired length, specified in a word count which is then translated to column inches. The other requirements are more stylistic in nature, which we review later in this chapter.

We will address the technical concern of story length first. Not only is it an easy concept to cover, it also reveals why so many of the stylistic choices exist. In a larger sense, many of the style choices used by newspaper and magazine writers today are based on money.

When people think of a newspaper or a magazine, the immediate reaction may be that the stories are the first materials laid onto the blank page. The truth is quite different.

Newspapers and magazines are businesses that require advertising revenue. Ads are sold by the amount of the page that the ad will cover. A ¼ page ad, for example, means that the ad will take up one-quarter of the page. Ads can also be sold based on column inches; this is simply the number of vertical inches that a specific ad will fill. If an ad is four column inches, it will measure four inches tall and one column wide (for a vertical ad) or one inch tall and four columns wide (for a horizontal ad). The other option is a two-inch-tall ad that spans two columns, so it looks more like a square and still totals four column inches.

The placement of the ad itself also impacts the cost. Ads on the right-hand side command higher rates, as readers tend to see the right-hand side first when they open the paper. Advertisements in Sunday papers, ads that are in color, or those placed in highly desired sections always cost a bit more. The real estate section on Sunday, for example, costs more than the lifestyle section on Tuesday.

Magazines are much the same, although more full-page ads exist than in newspapers. Some fashion magazines have forty pages of ads before any written copy appears. Still, the editors are keenly aware that the advertisements are laid in first, followed by the stories submitted from the writing staff.

Once the advertising department determines the number and size of the ads, they are placed in the periodical. This crucial step occurs before the news is written. Simply stated, without the ads paying for the newspaper, there would be no newspaper to put out, so the ads are the first items laid onto the pages.

The partially blank sheets (with ads already inserted) are now ready for the news editorial team. The remaining empty portions of the pages make up the *news hole*. This is the amount of column inches that will physically fit into that edition of the newspaper. When an editor asks for 20 column inches, that means there are only 20 inches available before the story runs out of room. If a writer offers a story of 26 column inches for that 20-column inch news hole, those bottom six inches are on the chopping block. For this reason, writers are urged to put the important points of the story into the lead paragraphs.

Style

Putting the most vital elements of the story into the top of the piece so they will not be cut is a simple premise. Once this single technical specification is achieved, the other concerns for the writer are those dealing with style. These include crafting compelling leads, writing in the active voice, using delayed attribution, writing with the correct descriptors, and checking wording for neutrality. We will step through each of these important attributes in turn.

Leads

The lead is the first sentence of the story. Many readers merely skim articles on the printed page, so having an attention-grabbing sentence is important to get their attention. Like broadcast news, there are different types of leads that are used to make someone want to read more. The primary type of lead is the hard lead.

The hard lead starts the story with immediate information, much like the old telegraph stories in the 1800s. Readers quickly get to the who, what, where, when, why, and how of the story with a hard lead. Not all of these elements will be in the first sentence, but enough important facts will be there to pique the reader's interest so they read more. An example is:

> The IRS says two million more households will be audited this year.

The soft lead offers an extra sentence before jumping into the information. This is a luxury that is not granted to all stories, but it breaks up the rapid-fire tone if all of the page's stories have hard leads. Expanding from our previous example, a soft lead would be:

> The IRS wants to make sure everyone is paying their fair share in taxes. The agency will audit an additional two million households this year.

A question lead is sometimes used to hook a reader into a story. The trick with a question lead is that the query must be immediately answered with the second sentence, like:

> What are the odds that your taxes will be audited? The IRS says it will audit an extra two million households this year.

Finally, the trivia lead uses a tidbit of information that is factual but not necessarily the main thrust of the story. It is used sparingly as most stories need to get to the point to save column inches. However, it can be employed to great effect, such as:

> The IRS says the average household underreports its income by nearly $2,000. That's why the agency will audit an extra two million households this year.

Once a strong lead is delivered, the rest of the story follows with pertinent information followed by details that become of lesser importance. Leaving less important items toward the bottom of the story allows an editor to easily trim the story if needed.

Active and Passive Voice

Since newspaper and magazine stories are limited by their column inches, writing in the active voice saves space while also making the sentences more dynamic. This deals with putting the subject and the object of the sentence in the correct order. We will first look at sentences written in the passive sense, like:

- The cat was chased by the dog.
- The seven hotdogs were eaten by the boy.
- The filet mignon was created by the chef.

Rewriting these sentences in the active voice results in cleaner copy that saves precious column inches on the page. The revisions are:

- The dog chased the cat.
- The boy ate the seven hotdogs.
- The chef created the filet mignon.

Attribution

Attribution is a key element of any written article. Simply defined, it is when the writer tells the reader where the information comes from. When it is a quote, the attribution is delayed until after the quote is presented. For example:

> "The state lottery payout exceeds five million dollars," said Mega Millions spokesperson Janet Wade.

This delayed attribution is common in newspapers, as the news reader is more interested in the quote itself than in the person who says it. By placing the important information at the start of the sentence, the reader is more likely to continue with the article. This is in contrast to broadcast style, in which the quote is listed after the speaker. Using the previous example, the broadcast style would be:

> Mega Millions spokesperson Janet Wade says the state lottery payout exceeds five million dollars.

This difference is due to the way the information is consumed across the two media sources. Newspapers are written for the eye, so the reader sees the information with the more important facts earlier in the sentence. Television and radio are written conversationally for the ear; thus the sentence is structured how the average person would simply tell the story aloud.

Other examples of delayed attribution would be:

- "It is shameful that Rhea Seehorn did not win an Emmy," said one fan after the awards ceremony.
- "This is the worst tattoo I've ever seen," cried the trucker after he saw the new Daffy Duck image inked onto his calf.
- "My administration will never raise taxes," promised the presidential candidate.

None of the above sentences, if spoken aloud, comes across as conversational. However, the delayed attribution is a foundation of newspaper and magazine writing, placing the quote at the start of the sentence to emphasize its importance.

Descriptors

A descriptor is used to identify a person's position in a story to give them relevance. This is done through a number of different attributes, such as their age or job. Newswriting style offers the person's name first, then the descriptor. The result looks like this:

- Bobby Houston, 41, says his food truck is the best in the business.
- Andi Rigos, an electrician, says the job should not take more than a day.
- Tommy Thompson, a Navy veteran, says he will run for City Council.

These are not written in conversational broadcast style, which puts the descriptor first before the name. That is because print writing is for the eye, not the ear. Newspapers and magazines put the name first, as it is the most important element of that person; the descriptors are secondary.

Objectivity and Subjectivity

Objectivity is the concept of presenting a story from a neutral point of view, without bias. The opposite idea is subjectivity, in which the reporter actively promotes one candidate, agenda, or social viewpoint over another. It is difficult for any reporter to be purely objective, as each person has their own individual background that can subtly appear in their writing.

The most neutral word that can be used at a press conference is the word "said", as in:

- The mayor said she would not raise taxes.

However, the tone and impact of that sentence can be altered dramatically if the writer merely changes the verb to one of the following:

- The mayor screamed she would not raise taxes.
- The mayor vowed she would not raise taxes.
- The mayor joked she would not raise taxes.

Simple changes in the verbs, adjectives, or adverbs can radically skew the neutrality of an article. Saying that someone "tersely" responded to an accusation is much different from "calmly" or "solemnly". All words should be checked to insure they do not convey an unintended feeling.

It is noteworthy that the use of the telegraph some 150 years ago contributed to news reporters writing more objectively. Since telegraph lines were "open", anyone on the line could intercept the transmissions. It became standard practice to lessen their individual biases and present the information clearly and objectively.

One area of the newspaper (or magazine) that expects no basis in objectivity is the editorial page. This space is reserved for opinions about current issues as viewed by the writing staff. These opinion pieces are usually written by an editor and may represent the views of the entire editorial staff. Rebuttals for these pieces are given by an opposing editor, an outside expert, or a reader in the community. These rebuttals appear as letters to the editor, which are printed as a direct contrast to the editorial.

In addition to the actual written story, there are other editorial elements that appear on newspaper and magazine pages. These are headlines, photos (or cuts), and cutlines.

Headlines

A headline appears at the top of the story and consists of just a few words. It should summarize the story, be straightforward, and prompt the reader to continue to read the article. It is important to write headlines with a sense of emotion to engage the reader. The following headline is flat, without any compelling information:

President Biden offers budget to Congress.

By targeting more specific elements that are within the story, the editor can come up with a stronger headline:

Biden's budget pushes green energy.

If the focus is the Congressional reaction to the budget, then that becomes the headline.

Republicans slam Biden's budget.

Even though it seems a difficult task to write a headline in just a few short words, some of the most powerful headlines were incredibly concise. "Dewey Defeats Truman" was the notoriously incorrect *Chicago Daily Tribune* headline that called the wrong election result in 1948; "Shuttle Explodes" topped the *Daily Record* after the 1986 Challenger disaster; and the *Los Angeles Times* simply headlined its front page with "Kobe Bryant dies in crash" after his tragic death in 2020. Editors generally write the headlines, but the reporter is often called upon to offer suggestions for the words that will introduce their story.

Cutlines

The cutline is an often overlooked yet essential part of scripting for printing media. This refers to the text that appears below a picture, describing what is happening in the image. A cutline is not a mere title or caption but conveys information about what the reader is looking at. Since the photo accompanies the story, the cutline's purpose is not to repeat what appears in the story itself. Instead, the cutline concentrates on only explaining what the readers is seeing in the photo.

Effective cutlines are written like miniature versions of the story, in that they contain the five Ws of relevant information. They may be longer than one sentence, but the first sentence should always be written in the present tense. Since the picture is showing the moment that news happened, the cutline should reflect that immediacy.

Let's use a standard photo of a local business opening its doors in a ribbon cutting ceremony. The photo shows Nick Rozier holding an oversized pair of scissors and snipping the ribbon to open Nick's Especial Taco and Burrito Barn in Wheatland, Missouri. The cutline reads:

> Nick Rozier opens his new restaurant, Nick's Especial Taco and Burrito Barn, in downtown Wheatland this morning.

Finally, the end of each cutline should identify the photographer with a photo credit. Newspapers are hesitant to use photos without crediting the photographer, as the editors want to make sure they have the legal right to publish the photo.

Advancing Stories

Stories are snapshots of events that have happened, but good writers always focus on what is next. If a bank robbery has been committed, has a suspect been arrested? If a snowstorm has knocked down the power lines, when are the utilities expected to be back online? If an aging company announced that it will close because of a bad economy, what will happen to the current employees?

Advancing stories allows the writer to push the narrative forward by identifying how the story will impact the audience. Readers will invariably wonder "how is the story going to affect me?". A gruesome murder in a neighborhood is bad enough, but the local readers want to know if the suspect is off the streets. Raising federal taxes by a few billion dollars is a stunning headline, yet the concern for the reader is how much will be coming out of her paycheck.

Extreme examples abound in the world of sports. When a team claims a national championship, it is unfair for a reporter to immediately ask the coach if the team will be able to do well next season. Sometimes a story is allowed to stand on its own and advancing it serves no immediate purpose. When a college player leads his team to victory, it is fine to let him enjoy the moment without hounding him if he is about to turn pro.

Newspaper Versus Magazine

Newspapers and magazines are both printed periodicals, but there are substantial differences between the two. Newspapers are geographically based, focusing on the news and events of just one city. The *Atlanta Journal-Constitution* covers Atlanta, the *Las Vegas Review-Journal* provides news about the Las Vegas area, and so forth. Newspapers are printed daily for their select market with very little distribution outside of their specialized area. The only exceptions are a handful of papers with a more national reach, such as *USA Today* or *The Wall Street Journal*. Newspapers are also meant to be read and discarded quickly because of their frequent publication.

Some magazines are geographically based, such as *Kansas City* or *The New Yorker*. But most magazines are created for certain demographics or psychographics. Demographic based magazines target those readers in certain age groups or genders; *AARP* (for seniors) and *Men's Journal* (for men) are two popular examples. Psychographics focus on interests and hobbies of a broader reading population that span generations and genders. Readers interested in sports will gravitate toward *Sports Illustrated*, video game enthusiasts will grab *Game Informer*, and so forth. Magazines may also be collected by a small percentage of readers.

The difference in audiences means the writing style varies greatly among newspapers and magazines. Newspapers ideally deliver the news in an objective manner without bias; some critics may argue that the press is skewed politically in one direction or another, but the ideal is that reporters and editors maintain neutrality in their stories. Magazines have full rein to advocate for specific points of view as they target readers with a similar mindset. Readers of *Modern Cat*, for example, will be cat enthusiasts who want definite "pro-cat" articles. *Model Railroader* will champion developments in the model train industry, *Bake From Scratch* will promote baking in home kitchens with wholesome ingredients, and so forth. This subjective reporting is welcomed in magazines, as it reinforces the reading audience's mindset and keep them subscribing to future editions.

Looking Forward

The scripting formats for periodicals are not expected to change dramatically in the coming years. The basic concept of putting the most important information in the lead sentence will be reinforced as readers have more options in more digital formats. Simply put, the accelerated delivery of news through new sources will allow readers to pick and choose which stories they want to read. Shorter stories, punchier headlines, and tighter leads will become the norm.

Formatting within the printed newspapers and magazines will evolve as well. A number of publications have closed shop in the past 20 years due to declining readership. Periodicals are already shedding pages and scaling back on their publication frequency. No matter what changes are made, the tenet of putting advertisements first, then filling the news hole with copy, will continue as long as the newspapers and magazines are published.

Exercises

1. Purchase your local newspaper (not the online edition, but the physically printed version). Using a ruler, measure the column inches of the news copy versus the advertising copy in the front section of the newspaper. How do those numbers compare to one another?
2. Using the same newspaper, read each story from the front page. These tend to be harder news stories rather than features, so they are more likely to follow the inverted paragraph form of writing. In how many of those stories can you determine the who, what, where, when, why, and how of the story in the opening paragraph?
3. Search online to find the magazines that enjoy the greatest number of subscribers (one such list is at www.magazineline.com/blog/most-popular-magazines-in-the-us). How many magazines on that list have you heard about? How many have you physically seen?
4. Track a national political story in two different magazines or newspapers (these can be online or physical copies). Examine the word choices used in each story. Can you determine the editorial bias of the article by the words that were used by the writer?

5. Name as many members of your family, including yourself, that still subscribe to a daily newspaper. Then name how many people in your family subscribe to a magazine.

Chapter Essentials

- The editorial staff assigns each story to a number of column inches, which is the space that story will occupy in the news hole.
- The inverted paragraph system of writing places the most important elements of the story in the lead paragraphs. These elements are who, what, where, when, why, and how.
- Style concerns include leads, writing in the active voice, using delayed attribution, writing with the correct descriptors, and checking wording for neutrality.
- Attribution is when the writer tells the reader the source of the information.
- The four main types of lead are hard, soft, question, and trivia leads.
- A descriptor describes an attribute of someone in the story and is written after the person's name.
- Neutral words do not convey unwanted emotion in a sentence's phrasing.
- A cutline is the text that appears below a picture, describing what is happening in the image.
- Advancing the story means informing the reader what will happen next that might impact the story's people and the reader's situation in the future.

Online Links

Asme.media. This professional website spotlights the work of the American Society of Magazine Editors. ASME features contests, a job board, and editorial guidelines for editors and publishers, thus framing what writers should know when preparing copy.

Columnists.com. This website for the National Society of Newspaper Columnists provides links for columnists and bloggers. It also features contests and conference information.

Newspapers.com. The largest online newspaper archive contains access to more than 22,000 newspapers in a searchable format. Ideal for researchers, this site also allows users to track the evolution of newspapers since the 1700s.

4 Graphic Novels

Key Words

Back-and-Forth
Caption
Gutter
Off-Panel

Panel
River
Speech Balloon
Thought Bubble

Historical Overview

Graphic novels and comic books are terms that are often used interchangeably, although they are not the same. The primary difference is that a graphic novel is a complete book that contains a beginning, a middle, and an end. These works can span hundreds of pages and merge multiple storylines into one cohesive story. They are bound like traditional books and can stand vertically on a bookshelf. *From Hell*, *Watchmen*, and *Alice in Sunderland* are three examples of graphic novels that tell complete, epic stories. *Maus* is the most famous graphic novel of all time, becoming the first and so far only graphic novel to win a Pulitzer Prize in 1992.

Graphic novels can be either nonfiction (biography, history, true crime, for example) or fiction (like adventure, science fiction, or superhero). The target audience of graphic novels is also divided into middle grade (ages 8 to 12), young adult (ages 12 to 18) and adult (over 18). There are also subsets based on where the work originated, like manga from Japan or manhwa from South Korea.

Comic books are more familiar, with DC and Marvel superheroes having migrated from the printed page to feature film success. Superman, Batman, Avengers, Fantastic Four, and a host of others demonstrate the success that a comic book can provide. Their stories are ongoing, with each comic book story building on the previous edition. A good parallel is the ongoing series from Marvel Studios, where early films about Iron Man and Captain America lead to later stories with the Avengers joining forces.

Newspapers added comic strips to their printed editions more than a century ago. These early comic strips were then assembled, reprinted, and issued in a magazine format to create the first comic books. The earliest comic book, *The Yellow Kid in McFadden's Flats*, debuted in 1897. Other forerunners included *Buster Brown*, *The Katzenjammer Kids*, and *Mutt & Jeff*. The earliest monthly comic book, *Comics Monthly*, debuted in 1922.

Superman debuted in *Action Comics No. 1* in 1938. Not only did it prove to be immediately popular, but if a mint condition edition surfaced today, it would be worth nearly $10 million. Batman followed less than a year later with other superheroes, like Captain Marvel, Flash, and Green Lantern quickly following suit. The period from 1938 through the mid-1940s was the peak of comic book readership, with some comics selling 1.5 million copies every month. Each of these comic books followed the same formula; tell stories in a magazine format that are released as individual issues, thus creating a demand among readers for the next edition.

Graphic novels emerged decades after comic books, but which graphic novel is the "first" of its kind is still debated. 1976's *Bloodstar* and 1978's *A Contract with God* were early works that branded themselves as graphic novels, while other works about Doctor Strange (1965–1966) and Black Panther (1973–1975) may also be considered for the distinction. Some even argue the very first graphic novel was the 1837 publication *The Adventures of Mr. Obadiah Oldbuck*, which came out decades before the first comic book.

For simplicity, we will use the term "graphic novel" to refer to scripting techniques for both graphic novels and comic books throughout this chapter. While their distribution patterns and narrative story arcs differ, the technical elements of formatting both graphic novels and comic strips are similar. It is worth noting that writers in these media frequently use their own unique systems to write their stories. However, the formatting here can be used to create submissions that are recognizable to agents and publishers in the industry.

Technical Specifications

Before we delve into comic books and graphic novels, a quick overview of comic strips is necessary. After all, the first comic books were just collections of reprinted comic strips that originally appeared in newspapers. Comic strips use the same terminology of comic books and graphic novels although the size limitations are much more restrictive. They also appear in daily newspapers, so while comic strips are much shorter, they must be created much more frequently.

Comic strips are typically three panels (or boxes) that tell a quick joke with a beginning in the first panel, the middle in the second panel, and the punchline in the third panel. This three-act structure evolved from theater as a way to set up a story, develop it, then have it come to a resolution. *Calvin and Hobbes*, *Peanuts*, *Garfield*, and *Dilbert* are examples of popular, long-running comic strips that relied heavily on three panels. Sunday comic strips can provide more panels and the opportunity to tell more in-depth stories, but the weekday and Saturday strips are consistently offered in the three panels format.

The other option is the single panel strip. This one box limits the story even further, but talented writers like Gary Larson of *The Far Side* or Bil Keane with *The Family Circus* show that a good joke can be delivered succinctly. The highbrow publication *The New Yorker* prints a timely single panel comic with each edition, but the writer and style of that single panel strip changes each time; *The New Yorker* simply chooses the best panel for that issue regardless of who created it.

Comic strips were the forerunners of the modern comic book and graphic novel. While the strips are just one or three panels, the longer formats expanded storytelling to sagas that ran for hundreds of pages. Still, writing a comic strip or graphic novel means concentrating on one page at a time. Each page of a graphic novel contains individual *panels*; think of these as frozen images on a television screen. The clear spaces between the panels are *gutters*; these provide frames for the individual panels and separate them from each other.

Each panel will contain a different visual element and look like a photograph. A vista of an exploding volcano, a detailed close up of a finger squeezing a trigger on a plasma gun, or an image of a victorious hero on a grim battlefield are just examples of visuals that may fill an individual panel. This imagery can be stark black and white imagery, like Frank Miller's classic *Sin City* work. The other extreme is a highly detailed, full-color image as found in countless Marvel and DC works. Most graphic novels are issued in full color, but the color palates can range from bright neon colors to subdued watercolors.

The size of the panel can also vary and should be noted by the writer. The largest panel is a double-page splash which covers two full pages. Other panel sizes include wide, tall, and small sizes, each of which is used deliberately to tell the story. If there are panels that contain spectacular action sequences, you will probably only get three or four panels per page.

Traditional reading in the English language means we start from the top left of the page and move to the bottom right; thus, the panels are laid out in a logical flow (sometimes called a river) for the eye to follow the storyline. Even the width of the gutters between the panels are meticulously laid out for the reader to better follow along. Working closely with the artist to make sure the script works with the images is understandably critical; there can never be a question of which panel should be read next in the river.

Graphic novels use images to tell most of the story, not the words. Still, words are used to move the plot along. These words can be what the characters are saying to one another, what they are thinking to themselves, or what the narrator is describing to the readers. Panels are limited in space; thus, brevity is vital when writing for graphic novels. Every word must count, since too many words can bury the artwork. If you are writing a few dozen words per panel, you need to scale down the word count and let the images tell the story. The text should be concise, compelling, and complement the artwork.

Although there is no standard formatting for graphic novels, there are two formats that have emerged as industry standards for dialogue: single column and double column. Dark Horse Comics requires single column format, which we will show below. Toward the end of this chapter, we will show the double column variation. This has been popularized by comic book writer Fred Van Lente and is used by a number of sites, including Jericho Writers. Again, graphic novelists are free to use either style or develop one of their choosing; as long as it is clear for the creative team and the publishing house, broad latitude is granted in this field.

This is also a good time to note that not all panels will have words, as many of them will rely solely on the visuals to advance the story. When you have such a panel, just write the words "No Copy" in all caps under the panel description, like this:

NO COPY

When words are used, they can be shown in one of three ways: captions, speech balloons, or thought bubbles. Again, English readers will follow the content from the top left to the bottom right, so any words must be laid out carefully. We will use a simple panel featuring our hero SteveRabbit to illustrate the difference among these three options. Visualize SteveRabbit (he's basically a large rabbit) in a backyard setting. The text is one simple sentence:

A storm is coming.

Captions come from a voice outside of the panel, like an omniscient narrator or as a voice-over from the character. They provide commentary and help move the action along. To format a caption, you type the word CAP, followed by a colon, on the left side of the page. You then write the captioned words as a sentence directly underneath that heading. The end result is this:

CAP:

A storm is coming.

Speech balloons are drawn within the panel and contain the words spoken by the character. If a character's dialogue exceeds one sentence, then they can have more than one balloon trailing one after the other. Of course, the layout here is still important so the reader will follow the dialogue from one bubble to the next without skipping to the wrong bubble.

Even the outlines of these simple bubbles can convey the emotions of the words. A jagged speech balloon shows that the speaker is under stress or that the voice is coming from a computer or over a telephone. A square speech balloon is more robotic, versus a softer tone depicted from a round balloon. To format a speech balloon in the single column format, write the character's name in all caps, left justified, and followed by a colon, like this:

STEVERABBIT:

Write the dialogue underneath the character's name without quotation marks. These are the words that will appear in the character's speech balloon. If SteveRabbit has a comment about a storm coming, it should be written as follows:

STEVERABBIT:

A storm is coming.

A thought bubble reveals the inner thoughts of the character. These are also like a voice-over in film, but instead of providing information for the entirety of the panel, they are limited to only what one person is thinking. Like the outline of the speech balloon, changing the shape of the thought bubble can also convey an emotion; a jagged thought bubble represents pain, anger, or another heightened emotion. Let's say SteveRabbit is merely thinking a storm is coming and doesn't say the words aloud. A thought bubble is appropriate, and scripting is a simple matter. Just insert the word (thought) after his character name, like this:

STEVERABBIT (thought):

A storm is coming.

Regardless of where the words appear, the format of the text can easily change the meaning of a sentence. Let's take a basic sentence to be uttered by our graphic novel hero SteveRabbit. The only change we will make is shifting the boldface type of a different word in the sentence. The scene has SteveRabbit talking to his colleague SquirrelJenny. They are talking about their archenemy JayBirdBeast when SteveRabbit says:

JayBirdBeast took every drop of bird food that we had for the baby birds.
JayBirdBeast took **every drop** of bird food that we had for the baby birds.
JayBirdBeast took every drop of bird food that we had for the **baby birds**.

Another option is to underline the words instead of putting them in bold text; this is a matter of personal preference, but the outcome is the same.

JayBirdBeast took every drop of bird food that we had for the <u>baby birds.</u>

Either way, it shifts the emphasis of the sentence. Tricks like making a speech bubble jagged, putting a few words in bold type, and using the right words are important to scripting a graphic novel. Since the room for the written words is so limited, any formatting shortcuts that convey emotion without taking up space are professional traits when developing individual panels.

For our example, we will create a scene with SteveRabbit and SquirrelJenny. These two crimefighters are challenged by the nefarious JayBirdBeast, an oversized Blue Jay that is terrorizing the backyard birdfeeder. We will create a page of four panels that introduce the characters and the plot. The top left corner of the page will indicate the number of panels on that page. This is done by writing the page number in all caps, underlined on the left side, such as:

<u>PAGE ONE</u> (four panels)

This indicates that four different panels appear on the first page. Each panel is then numbered and typed in regular upper and lower case. After the panel is numbered, we start a new line and type in the action lines. Each panel is limited by physical space, so a choice must be made between having a great deal of action or a lot of dialogue. Action is depicted by the art in the panel, so any dialogue would lay over that and obscure it. For the first panel, we will concentrate on action and no dialogue, like this:

Panel 1.
Backyard. SteveRabbit crouches under a tree, peers through binoculars. The reflection in the lens shows a distorted JayBirdBeast rifling through the now-empty birdfeeder. A sneer is on SteveRabbit's lips. An open compass is to his side.
NO COPY

For the next panel, we will add dialogue. Note that character names are in all capital letters, flush left, and followed by a colon. The dialogue is then written in the line immediately following the character name. The reason the dialogue is placed beneath the character's name (and not on the same line) is because it is easier to copy and paste the dialogue onto the graphic novel page if it's on a line by itself.

Some characters' voices may be "heard" before the character appears in a panel. In movies, this is called off-screen. In graphic novels, this is off-panel, as the action is literally limited to one panel at a time. To illustrate this, let's have SquirrelJenny's voice speak off the panel to SteveRabbit:

Panel 2.
SteveRabbit still holds the binoculars but his gaze is now on the compass. The compass arrow points to the north. He seems to be thinking.
SQUIRRELJENNY (OP):
Mapping out an attack?

That dialogue shows that we hear SquirrelJenny but we don't see her yet. The precise layout of the panel will be done by the artist, but if something specific is desired in a panel, it should be written in the description. In the above panel, SquirrelJenny's voice will appear as a dialogue box over the action. If you want it coming from a particular direction, specify that. Otherwise, the artist will insert the words over the images to the best of their ability.

For the third panel, SteveRabbit will speak and we will add a new dialogue element. He is whispering back to SquirrelJenny, so the lettering within his dialogue box will reflect that. Other standard options for modifying speech balloons are (small), (burst), and (weak).

Panel 3.
Close on SteveRabbit's face with a furrowed brow and an angry expression. He glares at SquirrelJenny.
STEVERABBIT (whispers):
Quiet, you fool! JayBirdBeast has emptied the birdfeeder! If he breaks it . . .

For the fourth panel, let's shift our attention to JayBirdBeast and yes, he will break the empty birdfeeder. We will introduce the sound effects in this panel, which are abbreviated as SFX. Like CAP (for caption) or character names, the SFX is left-justified and followed by a colon. They can also be in all capital letters if the action calls for it. If JayBirdBeast causes a birdfeeder to crash to the ground, it is scripted like this:

Panel 4.
JayBirdBeast raises his wings in triumph as the empty birdfeeder shatters on the ground below.
SFX:
CRASH!

These four panels comprise everything that is on page one and provide an overview of how basic formatting is established. But let's add some more advanced elements to the narrative. This includes back-and-forth dialogue sequences, pauses, and the double column format.

Back-and-Forth Dialogue

Two characters are needed to form a back-and-forth dialogue panel. More can be added, but for simplicity, we will just use two characters. Back-and-forth dialogue happens when the first character makes a comment, the second character responds, and then the first character says a counter-response. The number of words in this panel will infringe on the background art, so the comments should be short and to the point.

42   Graphic Novels

Special formatting helps with such dialogue. To make the interplay work between the two characters, we will use a set of double dashes, which look like " – –". This double dash indicates that dialogue will carry over from one balloon to another or from one panel to another. For our characters SteveRabbit and SquirrelJenny, the dialogue would look something like this:

STEVERABBIT:
The bird feeder is only the beginning. I think – –
SQUIRRELJENNY:
– – that JayBirdBeast is making another stop – –
STEVERABBIT:
– – right at the birdbath!

The double dashes also depict when a character breaks off in their dialogue, like when an action interrupts them. Imagine that SteveRabbit is pondering JayBirdBeast's next move. In the middle of his line, a SFX stops his train of thought, like this:

STEVERABBIT:
JayBirdBeast doesn't know how to shut the back door. Unless – –
SFX:
SLAM!

Interestingly, the double dash is the standard for such interplay or when a character trails off. The long dash and the semicolon aren't used in graphic novel formatting.

Pauses

Superheroes tend to talk to themselves a lot. These monologues move the story forward and provide an insight into what the character is thinking. But sometimes the hero will trail off, as if they have just figured something out. This is different from the double dash, which shows that their dialogue is interrupted. Instead, when SteveRabbit is lost in thought and trails off, the ellipsis of three periods is used, like this:

STEVERABBIT:
JayBirdBeast may not like sunflower seeds now, but if I mix them with nuts . . .

The other use for an ellipsis is when the character makes a dramatic pause within a sentence, such as:

STEVERABBIT:
Maybe the birdbath is his next target . . . or he's going to just fly the coop.

All of the above examples illustrate how to use a single column format. A double column format is also acceptable, as long as the writer chooses one format and stays with it consistently through the work.

Double Column Format

For the double column format, the character's name is in ALL CAPS. The difference is that the names are numbered, like this:

1. STEVERABBIT:
2. SQUIRRELJENNY:

The dialogue is placed in a second column that aligns with the character names. To have another scene using these characters, it would look like this:

1. STEVERABBIT: JayBirdBeast hates that gnome statue!
2. SQUIRRELJENNY: Oh no! He has a rock!
3. SFX: CRASH!

The other parts of the graphic novel, like the scene descriptions, are still written in standard paragraph form. It is only the characters and the dialogue that are formatted into double columns.

Final Page Count

Once you outline the story and start work on a graphic novel, the question becomes how many pages you should create for a complete work. If you assume four panels per page and 100 pages in your graphic novel, you are responsible for 400 separate panels.

Comic books are pages that are stapled in the center fold, so multiples of four are the best rule of thumb for a page count. Imagine a standard piece of paper. Lay it horizontally, then fold it in half, like a book. You will have four "pages" from that single piece of paper. Adding another sheet gives you an additional four pages, another sheet is four more pages, and so on. 32 pages is a common final page count for a comic strip (eight sheets times four yields 32 pages). A comic will have an introductory page of acknowledgements, plus there are pages of advertisements, so the actual story will span 20 to 30 pages.

Graphic novels have a higher page count and are bound like books. There is no set minimum or maximum number of pages, but 80 pages of story will allow the book to easily stand up on a bookshelf, plus it is thick enough to print a title on the spine. A page count of 120 or more will allow more vibrant artwork and graphics on the spine. But if a graphic novel is too thick, it is harder to hold, much like a 600-page hardback book. If the story warrants a few hundred pages, that's fine. Once you approach the 500-page mark, it may be time to consider breaking the story into two parts.

Looking Forward

The broad market of superhero films, television shows, and lines of merchandise indicates that the characters created in graphic novels and comic books are immensely profitable. The scripting formats used for these stories have some latitude depending on the writers and artists. The template of breaking the pages into individual panels and using a blend of strong imagery and supporting text is universal to everyone creating this type of media.

Expect slightly more codified outlines in the coming years as scripting platforms embrace graphic novels as a unique style. Final Draft, the de facto leader in scripting software, now offers graphic novels as a template for easier formatting. As more writers begin to use such a standardized template, graphic novels will gain even more popularity among creative individuals. There will always be room for experimentation in writing this format, but professional guidelines will help beginning writers make their way into this industry.

Exercises

1. Name as many current movies and television shows that you can that are based off graphic novels and comic books. How many of these movies have you seen? Which ones did you like the best and the least?
2. Outline a four-panel sequence of a new graphic novel. The characters should be any pets that you've ever had (if you haven't owned a pet, feel free to use anyone else's pet that you've met in the past). The scene is that two pets are hungry at night and manage to find a dozen donuts on the kitchen counter. They can either successfully retrieve the donuts or fail in their attempts. Without drawing any of the action, briefly describe what happens in the four panels and what dialogue you would use.
3. Read a comic book or graphic novel. Identify the panels, gutters, and different word boxes that are present. How do these elements work together to tell a story?
4. Find the comic strips in your local newspaper. How many strips are one panel versus three panel? Do you think the one panel strips are as effective in delivering the joke as their three panel counterparts? If you were a comic strip writer, in which format would you prefer to work?
5. Take a field trip to a local comic books store. Compare how many of the titles are familiar to you against the number that are completely new to you. Explain what titles (if any) pique your interest.

Chapter Essentials

- Early comic strips were reprinted and collated into the first comic books.
- Graphic novels and comic books differ due to the stories in each issue. A graphic novel is longer and contains an entire story while each comic book is part of a longer ongoing story.
- Formatting for graphic novels and comic books is similar. Both rely on a blend of the written word and strong artistry to tell their stories.
- Each frame of artwork is contained within a panel. These panels are separated on each page by gutters. The panels can be different sizes and the gutters can be different widths.
- Text is conveyed through one of three ways: captions, speech balloons, and thought bubbles. Placing the words in irregular type, like bold to represent emphasis or small to show someone whispering, helps convey emotion.

- Characters and their dialogue may be written as either single column or double column. This choice is at the discretion of the writer.
- Back-and-forth dialogue, double dashes, and ellipses are all specific formatting tricks used by graphic novelists.

Online Links

Comicbook.com. A comprehensive website that covers news in Franchises, Movies, TV, Comics, Gaming, Anime, Podcasts, and Video. For those interested in the different avenues where scripting for comic books can lead, this site offers a wealth of ideas.

Comichron.com. The greatest attribute of this website is the financial numbers it provides for comic books and graphic novels. This large database of sales figures shows the potential for new writers to enter this field.

DC.com and Marvel.com. These two websites are the official homes of DC and Marvel Comics, respectively. News about comic books and their characters, plus the related movies, video games, and television shows are all accessible in these two sites.

5 Advertising

Key Words

AIDA
Call to Action (CTA)
Column Inches
Closings

Demographics
Psychographics
Tagline

Historical Overview

Advertisers have always faced unique stress due to the very nature of their profession. The advertiser's job is to persuade someone they have never met to take an action they didn't expect to take. Moreover, most of these actions require people to spend money to purchase a product. This is like walking up to a stranger, telling that person about a product they didn't know about a moment before, and convincing that person to then give up their money to purchase it. It's a difficult challenge, yet advertisers pull it off every day in print, audio, visual, and digital ads.

Advertising is thousands of years old and has evolved depending on the technology being used to spread the message. Carved signs and flags in front of stores were the first true advertisements, but the first written ad was created on papyrus in 3,000 BC in Thebes, Egypt; it was written by a slaveholder looking for a runaway slave while it also promoted the slaveholder's weaving store.

Ads evolved slowly over the next few thousand years. It wasn't until the first newspaper ad appeared in 1704 that advertising took a leap forward from storefront messages. A humble real estate ad in the *Boston News-Letter* marked the first true newspaper ad. Since that time, newspaper ads have become standardized with their dimensions and verbiage. Print ads have also taken hold in magazines with full-page glossy color and even fold-out ads that span multiple pages.

Fast forward to the early 1900s when radio was attracting audiences and we find the first radio advertisement. The first paid radio ad appeared on WEAF in New York in 1922. Direct selling over the air was prohibited at the time, so Hawthorne Court Apartments simply paid $50 for a ten-minute broadcast about the happy life of living in the suburbs of Queens. Such long ads are unheard of today since most radio spots are 30 seconds long; some very short ads have run times of just five to ten seconds each.

Less than 20 years later, the first television commercial aired in 1941. This ten-second spot for Bulova Watches aired on New York station WNBT during a baseball game between the Brooklyn Dodgers and the Philadelphia Phillies. The black and white ad shows a watch face over an image of the United States; the audio is an off-screen announcer saying "America runs on Bulova time." TV ads are now awash in graphics, ongoing characters (Flo from Progressive Insurance or Lily from AT&T), music beds, sound effects, and a host of camera moves. Putting the company's website at the end of the spot is also common. Most of these ads are 30 seconds long, although they may run 60 seconds or longer for special events like presidential elections. Some ads are just a brief ten seconds and are dropped in during fast-paced events like football games.

The similarity among many advertisements is that they end with a *call to action*, or CTA. This is the hook for the advertiser to get the consumer to behave a certain way. It can be as simple as the words "Buy Now" on a digital computer ad. However, not all CTAs focus on money. A political ad aims to steer the consumer to vote a certain way while a non-profit ad will spur people to donate blood or give money to a charitable cause.

Finally, another purpose for ads is to retain awareness for popular brands. The Ford Motor Company, Pepsi Cola, and Nike Shoes have each attained a position in consumer consciousness that they could halt advertising and people would still know they exist. But ongoing ads reinforce their brands so consumers keep their products in mind. No one needs to be reminded that Toyota makes cars or Coca-Cola makes soft drinks, but ongoing advertising reinforces their products for consumers.

Technical Specifications

Finding the right audience is always the first task that faces any advertiser. This is done through targeting a specific buying group with the use of demographics and psychographics. These factors must be evaluated before the ad copy is written; putting an ad for snowshoes on a television station that only airs in the Sahara Desert is a colossal waste of money and effort. The key to good advertising is getting past such obvious examples and hitting specific target audiences.

Demographics look at potential buyers through factors like age, income, gender, and marital status. Airing an ad for Harley Davidson motorcycles during a commercial break during *SpongeBob SquarePants* is pointless, since the viewers of that cartoon are far too young to hop on a motorcycle. Demographics divide the audience into broad categories that advertisers can target with a well-placed ad. These categories are sometimes blended, so an advertiser will seek a male, 50+, college educated earning a base salary of more than $50,000. This audience will likely see ads for an expensive car. The other extreme would be a younger audience between the ages of 18 and 25 with little disposable income; this audience is perfect for a commercial touting a cheap fast-food meal.

Demographics divide people into categories of largely physical characteristics. More advanced audience segregation is in the form of psychographics which target attitudes, opinions, and interests of a certain population. For example, a printed ad in a hunting magazine might offer a new kind of camouflage. The interest in hunting already led the reader to that periodical, so it makes sense that they would be receptive to hearing more about an accessory for their hobby. This attitude is regardless of their gender or age group. Other examples are energy drinks airing during basketball games, golf clubs advertising during golf tournaments, and ads for kitchen appliances airing during a cooking show. The common thread among the audience members is not their age or gender, but their interest in that hobby.

Knowing your audience allows you to create an ad that will target them effectively. There is a consistent workflow to designing a successful ad campaign regardless of how it will be delivered. We will first look at how the workflow applies to create any advertisement. After that, we will specifically focus on how to market a new cola in the print media, in a radio ad, in a television spot, and as an Internet banner ad. The product, Slurp Cola, will be consistent across all the media outlets. The workflow before designing any successful ad campaign is as follows:

- Identify client needs
- Research your product
- Target your audience

For this chapter, we will advertise a new cola called Slurp. It has triple the caffeine of a regular soda and comes in a unique guava flavor. Based in Miami with a strong following in south Florida, it is popular among beverage drinkers in their teens and 20s. Several athletes have commented on how the extra caffeine helps them in game situations, while a handful of singers praise Slurp for helping them hit their high notes on stage. There is no scientific evidence that Slurp actually makes singers or athletes perform better, but there are celebrities who will happily endorse the drink. Finally, the client wants the tagline at the end of each ad to be "Go Slurp!".

Let's put this product information into the workflow.

- Identify client needs – The client wants to expand their marketing base beyond Miami and south Florida.
- Research your product – Slurp has several attributes that can be used in advertisements. It is high caffeine, a guava flavor, and has several celebrities who would like to endorse it.
- Target your audience – The target audience for Slurp is a younger crowd in their teens and 20s.

The workflow helps you define what your client wants, what your product offers, and who makes up your target audience. These are all vital pieces of information to help you shape your advertisement. Now that we understand the product's unique characteristics, what the client wants, and who the audience is, we can build the advertisement.

The ad industry relies on a simple four-step process in crafting commercials. This process, known as AIDA, means Attention, Interest, Desire, and Action. This process applies whether the ad is read in the newspapers, heard on the radio, seen on the TV, or found on an Internet page. The AIDA rules mean the following should happen:

- Attention. The ad must stand out from the rest of the commercials to get the attention of the potential customer.
- Interest. The ad must now engage the customer to the point that they are keenly interested in the product.

- Desire. This step is tricky, as the ad must make the potential customer decide to make the purchase. They know of the product, now they must have it.
- Action. The customer is motivated to buy the product.

AIDA is a cornerstone of a successful campaign, as the process addresses the essence of advertising. It is not easy to ask someone to suddenly part with their money for a product or service. Following the AIDA steps is a proven formula. Of course, it all starts with the writing.

Writing Tips

We will assume that basics, such as spelling and punctuation, will be perfect from the onset. A misspelled word in a multimillion-dollar ad campaign is unforgivable, especially when spellcheck is readily available on word processing programs. Besides that, some writing techniques are consistent regardless of the media platform. These include:

Conversational language. An advertisement is not a grandiose master's thesis in which you pull out the thesaurus and unleash obscure words with complicated sentence structure. An ad aimed at teens will use different terms than one aimed at senior citizens; it is important to match your ad's language with your target audience.

Action verbs. Words are precious in limited column inches or a finite number of seconds in television or radio. Not only should every word count, but they should be dynamic and compelling enough to motivate the potential buyer.

Talk to "you". Your ad is aimed at people who are bombarded with countless ads daily, so speaking to them as an individual is an immediate way to make a connection.

Offer solutions with your product or service. The goal of your ad is to convince the buyer that your product will solve their problem. Bad phone? Buy this one. Hungry for lunch? Eat at this restaurant. Your solution should directly lead the customer back to you.

Give the next step, where to go, how to reach you. The final step is the call to action that shows the audience how to find you. This is done by posting website addresses, phone numbers, or any other way that allows the potential buyer to connect to you.

Formatting for Print

Several factors limit print ads. The first is the physical space, or column inches, that are allocated to the ad. Smaller ads obviously will not offer the flexibility to pack in extra words and illustrations, so brevity is key. The second limitation is that the messages are constrained to what can be on the printed page. There are no audio cues, nor are there any moving visual images to capture the viewers' attention. Each written ad demands that the reader focus their attention exclusively on the ad itself. Capturing the reader's attention requires skillful ad copy. Although your ad may be a small two inch by two inch square in the bottom corner of a newspaper, it still must convey enough information to motivate a reader to pay for the product.

Let's develop a written ad using Slurp Cola as our example. Since it is targeted to a younger audience, it will likely appear in a full-color ad with illustrations and graphics.

50   *Advertising*

To get the readers' attention, we will hire a popular Miami hip hop singer, Janine Nouget, as the spokesperson. The ad will feature a single frame picture of Janine holding a Slurp Cola while she smiles at the camera. The tagline, "Go Slurp!", will appear in bold letters across the bottom of the image. This alone is enough to create a simple version of the ad. The product is shown with a celebrity that appeals to the target audience, the tagline is prominently displayed, and the ad will be placed in periodicals, like *Cosmopolitan* and *Sports Illustrated,* that are read by that demographic.

Of course, the ad can be tweaked to go beyond the basic visual of Janine holding the product. The picture itself can be changed so she holds a microphone in one hand and a can of Slurp in the other. Or she can hold the can on stage in front of a crowd of adoring fans. Even her caption can be improved, where the words say "Want to hit the high notes like I do?". Below that, in larger type is the tagline "Go Slurp!".

Once the ad is approved by the client, it is sent to the targeted periodicals and printed in the next issue. That ad may be the start of a series featuring similar celebrities or it could be the first of many Janine Nougat ads. Tying a celebrity to a product is nothing new; Shaquille O'Neal has appeared in many different ads for Papa John's, just as Patrick Mahomes shows up repeatedly in commercials for State Farm Insurance. If the celebrity endorser brings awareness and sales to a product, a long-term relationship is good for the brand and profitable for the celebrity.

Formatting for Radio

Radio ads last only 30 seconds, so capturing the audience's attention, making them aware of the product, and motivating them to purchase it must be accomplished quickly. Adding to the challenge is that many listeners are driving in their cars, so the ad must be delivered while the potential client is navigating a two-thousand-pound vehicle in traffic. Skillfully blending voices, sound effects, and music beds into an effective ad can be mastered by following industry scripting techniques.

A typical radio ad will have a printed one-sheet, which is the basic script that can be read, reviewed, and edited. As noted in Chapter 6 (Radio), the spots are written in a simple format. Sound effects (abbreviated as SFX), music, character names, and the narrator are in all-caps, left justified. The script will have the basic information in the top left corner, which looks like this:

Product:	Slurp Cola
Client:	Slurp Beverage Products
Ad Title:	Miami Heat Wave
Writer:	C. Frazier
Length:	30 seconds

After that, the commercial is written in the body of the page. Like the print ad, we will use popular hip hop singer Janine Nouget as the spokesperson. A sample radio ad could be:

SFX:	A LARGE AUDIENCE CHEERS WILDLY.
NOUGET:	You hear that? That's my crowd waiting for me. And they all want to hear me sing.
MANAGER:	Ready when you are, Janine.
NOUGET:	But my show doesn't start without one more taste of Slurp. That extra caffeine gives me the push I need. The unique guava flavor goes down easy. And Slurp helps me hit the high notes night after night.
SFX:	THE AUDIENCE STARTS TO CHANT HER NAME.
NOUGET:	Looks like they're ready for me. And you know what?
SFX:	JANINE TAKES A SWIG OF SLURP.
NOUGET:	Ahhh. Now I'm ready for them. So be like me, Janine Nouget. Find Slurp at your nearest store. And do what I do! Go Slurp!
SFX:	THE AUDIENCE BURSTS INTO APPLAUSE.

Like the printed ad, the radio commercial will quickly find its way to the right demographic audience. Janine is a hip hop singer, the target audience listens to hip hop music, so the obvious radio station choice will be those that play hip hop. This ad will likely miss audiences on a country music station because listeners won't connect with the celebrity. Instead, you would use Carrie Underwood there. A radio ad is only as effective as the audience to which it is targeted.

Formatting for Television

For our television ads, we will focus on the popular 30-second format, since there are very few ads that deviate from this standard length. Ads for candidates during an election season may span several minutes, while shorter 15-second spots are appearing more frequently during sports events. The standard 30-second spot is still the norm in the advertising industry.

We will again rely on Slurp Cola, use hip hop singer Janine Nouget as a spokesperson, and will use a split-column format. This two-column format conveys the video in the left column and the audio in the right column. The video column shows the visual imagery, including the graphics, setting, and action. The audio column includes all voices done by the actors, narration, sound effects, and music. A typical television ad will have a printed one-sheet, which is the basic script that can be read, reviewed, and edited. We will use the same language as the radio ad for simplicity. The format for these scripts follows these industry standards:

Product:	Slurp Cola
Client:	Slurp Beverage Products
Ad Title:	Miami Heat Wave
Writer:	C. Frazier
Length:	30 seconds

Video	Audio
Exterior – Night shot of concert venue	SFX – Offstage crowd cheering
Dissolve to Interior – Janine in a backstage dressing room	Janine – You hear that? That's my crowd waiting for me. And they all want to hear me sing.
The Manager quickly ducks in	Manager – Ready when you are, Janine.
The Manager exits. Janine grabs a Slurp.	Janine – But my show doesn't start without one more taste of Slurp. That extra caffeine gives me the push I need. The unique guava flavor goes down easy. And Slurp helps me hit the high notes night after night.
Janine holds Slurp to camera	SFX – Offstage crowd chants her name
Janine smiles	Janine – Looks like they're ready for me. And you know what?
Janine takes a drink, then holds Slurp to camera	Janine – Ahhh. Now I'm ready for them. So be like me, Janine Nouget. Find Slurp at your nearest store. And do what I do! Go Slurp!
Janine winks at camera. Graphic: GO SLURP!	SFX – Offstage crowd roars

Formatting for Digital

Twenty-five years ago, ads for digital didn't exist because the online websites were still being developed. The technology has matured quickly, with a variety of ads that can be quickly tailored for any audience and budget. Where the ad is placed on the computer screen helps determine what can be placed in the ad. The options are:

- **Banner ads.** These ads are horizontal and can appear on either the top or the bottom of a webpage.
- **Sidebar ads.** These vertical ads are placed on the sides of the page, so the wording tends to be choppier with shorter words and sentences. A skyscraper ad is tall and narrow with the ability to run up the entire side of the webpage. A block ad is more of a square shape, akin to what you might find as a newspaper ad.
- **Popup ads.** These can be any size, from a small box to an ad that covers the entire page. These have fallen out of favor because they randomly appear and frustrate computer users. After all, who wants to be associated with an advertisement that suddenly appears and takes up the entire screen?

Building digital ads requires maintaining a hierarchy among the components within the ad. The company logo should be included to maintain brand awareness, the value proposition (like "limited time offer" or "50% off") should be dominant and attract the customer's eye, and there should be a call to action readily available. This CTA should be a clickable button with text like "learn more" or "watch now".

Digital ads must be clear, concise, and convey a message quickly. Most users try to avoid ads on their computer screens, so there is an inherent bias working against the advertiser. The good news is that digital ads can be targeted to users who are already interested in the product. Placing a banner ad about a new screwdriver set on a handyman's website is smart marketing.

There is also research about the components that make up the look of the ad. The color scheme is important, as studies have shown that blue conveys safety and trust (more than half of all Internet ads have blue in their logos) while brown is a natural, masculine background color. Other colors (black is exclusive, purple is luxurious, yellow is cheerful) have their uses as well. Cursive and extremely thin fonts are hard to read and should be avoided.

With all these design elements in play, the goal of a digital ad is to prompt the user to pause for an extra moment to start a call to action. Not only will these ads become more sophisticated, expect them to become more targeted to specific users' browsing histories. For our digital ad for Slurp Cola, Janine Nougat will hold a can near her face in a close shot with the tagline "Go Slurp!" in the bottom third of the image. Like our original print ad, this spot will be clean, easily defined, and tie our spokesperson to our product.

Closings

The federal government mandates some legal qualifiers at the end of certain advertisements. Car commercials are notorious for having lengthy disclaimers about financing at the end of their TV spots, while financial companies, medicines, casinos, and alcoholic beverages all face similar legal wording. The guideline is that the legal disclaimers within the ad must be clear and conspicuous. A reasonable person should be able to read the fine print, even if they need to pause the television ad to do so. They must be given an opportunity to get all the information.

The other items that may be required in an ad are slogans, logos, and signatures. These are required by the individual company, not by the federal government. Putting a consistent icon is vital to maintaining brand awareness. After all, the Nike swoosh or the Mercedes Benz logo are well-known; it is only common sense to reinforce a company's brand in its advertisements.

Looking Forward

Advertising will exist as long as sellers need buyers for their products and services. Luring in customers with a call to action through enticing ad copy and dynamic visuals will continue regardless of what types of digital media are developed in the future. The form of advertisements will likely become shorter and smaller; expect television ads to shorten from the 30-second standard format and online ads to become more frequent.

The greatest evolution will be in how ads are targeted at individual consumers. Demographics once divided people by categories like gender and age. Psychographics then elevated the modeling to consider an audience by their interests and hobbies. Advertising to individuals will become the norm, particularly as websites monitor consumers' browsing histories. Regardless of how the audience is targeted, there will always be a need for writers to create advertising copy across the media spectrum.

Exercises

1. Try to remember how many advertisements that have already tried to make you purchase something today. This can include Internet ads, television and radio commercials, and printed material in newspapers and magazines.
2. What are some famous taglines from commercials that stand out to you? Take a minute and list as many taglines as that you can remember from famous products, like "Do The Dew" (Mountain Dew) or "They're Gr-r-reat!" (Kellogg's Frosted Flakes). Can you define what makes a tagline memorable?
3. Coca-Cola is a world-famous soft drink brand, yet the company still spends millions of dollars each year to promote its products. Discuss why it is important for popular brands to continue to spend money on advertising.
4. What are the five writing tips that are used to create a successful ad?
5. Watch a television program outside of your age demographic; if you're a teen or in your low 20s, find a show that appeals to senior citizens. What kind of ads run during that program? Next, find a cartoon aimed at children. What sort of advertisements run on that show?

Chapter Essentials

- Advertising is driven by sellers who want to reach a buying audience for their products and services.
- Demographics divide people into largely physical characteristics like age and gender. Psychographics target attitudes, opinions, and interests of a certain population.
- The workflow before designing any successful ad campaign is identifying client needs, researching your product, and targeting your audience.
- The ad industry relies on the four-step AIDA process when crafting commercials. This acronym stands for Attention, Interest, Desire, and Action.
- Radio ads are written on one-sheets, which is the basic script that includes character names, narration, sound effects, and music.
- Television ads are written in a two-column format that shows the video in the left column and the audio in the right column.
- Digital advertisements are placed as banner, sidebar, or popup ads.
- Some products, like alcohol or casinos, must carry federal disclaimers for consumer awareness in their advertisements.

Online Links

Aaf.org. American Advertising Federation's site provides reports on the advertising and marketing industries, legislative news, and internship opportunities for students looking to make corporate connections. AAF sponsors Alpha Delta Sigma, the only collegiate national honor society in the field of advertising studies.

Adage.com. Advertising Age's massive website features news, blogs, and employment information about the advertising industry. Special features on Super Bowl advertising, industry webcasts, and notices of upcoming events are available as well.

Adweek.com. This site categorizes news articles into areas such as agencies, brand marketing, convergent TV, and social marketing. A wealth of up-to-date information is available in all areas of this website.

6 Public Relations

Key Words

Community Relations
Crisis Communications
Internal Communications

Media Relations
Press Release
Strategic Communications

Historical Overview

This history of public relations either dates back thousands of years or just a bit longer than a century, depending on how one defines public relations. One school of thought argues that PR dates back to Ancient Greece, when the philosophers Aristotle and Plato taught the art of rhetoric to influence an audience to see their point of view. This swaying of public opinion was based largely on their oratory and persuasive skills. While crafting arguments may be the foundation of public relations, actually using these techniques on behalf of a company evolved much later.

In the early 1900s, Ivy Lee was a reporter for *The New York Times*. He noticed that industrialist John D. Rockefeller Jr. was suffering from a poor image because of a very public strike among his coal miners. Rockefeller's Standard Oil company was seen as oppressive and uncaring, so Lee advised Rockefeller to visit the miners. This quickly boosted the public perception of Standard Oil in 1903. Just a few years later, Pennsylvania Railroad sought out Lee after a major train crash occurred on one if its rail lines. He wrote a press release to help salvage that company's reputation; Lee's statement was published verbatim in *The New York Times* in 1906. These two early instances of public relations showed that the right communication skills could dramatically alter the public perception of a company. Lee later went to work as the publicity director for the American Red Cross during World War I.

Public relations took a giant leap forward in the 1920s with writer Edward Bernays. The nephew of psychoanalyst Sigmund Freud, Bernays applied his uncle's theories of behavioral psychology into modern PR strategies. He viewed public relations as a science and explained his concepts in the seminal 1923 book *Crystalizing Public Opinion*. During World War II, he theorized that how governments used PR to sway public opinion could serve as a template for corporations to subtly influence the public as well. In 1945, he wrote *Public Relations*, which defined how an organization could release information to the public in the manner that best suited the organization. *Life* magazine later named him one of the most influential people of the 20th century.

Public relations has since evolved into its own field of expertise. Digital media platforms now provide a wealth of new opportunities for PR managers to promote their companies, political agendas, or points of view. Unlike advertising, PR is not designed to raise sales of a product. Instead, a strong public relations campaign is created to elevate a company's overall brand. The scripts for these public relations offices have their own specific templates that are used by the professionals in the PR industry.

Technical Specifications

The public relations process can be streamlined into a four-step RPIE process: research, planning, implementation, and evaluation. Each of these steps serves a critical role in any PR campaign and warrants further examination.

- Research. Much of a PR professional's daily schedule is spent analyzing data. Before a PR campaign is launched, the practitioner must know who they are trying to reach, what messages they want to deliver to the audience, and what result they want from the audience. This involves Internet searches, focus groups, interviews, and other research methods as needed.
- Planning. A successful campaign has specific goals with a defined audience in mind. Once the objectives are set, the public relations officer must determine which strategies will work best for the campaign.
- Implementation. This step may also be called the Communication step. This entails getting the message out with the different available media. A budget is used at this step to make sure the company is spending its money wisely.
- Evaluation. An important outcome for any PR campaign is knowing whether it succeeded or not. Counting hits on the website or tallying the number of people who attended a community event are just two examples of checking a campaign's effectiveness. These results will impact the company's future PR strategies.

Public relations is not just limited to communication that flows from a company to an external audience. To examine public relations even further, the modern PR industry can be divided into five different areas: strategic communications, community relations, media relations, internal communications, and crisis communications. Each of these fields has subtle nuances as the target audience for the message, as well as the purpose of the message, is different. We will discuss each of these in turn.

- Strategic Communications. This broad form of outreach is when an organization uses any form of communication to satisfy its mission. This is done by researching marketing trends, changes in culture, and the shifting dynamics of consumer behavior. It is especially effective when a business has a new product or service to promote.
- Community Relations. This function of public relations can best be illustrated by community outreach, like when a business hosts a blood drive or a fundraiser for local tornado victims. The outcome should be mutually beneficial, so the community reaps the reward (more funding or awareness) while the business receives more respect.
- Media Relations. The in-house PR office will frequently entice local reporters with stories about the business's new products, services, and nonprofit causes. When the

local branch launches a grand opening, unveils a revolutionary product, or celebrates 20 years in the community, media relations is in charge of spreading the word.
- Internal Communications. Not all public relations are meant for the general public. This communication form focuses on a company's employees and is meant to keep workers up to speed on breaking developments. Recognizing a worker's longevity, boosting morale, and providing information about pending leadership changes are all parts of PR that are directed within a business' own walls.
- Crisis Communications. When accidents or crimes occur, a company needs to immediately respond to reassure customers, suppliers, and the local community. This requires a PR team to be able to answer immediate questions during evolving situations, like a hurricane threatening a car dealership or a fire destroying a bookstore. Successful crisis communications can allow the company to get in front of the story.

Each of these five types of public relations relies on getting the word out quickly, professionally, and in a delivery format that can be accessed by the audience. This means the PR office should be well-versed in writing copy, working with audio and video, and delivering messages via social media. In one form or another, each of these communications starts with the humble press release.

Press Release

Much of the work handled by the PR specialist is in the form of a basic press release. These are delivered to the local media to make announcements, provide information, or make official statements on behalf of the company. A press release is usually just one page long, but they can be lengthier if there is a great deal of information within.

No press release ever happens by accident. They are generated by a company that wants to promote a project, an expansion, or some other newsworthy achievement. Large businesses will have in-house public relations teams to generate press releases; alternatively, a business may contract with an external agency to handle their press releases and other community outreach. A small business may have just one person handle press releases in addition to performing other tasks.

Regardless of the size of the company, there is a six-step process in how press releases work.

- A business has an upcoming event and wants to generate media coverage to promote it to the public.
- The PR team inside the company (or the boutique agency that is on retainer) will create a press release.
- The press release will be distributed to local media outlets. This is typically done via email, although hard copies of press releases are still sometimes mailed or faxed. Social media outlets (like Facebook or LinkedIn) may be used to send the message out to the general public, but a true press release relies on a news outlet relaying the information to their audience.
- A journalist at a news outlet reads the press release, decides it would make an interesting story, and receives approval to pursue the story from their editor/producer/news director.
- The journalist uses the contact information on the press release to connect with the company spokesperson for further information. This can range from a simple phone call to a request for an on-camera interview for a television program.

- The journalist then creates the story and runs it on their newscast (television and radio) or in the local newspaper. The story will also be carried on their website.

The competition for a press release to stand out from all the others is immense. Since a newscast only has a finite amount of time for stories (and a newspaper similarly has limited space to run stories on a given day), a press release must provide compelling information that intrigues the reporter. It must be clear and contain all the relevant facts, plus it must be written in an approachable style.

One intriguing element for a press release is that it must serve two competing functions simultaneously. On the one hand, it should contain all the information needed for a reporter to craft an independent story; literally, the who, what, when, where, why, and how of a story should all be there. If a reporter reads a press release and decides that the story is worthy of pursuing, she can write the story directly from the release.

Conversely, the press release may prompt a phone call from the reporter to make the story "bigger". The basic story for a television newscast is a reader. This type of story entails the news anchor reading some information directly to the camera for about twenty seconds. Any press release should readily provide ample information for the reporter to write such a basic story. But a great press release will entice the reporter to call in for more information, setting up an on-camera interview and shooting footage of the event.

This explains the duality of the press release. It must contain enough information so the reporter can craft a story just from that page. At the same time, it should be so compelling that the reporter deems it worthy of reaching out to the PR team to expand the information into a bigger story.

Written Press Releases

Press releases may be used for a variety of business communications. If a new cell phone feature is about to hit the market, a press release is sent out. This type of update is crucial when new products launch, when updates go on sale, when a grand opening is scheduled or when a new business partnership is announced. Other press releases deal with more mundane items that may be of interest primarily to those within the company. For example, the promotion of Gordon Walker from Assistant Quality Manager to Associate Quality Manager may not intrigue the general public, but the company's internal audience will appreciate the notice. Similarly, if Gordon Walker goes on to win Associate Quality Manager of the Western Division for the Year, that award announcement would also be more interesting to his colleagues than to anyone not affiliated with Walker's company.

Regardless of target audience, all written press releases adhere to a standardized format. These are:

1. Contact Information
2. The heading FOR IMMEDIATE RELEASE
3. Strong opening line for news reporters and editors
4. Two to three paragraphs with supporting information
5. A description of the company
6. Three pound symbols, ###, centered at the bottom of the page

Each of these elements is necessary and worthy of further explanation. Let's step through them to highlight why they are so vital in a standard press release.

1. Contact Information. This section gives the name, title, phone number and email of the person responsible for the press release. This provides a sense of authority to the press release since it allows a journalist to get in touch with the writer. Nothing is more infuriating to a reporter than receiving a bit of information without the means to follow up for more details. Anonymous press releases are usually dismissed as either fake news or rumor.
2. The heading FOR IMMEDIATE RELEASE. Once this appears on the press release, it relays a sense of urgency to news outlets to spread the word quickly. Occasionally, the heading will ask for more time, such as FOR RELEASE NO SOONER THAN FRIDAY, AUGUST 13TH, AT NOON EST. This practice may be used in entertainment or sports releases to build hype for an impending announcement. In reality, asking reporters to "hold" news announcements for a future date may not work if competing outlets are trying to get the scoop on each other.
3. The opening line. This sentence must be dynamic, attention-getting, and draw the reader into the rest of the press release. News reporters and editors receive a number of press releases every day, so they do not read each word on the page. It is crucial that this sentence give as much pertinent information (who, what, where, when, why, and how) as possible. If the opening line doesn't hook the person into reading more, the press release is discarded.
4. Two or three supporting paragraphs. This area further develops the story and provides more background for the reader. Quotes from company officials are inserted in this section, lending a more personal touch to the press release. The information in these paragraphs, when combined with the facts from the opening line, should be more than enough for a reporter to write a short news story.
5. The company description. This is boilerplate information that will stay consistent across all press releases. The year the company was founded, the number of employees or branches, and similar "About Us" wording should be placed here.
6. Three pound symbols (###). These marks have served as the standard for press releases for decades. When three of them are centered at the bottom of the page, they indicate the end of the press release. Since a press release may span more than a single page, the ### mark shows the true end of the information. The symbols have evolved to become known as hashtags on social media, but in press releases, they are still referred to as pound signs. In the UK, where the term "pound" refers to their money, these symbols are called hashtags or number signs.

A sample press release looks like this:

Jason Newbury
Vice President of Marketing
Wheatland Fifth National Bank
1–888-WHEATLAND
jnewbury@wheatlandfifth.com

FOR IMMEDIATE RELEASE

Wheatland Fifth National Bank Celebrates Two New Branch Openings

WHEATLAND, MO. Feb. 29, 2023 – Wheatland Fifth National Bank, a regional financial institution serving eleven counties in mid-Missouri, announces two new branches to better serve its customers. Ribbon cutting ceremonies for the new branches in Stockton and Weaubleau are scheduled for April 1st of this year.

"It's an exciting time to offer our services to more clients across mid-Missouri," says Bud Collins, Wheatland Fifth National Bank President. "These new branches will provide another 32 jobs to these communities. More importantly, our locations are always eager to provide local, professional financial services to the agricultural communities that we so proudly represent."

The April 1st ribbon cuttings will take place at 8am in Stockton and at 10am in Weaubleau. The public is invited to meet with banking representatives and to tour the facilities. Refreshments will be served.

Wheatland Fifth National Bank (WFNB) is a bank and an investment services company headquartered in Wheatland, Missouri. Founded in 1952, WFNB employs more than 200 financial experts in Bolivar, Buffalo, Clinton, Lake Ozark, Lincoln, Lowry City, Macks Creek, Phillipsburg, and at its Wheatland headquarters.

However, the tone of a press release can vary. The previous example of a bank expansion is fairly straightforward and is designed for financial and business news reporters. If your audience leans more toward entertainment and lifestyle news, the tone of the press release will be more casual. The following example spotlights a new superhero movie, so the overall attitude is geared toward a more youthful audience.

Elliott Fitzsimmons
Vice President of Distribution
Ninth Holiday Entertainment
1-877-HOLIDAYENT
elliottf@nintholiday.com

FOR IMMEDIATE RELEASE

SteveRabbit And SquirrelJenny Team Up Against JayBirdBeast!

LOS ANGELES, CA. May 20, 2023 – Fur and feathers will fly in movie theaters this June! The superhero team of SteveRabbit and SquirrelJenny are teaming up to protect the backyard feeders from the nefarious JayBirdBeast! This new villain is an oversized Blue Jay who became evil after an accidental power surge at the neighborhood bug zapper. The new film, *The Dawn of JayBirdBeast*, is sure to smash box office records.

"We are thrilled whenever these two backyard heroes team up," says Shonda Dominica, the animation visionary who created the two main characters. This marks the third feature-length film for our two beloved heroes. Previously, the duo starred in *Curse of the Poodle Yappers* in their debut film, followed by *Gopher Invasion* last year. Both movies grossed more than $250 million worldwide and received Academy Award nominations for Best Animated Film.

Ninth Holiday Entertainment is a global entertainment company with a focus on producing and distributing quality animated and live-action films. Headquartered in Burbank, California, USA, Ninth Holiday is the creative force behind the SteveRabbit and SquirrelJenny series as well as *The Epic Adventures of Whiz Grass and Poot Berry, Terror in the Knight,* and *Schmoo and The Beans International Travel Series.*

###

In addition to announcing new products, press relations are valuable for promoting community outreach programs. Events like 5K benefit runs, neighborhood cleanups, and fundraisers for charitable causes are always needed by local stations and newspapers to bring attention to hometown efforts. They also promote a "feel good" tone with the local news as they spotlight regular people trying to make a difference. The tone of these nonprofit efforts is straightforward and urgent.

Elise Sheindlin
Regional Intake Coordinator
Wheatland Ambulatory Blood Services
1–800-BLOODISLIFE
elisesheindlin@WABloodSvcs.com

FOR IMMEDIATE RELEASE

Urgent Blood Need for Hickory County

WHEATLAND, MO. May. 21, 2023 – Wheatland Ambulatory Blood Services is calling for residents to roll up their sleeves and donate blood before the upcoming Memorial Day weekend holiday. All types of blood are needed, but O negative and O positive supplies are critically low. The Hickory County area typically needs 30 units of whole blood and 10 units of plasma during the holiday weekend.

"We're very low on blood right now," says Jenny Gooch of the Wheatland Ambulatory Blood Services. "We've reached out to the Kansas City Red Cross for emergency help but they are low on donors as well. If we don't get enough blood, then accident victims will need to rely on saline as a substitute during emergency surgeries. It's a poor solution for a problem that we should be able to solve on our own."

Wheatland Ambulatory Blood Services is located at 221 Rutherford Way in Wheatland. Donation hours are between 10am and 6pm Monday through Friday and 12pm through 4pm on weekends. Donors are encouraged to make appointments, but walk-ins are always welcome. Donors must bring proof of identification and weigh no less than 90 pounds to give blood.

Wheatland Ambulatory Blood Services provides emergency care for Hickory County and eight other counties in the mid-Missouri region. Founded in 1961, the organization is credited with saving thousands of lives in its 60+ years of existence.

Crisis Communications

Emergencies happen every day. Products malfunction, the weather wreaks havoc on supply chains, crimes occur in the workplace, and a number of unforeseen crises occur unexpectedly. Businesses must be fully prepared to deal with crime, environmental hazards, and random accidents by having an established public relations office. This is when the PR team becomes the center of the storm, juggling multiple requests from a variety of outside groups. Crisis communications is when an organization uses its protocols and media expertise to communicate during a threat to a business, a person, or their reputation.

A common strategy is to use a three-step process to deal with the ongoing crisis.

- React to the crisis
- Create an ongoing strategy
- Move past the crisis

We will step through this process using the following example. Let's imagine a worst-case scenario for our new Wheatland Fifth National Bank branch in Weaubleau, Missouri. Just as the grand opening was scheduled for Saturday at 10am, a Midwest Superchem Train derailed on the train track located three hundred yards behind the new branch. The public relations team, which moments ago was concerned with simply messaging a feel-good story, must now pivot into crisis mode. This means quickly reacting to the crisis by controlling the information that is going out to a number of various groups asking different questions, such as:

- Customers. "Is my money safe?" "When will the business reopen?"
- Employees. "Do I still have a job?" "When will it be safe to go back to work?"
- Law enforcement. "Is the area safe?" "How many people were hurt?" "Is this a criminal investigation or just an accident?"
- Management. "What happened?" "Was anyone injured?" "How long will our business be affected?" "Does the company have any possible exposure that could be used against it in a lawsuit?"
- Government regulators. "What government agency should investigate this?" "How is the general public impacted?" "What resources are needed for the business to fully recover?"
- News reporters. "What happened (who, what, when, where, why, and how)?" "Are there any injuries, deaths, or significant damage?" "How long until the area is safe for people to enter?"

Reacting to the crisis means some responses are immediate while others may be delayed. First, answers to some groups, particularly law enforcement, must be provided immediately. Second, a standard press release should be crafted from the material available. These press releases are living documents that will be updated repeatedly throughout the day. Since crisis communications deals with breaking news events, not every element of the "standard" press release template may appear.

Jason Newbury
Vice President of Marketing
Wheatland Fifth National Bank
1-888-WHEATLAND
jnewbury@wheatlandfifth.com

FOR IMMEDIATE RELEASE

Wheatland Fifth National Bank Safe After Chemical Train Derailment

WEAUBLEAU, MO. April 1, 2023 – All employees of the new Weaubleau branch of Wheatland Fifth National Bank are safe and accounted for following this morning's train derailment near the new location. The bank branch was undamaged in the accident and all deposited funds are safe.

WFNB is working with law enforcement officials at this time and will release more details throughout the day.

###

This brief press release provides enough information to the interested parties; everyone is safe, the money is secure in the bank, and the physical building was not damaged. Details of the train derailment and the chemical spill are not delved into deeply, as the bank is concerned with its own employees. The news media and the public would expect a press release from the public relations team of the Midwest Superchem Train for that information.

Messaging must be consistent. If it changes, make the correction immediately. And if you don't have an answer to a question, be upfront and just admit that you are waiting for more information from authorities. It is always better to delay giving the right information instead of telling the public something that is incorrect.

Crisis communications also relies on social media more than other forms of PR because of how fast events are unfolding. Quick updates can be delivered in seconds directly to the consumer, as many people use social media as a regular news resource. This underscores why businesses should maintain an active presence on platforms like Facebook and Twitter. Controlling the story and communicating directly and clearly to the public are important every day, but relaying urgent news is expected during a crisis.

PR Campaigns

A public relations campaign is a series of planned activities that are designed to promote a company's reputation. This can take the form of driving traffic to the company website, drawing attention to a noteworthy cause, or putting out information about a new product or service. The campaign spans different forms of media with a consistent message. More importantly, the goal of the PR campaign is not to sell a product or service. Instead, the goal is to raise awareness of the brand without marketing or sales pressure.

One excellent example of a winning PR campaign was the Airbnb.org for Ukraine Campaign. In 2022, Russia invaded Ukraine, forcing millions of Ukrainians to flee their homeland, only to scramble for housing in neighboring European countries. Airbnb quickly partnered with international nonprofits and governments, finding housing for up to 100,000 refugees. Not only did the company offer shelter free of charge, but more than 28,000 people signed up to offer temporary housing to the refugees. Additionally, Airbnb offered to match up to $10 million in donations.

This public relations campaign not only helped countless displaced families but it elevated the Airbnb brand. Travelers around the world began booking at Airbnb to support the company. Airbnb's position in the temporary housing market made its effort to help the Ukrainian refugees a natural fit. By aligning their community outreach with their own business platform, Airbnb delivered a compassionate PR campaign that helped countless refugees during a time of immense suffering.

Multimedia Campaigns

Written press releases will always be the cornerstone of successful PR campaigns, but the possibilities of audio, video, and digital delivery beg for inclusion in communicating to the target audience. To make sure the message receives the widest distribution possible, the PR office must take advantage of every possible way that the target audience might receive the news.

Let's take an example in the field of internal communications. The PR office may want to recognize Lenny Del Guardo for 20 years on the job at Wheatland Fifth National Bank. A standard press release is drafted. Then the PR team takes a camera and microphone over to Lenny for a quick interview. That footage is then cut into a PR story that runs on the company's website to boost morale. A mass email is sent to all employees' company email accounts alerting them to the news. A quick tweet is put out on the company's Twitter feed, a Facebook post is distributed, and a LinkedIn update is sent. The congratulatory message is largely the same but sending it to so many channels reinforces its importance. If an announcement is relevant enough for a company to post it on one outlet, it should also go out to as many platforms as possible. The essence of public relations is that it reaches the public; the duty of the PR office is to make that connection as easy as possible.

Looking Forward

The need for public relations will continue to expand in the coming years. As consumers are bombarded by countless messages from different media throughout the day, a quality PR campaign will be needed to stand out among the crowd. Brand reinforcement and putting a positive spin on a company will remain a busy field; those familiar with the various PR scripting templates will have ample opportunities to display their skills.

66 Public Relations

The digital distribution of text and videos underscores the need for PR professionals in crisis communications. Since accidents and tragedies can be recorded on cell phones and uploaded to the Internet quickly, a quality PR team will be needed to tell the company's side of the story. Keeping a social media presence and staying in touch with the public will be expected from businesses in the future.

Exercises

1. Name the six basic components of a written press release. Add a brief sentence to each component that explains their importance.
2. What are the three steps that can be followed in a crisis communication situation?
3. List at least five of the groups that should be considered in a crisis communication event. How is your messaging similar or different depending on which group you are addressing?
4. Name one successful PR campaign that you can recall that helped a company's brand. Prnewswire.com is a helpful website for locating such campaigns.
5. Describe why evaluation is so important whenever a public relations campaign is designed.

Chapter Essentials

- Public Relations is not designed to sell products, but rather to influence the public's perception about a company or person.
- Ivy Lee and Edward Bernays are considered to be the founders of modern public relations.
- All PR campaigns should follow the RPIE model: research, planning, implementation and evaluation.
- The five main areas of modern public relations are strategic communications, media relations, community communications, internal communications, and crisis communications.
- A press release should contain enough information for a reporter to create a basic story yet still compel the reporter to want to follow up for more information.
- Social media is a powerful tool in public relations; it allows the company to directly connect with the public. This is especially vital during crisis communications.

Online Links

Prnewswire.com. This site is a distribution network, allowing access to thousands of press releases in the areas of Business and Money, Science and Tech, Lifestyle and Health, Policy and Public Interest, and People and Culture. If you want to see how professional press releases are written in areas ranging from Aerospace to Wireless Communications, this site is easily searchable and comprehensive.

Prsa.org. The website for the Public Relations Society of America features PR strategies and tactics, a list of upcoming events, news updates, and job postings.

Prsa.org/prssa. A subset of the PRSA, the Public Relations Student Society of America offers scholarships, publications, and resources for collegiate PR students. If you are a PRSSA member in college, you can join PRSA as an associate member up to five months before or two years after you graduate. The dues for an associate member are $60 annually, which is a savings of nearly $200 per year.

7 Corporate, Training, and Educational Videos

Key Words

Educational Videos
External Corporate Videos
Internal Corporate Videos

Training Videos
Video Brief

Historical Overview

The purpose of corporate, training, and educational videos is to inform an audience about a specific point of view, method to complete a task, or educate people about a certain subject. Unlike many other forms of broadcast media, corporate videos are produced for a very specific audience. An educational video that teaches kindergarten students how to say "Hello" in French is tailor-made for that group of children. Similarly, a training film for ironworkers in a smelting plan on best safety practices is geared specifically for that audience.

Recent events made educational videos much more popular. The demand for educational videos skyrocketed during the Covid pandemic as teachers found new delivery methods to teach their students. Once these online classes found more acceptance in the curriculum, many schools continued to offer them. But the origin of educational videos reaches back more than 100 years.

One questionable theory maintains that the first educational films were shown to students in St. Petersburg, Russia, as early as 1897. This is debatable, since the Lumière Brothers in France did not create short films for public viewing until 1895. What is known is that the early newsreels in the 1900s proved the power of film beyond telling narrative stories; the messages could be educational as well.

In World War I, the US Army and Navy produced training films for incoming soldiers to prepare them for going into battle. In the 1930s, the Republic of China faced a surging population of illiterate students; educational films were rapidly produced to efficiently teach large classes who still could not read. In the next decades, educational films spread throughout classrooms around the globe, delivering materials at a cost-effective price.

The history of in-house corporate videos is not so easily traced. No one knows when the first corporate video was created, as their audiences were within the walls of the company. The range of corporate videos spans staff training, safety, onboarding for new employees, and event videos for company morale. Internal corporate videos focus

DOI: 10.4324/9781003274766-8

exclusively on an audience of the company's employees. Some of these are casual, like making a celebratory video to mark a corporate anniversary. Others are more formal, like job training or skills certification.

Corporate videos can be divided into several different categories. These include videos that focus on branding, internal communication, company profiles, promotions, industrial, social media, testimonial, recruiting, and training. Not all companies create videos for each category, plus there is overlap among the definitions. For simplification, let's divide corporate videos according to their target audience.

External corporate videos deal with how the company presents itself to the outside world. The first reaction many people have is that external videos are the commercials they see on television. But this category goes far beyond that. Promotional videos, branding, social media, marketing, and all forms of public relations fall into this category.

Internal corporate videos are geared to employees within the company. Training and safety videos are common in this area because company management wants consistency in its products and must adhere to local, state, and federal safety mandates. If there is an accident on the job, investigators will want to know if the worker was trained to handle the situation safely. Management relies on training videos to bring workers up to speed on safety, as well as to protect themselves from lawsuits when something bad happens.

Technical Specifications

For this chapter, we will focus on corporate videos that are created by an in-house production team. Many larger businesses employ video producers to provide expertise with projects like webinars and Zoom meetings. However, the relatively low cost of video production equipment has prompted more companies to develop in-house production departments. Additionally, the recent Covid outbreak showed corporations not only the utility of training videos, but also added in a safety element to productions. Simply put, a company that works with its own production team does not subject anyone to working with an external group that may not adhere to the company's health protocols.

Pragmatically, companies are building in-house production studios for three main reasons:

- Lower production costs. Corporations can save on travel time and expenses by keeping all productions within the building.
- Reduce turnaround time. Working with an external production house entails coordinating schedules and waiting for the project to be completed.
- Allow video creation for all departments. The dedicated studio encourages different departments to produce training videos, webinars, product demos, and much more.

These in-house production studios must be staffed by video professionals who are familiar with all phases of shooting and editing. Of course, they must be well-versed in how to write the media scripts. There are several steps to creating such a script, but it all starts with a video brief.

Video Brief

The video brief can be thought of as an outline for the project. Most corporate videos are assigned by a supervisor who often may not understand the nuances of scripting and producing. This is when a video brief comes in handy by offering the following elements in an easy-to-understand format.

- Purpose. Why is the video being created?
- Desired action from audience. What outcome is desired after watching this video?
- Who is the audience. Who will be watching this video?
- What value is being brought to the audience. Why are they required to watch the video?
- What distribution channel will be used. How will the video be delivered to the audience?

For this example, let's use our ironworkers who work with boiling metals and extremely dangerous conditions every day at the Mid-Missouri Iron and Steel Factory. We can write up a video brief for our training video, *Safe Slag Disposal for Ironworkers*. For clarification, slag is a byproduct of smelting ore. As an ironworker applies heat and a chemical reducing agent, the ore is decomposed, thus extracting the metal. The waste material is slag, which looks like lava and has a temperature of about 2800 degrees Fahrenheit, or 1550 degrees Celsius. It's nasty stuff and should not be treated lightly. The company administration wants to keep its workers safe, so a video brief for the project will look something like this:

- Purpose. The video is being created for two reasons. First, to provide additional safety training for the 45 ironworkers on site. Second, to comply with a recent OSHA mandate concerning best safety practices for ironworkers disposing of slag and the toxic gases it emits.
- Desired action from audience. The desired outcome is that our ironworkers will follow the best safety practices when disposing of slag.
- Who is the audience. The audience is the 45 ironworkers at our plant. The video will also be required of new employees to maintain OSHA compliance.
- What value is being brought to the audience. The ironworkers watch the video for updates on safe practices as well as to comply with the OSHA mandate.
- What distribution channel will be used. The video will be delivered via mandatory screenings on company property. This viewing will be on regular workdays, so workers are compensated for their time. Workers will view the video in shifts to make sure the plant's operations are not impacted.

Now that the video brief has outlined the rationale behind the story, it is time to write a rough draft. There will be revisions to the script, as each version will need to be approved by a number of stakeholders. First, the legal counsel for the company will thoroughly check the wording to make sure the wording complies with the OSHA mandate. Second, the work supervisors will have editorial input because they will be charged with making sure the safety steps are implemented. Human Resources will want to provide feedback, since all employees (both current and incoming) will be expected to watch the video. Finally, expect the corporate administration to weigh in to make sure the product has the appropriate "look" for the company.

The reality is that, even with all that input, there remains a kneejerk reaction against a company mandating a worker to watch a training video. The videos are frequently boring, can stray off topic, or not connect with the target audience. Being forced to watch a video about how to do your job can result in workers tuning out the message. To combat this, there are four rules of thumb that should be employed in every corporate video:

- Turn the message into a story.
- Speak in an understandable language.
- Keep it short and sweet.
- Use sound and visuals.

Each of these guidelines makes sense. Audiences can relate to someone telling a story, which is a communication technique that originated in the days of early theater. Speaking in an understandable language ensures the audience will readily connect with the story instead of tuning out the message. Keeping it short and sweet means the viewer can stay engaged for the duration of the video; a 20-minute video is manageable, but a three-hour mandated viewing is ponderous. Finally, using sound and visuals should be expected of all quality video productions.

Continuing with our ironworkers, let's start with a standard two-column script about the dangers of slag. The script format will be a split column format. This format offers two columns, video and audio, that are lined up next to each other. The video elements are typed into the left column, while the audio portions, like narration and interviews, are in the right column. Formatting in two columns allows the writer to piece together the audio while the video is playing, or lets the narration be written first while the video elements are then inserted. Setting up a split-column format in Microsoft Word requires the following steps:

1. Open a new document
2. Click Insert. A new submenu will appear.
3. Click the down arrow next to the Table icon.
4. Click Insert Table
5. Change Number of Columns to 2. Change Number of Rows to 2.
6. If you need to insert more rows, click Layout. Then click Insert Above or Insert Below, depending on your cursor.
7. Type Video in the top left cell. Type Audio in the top right cell.
8. Add Video and Audio in the cells below.

The result is a two-column grid that can be used for lining up video and audio. Extra columns may be added at any point, so if a safety liaison from Human Resources wants a place to make specific notes, that is a simple fix. For now, we will employ the two-column template. Our first-person narrator, Bev, will be an ironworker with 25 years of experience dealing with smelting and slag. We will join her in the plant, where she is wearing the required safety suit. She speaks directly to the camera.

Video	Audio
Interior – Shot of Bev at blast furnace Graphic – Safe Slag Disposal for Ironworkers	Bev – Does this look familiar? I'm working with a blast furnace and the slag is starting to accumulate. So, what are the best ways to dispose of this? I'm Bev Hodges and I'm going to step you through this.

Interior – Close shot of the blast furnace	Bev – We all know slag is basically liquid metal, so it's dangerous until it hits a cooling point at room temperature.
Interior – Tracking shot of discharge gases moving through exhaust pipes	Bev – There are two concerns here. The first is the heat of the slag. But something you may not consider are the toxic gases coming off the slag. It looks like steam but there are particles in there that can damage your lungs and respiratory system.
Interior – Shot inside workroom. Bev is now in regular clothing and stands behind a table showing safety equipment.	Bev – Until the slag solidifies, it's going to emit the toxic gases. The ratio is in parts per million, so any effects won't happen after just a few exposures. But over time, the accumulated effects can add up.
Interior – Closer shots of the breathing mask	Bev – That brings us to the new OSHA mandated safety feature. This is the Ryconite TriLevel mask.
Graphics provided by Ryconite for the TriLevel mask	Bev (VO) – This mask features three levels of micro filters, filtering particles that are less than one – one hundredth of a micron. And a micron is a millionth of a meter, so you're looking at a filter that takes that micron and filters it down to the 99th percentile.
Interior – Medium shot of Bev holding the mask	Bev – The mask is the first step in keeping you safe while disposing of slag. Not only are the filters in this mask medical grade, but they have an effective working life of 90 days. Your supervisor will maintain a filter replacement schedule and provide you with new filters every 80 days.
Interior – Closer shots of the breathing mask	Bev – You'll notice I said 80 days, not 90 days. That is a ten-day safety window that the Mid-Missouri Iron and Steel Factory has internally implemented to make sure that no filter even gets close to the end of its useful life.

Safety videos are just one type of corporate production that is made to satisfy government mandates. In addition to that, many government agencies have their own in-house production offices. For example, the US Department of Labor produces safety videos on an ongoing basis. These videos are highly specialized and produced for specific audiences in mind. For example, one video is titled "Controlling Respirable Crystalline Silica in Construction: Stationary Masonry Saws". Clearly, only those who are concerned about inhaling crystalline silica particles from stationary masonry saws at construction sites would be interested in that five-minute video.

Producing safety and training videos is a large industry that is relatively unknown. Governmental agencies, ranging from federal departments down to local municipalities, create instructional videos for their workers as well as for public outreach.

Corporations produce training videos for their workers as well as to remain in legal compliance.

Every training video follows a standard template of an introduction, a body, and a conclusion. These steps can be further defined as follows:

- Introduction. The start of the video introduces the purpose of the project, the narrator, and the desired result.
- Body. This is a step-by-step walkthrough of the process.
- Conclusion. This section summarizes what has been learned and what steps can be taken next. If the course offers a certification, this step shows how to print it out for the employer.

Human Resources Offices can require incoming employees to watch these training videos to set consistent standards for their companies. Let's create an example for Nick's Especial Taco and Burrito Barn. Headquartered in Wheatland, Missouri, Nick's has 27 locations ranging from Kansas City to Springfield, employing more than 500 cooks, servers, and other workers. Many of the employees are college students who do not plan to work at Nick's for more than a year or two, thus there is high turnover.

Nick's needs to have consistency across its 27 locations, so training videos are vital for incoming employees. Each new worker is required to watch eight videos that cover topics such as safety, sanitation, food preparation, and dealing with customers. These videos are in addition to hands-on training that the new workers will receive in the restaurants.

For this example, we will review how Nick's developed a video showing the steps to make their Burrito Classico. The project was produced at Nick's Wheatland location during the overnight hours when the restaurant was closed. The audience for this training video is incoming workers who are typically of college age. We will use the industry standard two-column template for the Burrito Classico training video.

Video	Audio
Exterior – Shot of Nick's Headquarters in Wheatland Graphic – The Burrito Classico	Nick (VO) – Hey everybody! Welcome to our headquarters here in Wheatland, Missouri.
Interior – Nick behind the prep counter in the test kitchen	Nick – I'm Nick of Nick's Especial Taco and Burrito Barn. Today, I'm going to show you how to build our Burrito Classico step by step. This is one of the mainstays of our menu and it's important to get this right every time.
Interior – Closer shots of the tortillas	Nick – The ingredients we'll be using can be found on any of our prep lines. From the left to the right, we'll start with our tortillas. You'll see there are two options, the wheat or white. Most of our customers pick the white, so we'll use that one today.

Interior – Closer shots of the proteins	Nick – Next up are the different proteins. You have chicken, pork chorizo, beef, or our Spanish tofu. The Classico uses one half cup of any of these. If a customer asks for double meat, that's a full cup of protein. And remember, this is the Classico. If the order is for a Grande, you will use two proteins, so a quarter cup of one and a quarter cup of another.
Interior – Closer shots of the veggies	Nick – A lot of variety here. These are done a quarter cup each. You have lettuce, black olives, red onions, white onions, mushrooms, corn, and yellow rice. Customers will mix and match these, so check the ticket before moving on to this step.
Interior – Closer shots of the cheeses	Nick – This is a really neat part of the assembly line. Most places offer one type of shredded cheese. Here at Nick's, we have three options. The shredded gold cheddar, the shredded yellow havarti, or my favorite, the shredded yellow gouda. We use a generous one-third cup on each Classico.
Interior – Closer shots of the sauces	Nick – Customers really like the choice of our sauces. Each of these are based around a different pepper. We have five here and each will be one-third cup. You can see the green tomatillo, the mild yellow bell, the zesty poblano, the spicy jalapeno, and the fire-hot Carolina reaper. Too hot for me, but a lot of our customers love it!
Interior – Nick behind the prep counter in the test kitchen	Nick – Those are the ingredients, now let's get to building the Classico. You're going to check the order on the ticket, get your prep gloves on, and get started. First step, we grab the tortilla.

The idea behind the two-column format is to visualize the story as it unfolds. Even if you don't know what ingredients make up a Burrito Classico, the step-by-step instructions are plainly laid out for the viewer.

Viewer Environments

One variable in training films is where the final product will be watched by the audience. Many training films are shown in a workroom at the employee's company, often in a group setting. Others are available online, so they are watched by workers on their computers at home. Either way, a methodology is in place to certify that the employee has indeed watched the training. A supervisor will typically oversee screenings at work and note which employees attended. The home option requires the worker to log in with a unique username and password, thus verifying that the viewing requirements have been met.

The other variable that may come into place is the physical size of the viewer's screen. An extreme example is a training film used by NASA astronauts while in space. These films are watched on very small iPad screens, so showing video with text bubbles and good writing is the best way to communicate new information. Camtasia is a professional software platform that allows producers to create video tutorials in such a manner. Not all videos will be restricted to such an unusual space, but writers should be aware that such conditions exist.

Defining the Audience

Educational videos are directed to a captive audience. The best parallel is to examine how children's books are divided by ages. Introductory board books are for newborns to toddlers up to three years old. Coloring and activity books are introduced after that, followed quickly by early reading books around age five. Books that are told in chapters are introduced when a child is between six or seven, followed by middle-grade books, then young adult (YA) novels that are introduced when a child starts their teen years.

Educational videos are much the same, as the targeted audience can be defined by the different ages, grades, or educational ability. The market for such educational videos is staggering. If a writer examines the number of individual school districts, then the number of classrooms at differing grade levels, then factors in the different school subjects (math, history, social studies, etc.) that make up the curriculum, the result is countless opportunities for quality educational videos.

Looking Forward

Corporate, educational, and training videos will continue to thrive for the foreseeable future. Using video to train people exploded when social distancing was enforced during Covid. Universities worldwide embraced online learning and offered courses to students who either could not or would not attend face to face classes. Once the threat of Covid waned, the demand for some online classes remained. Other options include hybrid classes that mix traditional classroom instruction with educational videos that can be watched according to the students' schedules.

Video production has also been formalized in corporate settings to comply with federal and state regulations. When a new employee joined a company in years past, the required training used to be done by an in-person supervisor. This was costly and inefficient. Today, videos can be produced once and shown if the information remains relevant. Scripting and producing these videos will continue to be a growing market for both in-house and freelance production houses.

Exercises

1. Think back to your classroom days in elementary, middle, and high schools. Approximately how many educational films did you watch during those years? Do any of them stand out to you? Why are they memorable or forgettable?
2. Many employers rely on training videos to teach incoming workers. Were you required to watch any such videos at your current or previous jobs? What were they?

If not, can you think of any situations where a training video could have been used effectively for you?
3. What are the four guidelines that should be followed when producing any corporate video? Why are these important?
4. The two-column format of video and audio is an industry standard, but some companies want more columns on their script. Explain some of the benefits of adding additional columns.
5. The viewers for a training video are often a captive audience that is required to watch the project from start to finish. What are some of the challenges that are faced by a producer confronting such an audience? What steps can be taken to make sure the audience watches the video?

Chapter Essentials

- The unique aspect of corporate, training, and educational videos is that the audiences are predetermined before the videos air.
- Three reasons for a company to build an in-house production studio are lower production costs, faster turnaround time, and allowing video creation within all departments.
- The five elements in a video brief are the purpose of the video, the desired action from the audience, who is the audience, what value is being brought to the audience, and what distribution channel will be used.
- The two-column format allows the client and production crew to visualize the final production before the video is shot.
- Corporate, educational, and training videos may be watched in a workplace, in a classroom, or at home.

Online Links

fluentu.com. This site for educational videos concentrates on foreign language learning and provides examples that show the power of this learning tool.

osha.gov/video. The US Department of Labor runs the Occupational Safety and Health Administration (OSHA). As one of the largest creators of workplace training and safety videos, this website gives examples of what is being produced in this field.

refseek.com/directory/educational_videos.html. Refseek offers a list of 25 online educational video websites. These include Big Think, Howcast, Math TV, and MIT Open Learning. This extensive array demonstrates the best practices in educational videos across a variety of subjects.

8 Documentary

Key Words

Documentary
First-Person
Linear
Nonlinear
Parallel Action
Point of View
Sequence
Shooting Ratio
Split Column
Stringout
Third-Person
Touch and Go

Historical Overview

Documentaries are symphonic. They are the only form of media that allow the producer to use any forms of visual and audio tools at their disposal, blending them in any fashion they see fit. Feature films are limited by not breaking the fourth wall to directly address the audience; when they do, the main character is often just delivering a funny quip for the audience's amusement. But documentaries have full creative license to blend first-person interviews, third-person narration, visual graphics, animation, music, sound effects, and recreations of historical events to tell a story. In no other media format is there such a broad array of tools coupled with such creative freedom.

The other perk for producers is the fluidity of finished running time. A short mini documentary that only runs on the web can be as concise as two minutes. The other extreme are documentary series on streaming platforms like Netflix or Hulu that can span eight episodes of an hour or more in duration. Ken Burns and Lynn Novick's epic documentary series *The Vietnam War* spans ten individual episodes that last a combined 18 hours.

Even the definition of a "short" versus a "feature" documentary is not clear among industry experts. A short documentary is typically thought of as between two and 25 minutes long for many film festivals. But the Academy of Motion Picture Arts and Sciences (AMPAS) says anything under 40 minutes is a short, while anything longer is a feature. Meanwhile, the Sundance Film Festival limits short films to 50 minutes. The PBS documentary series POV requires a broadcast length of 51 minutes and 50 seconds. The Screen Actors Guild defines a short documentary as under 75 minutes.

A documentary's running time is typically determined by the subject matter, the approach of the producer, and the budget. An overview of the battles of WWII is a massive project that will command an extensive crew, a generous budget, and long running time. On the other extreme, a short documentary about someone's puppy seeing snow for the first time can be shot and edited with little time and expense.

DOI: 10.4324/9781003274766-9

This leads to one of the beauties of documentary production; anyone can tell a story about their own life experiences, hobbies, or interests. The gear threshold to enter this field is surprisingly low since a short documentary can be shot on a cell phone and edited with free software on a laptop. The final hurdle of exhibition is easily surmounted as anyone can upload to YouTube, Vimeo, or their own website while also submitting to a host of independent film festivals.

The underlying premise about documentary production is that it is a story that just happens to be true. The first film, *The Sneeze,* can be rightfully viewed as the first documentary. Shot at Thomas Edison's Black Maria studio in 1894, the five-second film features assistant Fred Ott sneezing toward the camera. The film is silent, black and white, and consists of a single shot. Regardless, it captured a "real" event, thus one could argue that the oldest surviving film is also the oldest surviving documentary.

Capturing real-life events became the mainstay of early productions. Auguste and Louis Lumière pioneered documentaries in France by recording short films of everyday events. In 1895, the brothers hosted their first paid public screening, showing ten short documentaries to a captivated audience. Each silent film lasted less than a minute and concentrated on mundane events in everyday life. The films included workers leaving the Lumière factory, a baby eating breakfast, and a street scene of people walking near the Cordeliers Square in Lyon. None of these documentaries were scripted; writing scripts for real-life stories would come later.

Over the next decades, documentaries would become longer as the film technology improved. In 1922, *Nanook of the North* was the first feature-length documentary that received commercial success. Although it was silent, it was produced as a narrative that followed Nanook and his Inuk family in the Canadian Arctic. The story was tied together with written narration, allowing the audience to read passages before moving to the film's next vignette.

Different documentary styles emerged until present day. Michael Moore (*Roger & Me, Fahrenheit 9/11, Sicko*) inserts his own persona into each of his films by offering first-person political and social commentary. Ken Burns (*The Civil War, Thomas Jefferson, The Dust Bowl*) relies on an omniscient narrator interspersed with interviewed experts. Adventure documentary producer Jimmy Chin (*Free Solo, Meru*) is an on-camera presence in his productions but is often shown in a supporting role to other people.

There is no "right" way or "wrong" way to script a documentary. The subject matter may be contemporary or historical, the story may be linear or nonlinear, and the point of view (POV) may be first- or third-person; this last element impacts the narration choices (omniscient voice, self-narrated, a reliance on third-person experts, or a combination of these techniques). Let's examine these different elements to see how they influence how you would create a script.

Contemporary Versus Historical

A contemporary documentary takes place in the present day. This allows the producer to decide on the best approach of video, audio, and graphics. A project about local boys playing ice hockey would involve footage of the boys playing a game, which is an easy day of shooting. Other elements can be added or not. Do you want to include footage of them practicing? If one of the boys has a tough home life, do you bring the family into it? If the star player has potential for a collegiate hockey scholarship and then a future in the professional leagues, does that become your focus? Another consideration is the style in which you would shoot the footage; you can affix small GoPros to their helmets, retrieve footage from a local news station, or potentially pilot a drone around their practice rink. Even a basic contemporary documentary with readily available footage presents an array of choices in how to shape the narrative.

An historical documentary is even more challenging. Naturally, you cannot feature first-person narration for an event from more than a few decades ago since the key actors are long gone. Unless you rely on reenactments, the scripting must be third-person. Not only will this allow an omniscient (and often unseen) narrator, but it also lends itself to interview experts on the subject matter. These interviews are then interspersed with the narration.

For an historical documentary, the expert interviews are shot first. This directly impacts how the scripting is carried out. Their interviews are then transcribed, and the relevant portions are edited into the final cut. After these portions are placed into the audio track, the producer will write the script for the narrator. The narrator's voice is always written last. This is because the on-camera expert interviews cannot be altered but the narrator's script can be tweaked repeatedly before recording. This narrator script is written as a simple Word document for the narrator to voice in front of a microphone.

Linear and Nonlinear

The simplest documentary format deals with a linear narrative. Events happen on one day, these cause successive events to happen on following days, and so forth. The story telling arc is simple to script as the scenes are tracking the cause-and-effect of the events. For example, if the documentary is about a police investigator who is searching for an arsonist, the linear structure is straightforward. The crime is committed, the investigator is called in, she investigates the crime scene, looks for clues, closes in on the arsonist, and makes the arrest. This linear storytelling is commonly seen in feature films, episodic television series, and theatrical plays.

Nonlinear structure works by reframing the story with flashbacks and the occasional flashforward. This gives the writer more freedom to create sequences that are then inserted on the editing timeline as desired. Using the previous example of the investigator and arsonist, the writer may flip the story to concentrate on the day of the arrest. The opening scene could have the investigator approaching the house with the criminal inside, then the next scene flashes back to the initial crime. Back to the investigator knocking on the door, then jump back to her initial search of the crime scene. Jump forward to the arsonist running away, flash back to a clue that identifies him as the prime suspect, then make the final edit forward to her tackling the arsonist and making the arrest.

Shifting the time elements in these cases impacts how the writer creates the final script. The linear plot is easy to follow, yet the nonlinear may add dramatic tension through its storytelling arc. Either way, it is up to the writer to determine which tactic will create the best outcome. This decision should be made early in the writing process.

Point of View

The way the documentary is presented is tied to the point of view conveyed by the writer. First-person documentaries present the information from the writer/producer's point of view; the narration is voiced by this person, who slips into the role of the host. This allows the host to share the journey of the documentary, which is a powerful format if they underwent this experience. Projects on cross-country travel, medical issues, and social injustice often work very well with such a structure. The intimacy and emotion that are captured by a firsthand account can deliver powerful moments that are unmatched by a faceless narrator.

The other option is third-person narration. This format is helpful for historical documentaries when the actors have long since passed on. Stories that have multiple points of view, like political or economic issues, can benefit from having an authoritative voice to guide the viewer along. Finally, when a well-known celebrity wants to help a social or environmental cause, they may use their star power as a narrator. Meryl Streep (*Five Came Back*), Morgan Freeman (*30 For 30*), and Patrick Stewart (*Death Zone: Cleaning Mount Everest*) are just a handful of the celebrities who have lent their talents to documentary narration.

For clarification, there is no device that is second-person narration. First-person refers to someone talking from their point of view. Third-person features an omniscient narrator who provides information but is not directly tied to the story. Second-person refers to the viewer who is watching the documentary, so having that person narrate the project is impractical.

Once the documentary approach is decided (contemporary, linear, and from a first-person POV, for example), there are a few technical elements that will impact the scripting once the production is underway. These are the shooting ratio, the Touch and Go principle, and sequences. Let's address each of these in turn.

Shooting Ratio

A shooting ratio is how much footage you shoot for a documentary compared to how much of that footage you use in the final product. If you shoot five hours of field footage for a one-hour documentary, your shooting ratio is five to one, or 5:1. Shooting twenty hours of footage for that same one-hour documentary results in a 20:1 ratio.

This impacts scripting because too low a shooting ratio will force the writer into using whatever is possible of the available footage. Shooting 30 minutes of footage for a 20-minute documentary results in a 1.5:1 ratio, which is critically low. The writer would then need to structure the story around what is available or alternatively to look for graphics to supplement the video.

The other extreme is a high shooting ratio. If someone shoots 60 hours of footage for a one-hour documentary, the ratio is 60:1. This is an unwieldy amount of footage that must be culled through. The writer will accordingly need to edit down much of the script that deals with the 59 hours of unused footage.

There is no magic number for a shooting ratio, but 5:1 is a good rule of thumb for an absolute minimum (and even that number will present challenges). 10:1 to 20:1 is a solid range, while anything above that span can result in information overload.

Touch and Go

The adage of a picture being worth a thousand words is seen most clearly in a quality documentary. Since documentaries are based on real events, there is always a danger in the final product becoming too much of a long-winded speech. Audiences don't like being lectured at, especially in a medium that has so many visual options at its disposal. The stories should compel the viewer to watch, while the narration guides the story along.

This is where writers use the Touch and Go principle for documentary storytelling. Let's say there is a 30-second segment of a sailor knitting a scarf while he rests on the ship's deck. He is far from home and won't return for another three months, but his wife packed some yarn and knitting instructions for him. His name is Alan, her name is Alice, and they married just before he got onto the ship, departing from his Seattle home as a radio operator for a scientific research vessel. We have a sequence of shots of our sailor knitting, including a wide establishing shot, several medium shots, and a variety of close ups. A poor example of how to write this sequence is to write precisely what the audience sees, like this:

> Alan finds time to knit on the deck. He is making a scarf. Each stich must be carefully placed so the scarf will stay not unravel. He knits when he has spare time from his duties as radio operator. Another stich is done, followed by another. It takes a long time to make a scarf by hand.

The writer is referencing the video, but there is not enough new information relayed by the narration. Instead, the Touch and Go principle ties the audio to the first shot of the video sequence, then it expands to include information not shown on the screen. For example:

> Alan finds time to knit on the deck. His new wife, Alice, is waiting back home in Seattle. They were married for just four days before he set sail as the radio operator. By the time he gets home, he will have been at sea for three months. Although they are married, he spends more than 90 percent of his life away from her.

The first sentence remains the same, allowing the audio to "touch" the video. After that, the audio is allowed to bring in more background information, leaving the video to show the scarf being made. After the first sentence, there is no more mention of the scarf or knitting. Instead, the narration is free to "go" to moments that will better flesh out the characters and their individual stories.

Sequences

A sequence within a documentary is a series of video shots that are tied into a specific location or event. In the above Touch and Go illustration, Alan was shown knitting a scarf while on deck. This sequence contained various shots of Alan, such as the wide shot to provide an overview of his work, some medium shots, and a variety of close ups.

Sequences may be seen as pieces of a puzzle that can be moved around until they fit in the documentary correctly. Let's say there are two other isolated sequences, like the bosun monitoring the tension on the ropes and the captain plotting the course. Each of those sequences contains a wide shot to establish the scene, several good medium shots, and a handful of close ups. These three sequences all depict a typical slow day at sea, so they may be placed interchangeably in the finished product.

The other option is to intercut the sequences to depict parallel action. This means that two or more things are shown happening simultaneously. You have three sequences: Alan knits a sweater, the bosun checks the ropes, and the captain plots the course. You can easily cut these as three individual sequences, or you can start with a few shots of Alan, then the bosun, the captain, and intercut as needed. Tying the elements together can be done with simple narration, like:

> A quiet day on a calm sea means catching up on small projects. Alan takes a break from his radio duties to work on the scarf that he promised his wife. The bosun uses the time to check the ropes, while the captain plots the course for the next leg of the journey.

Each sequence has fewer shots but lends itself to a more holistic view of the ship's workings. This new sequence will be labeled "Afternoon Duties" and will merge the previous sequences of "Knitting", "Checking Ropes", and "Plotting Course". During postproduction, this sequence may be inserted on the timeline whenever it is needed.

Technical Specifications

Formatting documentary scripts is based on personal preference. Certain production houses and directors may opt for two column scripts, playing video in one vertical column with matching audio in a second column. Other producers write in block paragraphs, focusing on one idea to be supplemented with visual images.

The debate is best illuminated by which should be edited first, the audio or the video? Each technique carries advantages and disadvantages.

AUDIO FIRST
Advantages: Script can be "locked in" quicker
                 The overall running time is easier to adjust
Disadvantages: Once you hear the script, you may not want to make changes
                 Ignores the strength of video in a visual medium

VIDEO FIRST
Advantages: Relies on the power of video in a visual medium
                 Allows more freedom in cutting individual sequences
Disadvantages: Harder to gauge the overall running time
                 Audio elements may need to be rushed or lengthened to fit video

Instead of dictating an absolute right or wrong way to script a documentary, this text will offer several real-life examples of how award-winning documentary scripts were scripted in different fashions. Each script evolved differently, thus their back stories may provide illumination as to why they emerged in their own unique way.

The Hill of Witches

Shot in Lithuania, this 12-minute documentary examines a network of forest paths that feature hand-carved wooden statues. The sculptures range from six to 30 feet tall. Each of them depicts historic, pagan, religious, or cultural iconography that was chosen by the individual artists who carved them.

Production on this documentary spanned several weeks. There are two primary elements to the footage. First, there are interviews with several local experts; two of them, labelled as the Teacher and the Bioenergeticist, are shown in the script segment below.

The second element is the footage of the carvings. The shots are largely isolated video images of the sculptures from various angles at different times of day and under various weather conditions. There are also a handful of shots of the nearby beach along the Baltic Sea.

The script for this documentary is based on the "write audio first, insert video second" model. For this workflow, the interviews were transcribed, then selected quotes from those interviews were identified to tell the story: these are noted by the time signatures next to their names. For example, the first segment where the teacher speaks has a time of 06:29–06:53. This means that the teacher's quote can be found at 06:29–06:53 of the raw footage file.

Once the quotes were placed in a timeline, a narrator's script was written to provide context and to link the quotes together. The video was then edited to the audio track, following cues given in the script. When the teacher says her opening line about the path becoming dark, for example, a segment of video of the forest darkening because of a cloud passing over the sun is laid over that audio. When the narrator mentions the Curonian Spit, that thin, sandy peninsula is shown. The first few minutes of the audio script is below.

> Slow music montage to start, dissolves
> Title sequence – *The Hill of Witches*
> Teacher – 06:29 – 06:53
> One thing is really interesting. Once you start walking down the path, everything is so bright, all the surroundings, but at the halfway it gets dark all of the sudden. We have been wondering why. Later we talked with the masters and they said it is the point where devildom breaks loose. So, when I work as guide, I always tell people "Do not cross this line, or the hell will break lose. You might stumble upon something for sure."
> Narrator – Section 1 00:56 – 1:14
> The village of Juodkrante, Lithuania, is located on the Curonian Spit, a long, thin peninsula made of shifting sands on the Baltic Sea. Visitors enjoy the open beaches, just footsteps away from the nearby forest.
> (Insert brief music interlude here for scene change from beaches to Hill.)
> Narrator – Section 2 1:14 – 1:38
> The Spit is also home to the Hill of Witches, a forest containing 80 sculptures. Artisans crafted these wooden pieces by hand. But the story behind how the sculptures came to be is as unusual as the sculptures themselves. It began as a local movement in 1979 when Lithuania was still under the control of the Soviet Union.
> Bioenergeticist – 1:39 – 2:44
> Similar thoughts dictated a reason for the Union of Lithuanian Folk Artists, which back in the Soviet times was called the Association of Folk Arts, to found an ensemble of ethnographic sculptures exactly in this place. At that time permissions from the Communist party were needed for almost anything. However, as an ethnographic creative center for the poor, working-class people, it did not bother any of the Party's high officials, so the permission was granted. At first, it was not called the Hill of Witches. The name was simple – the ensemble of ethnographic sculptures. That is how it was designed and built. But no one thought about the theme. Woodcarvers were invited to come, they were provided with oaks and that was the whole offer – here, please carve ethnographic sculptures.

84 *Documentary*

Teacher – 2:45 – 3:26
As I mentioned before, back then I was a principal at the school. And so we put six metal beds and a cupboard in each class. There was only one restroom downstairs, for the sculptors to wash up. They received the food from a canteen in the center of the city and worked at the forestry, a kilometer away toward Klaipėda. And they had two weeks to carve and place the sculptures.

The other approach is to concentrate on the video elements first. This technique was used in *Antarctic Voyage: Imaging Unseen Earth*. This hour-long documentary focuses on a group of four University of Texas graduate students. The quartet joins a geophysical research team aboard the *Research Vessel Maurice Ewing* as it explores the Bellingshausen Sea along Antarctica.

The scripting of this project is straightforward, as the students follow a linear timeline. They are issued special cold-weather clothing and board the ship in the first few minutes. The ship leaves Punta Arenas, Chile, and heads south. They then encounter the Drake Passage, which is a notoriously dangerous passage of water between South America and the Antarctic Peninsula. After that, the scientific experiments begin, icebergs and penguins are encountered, and the ship eventually sails back to Chile after two months. Small vignettes, such as a dining sequence or the students taking turns on the rowing machine in the small exercise room, are sprinkled throughout the narrative as a counterpoint to the geophysical research.

Because the events unfolded in a straightforward timeline, *Antarctic Voyage* is an example of "edit the video first, then write the audio narration second". A common strategy in scripting a linear documentary is to create stringouts. A stringout is editing all the takes of a scene into individual segments. These stringouts are then compiled together for the production team to evaluate.

Let's look at how *Antarctic Voyage* was scripted. First, a quick montage of icebergs was desired for the opening title sequence. Then the following scenes were needed in order: introductory shots of the ship anchored in the harbor, the students obtaining cold-weather clothing from a local shop, the final provisions being loaded onto the ship for the two-month voyage, and then the *Maurice Ewing* departing from the port. The stringouts of those introductory scenes are then edited together. As the sequences begin to take form, the narration is scripted to lay over the video elements. For our example, Tim, who was one of the students on the Antarctica trip, serves as the first-person narrator.

Video	Audio
Exterior – Daytime shots of icebergs	Tim – Like most people, I rarely thought about Antarctica, the lone continent at the bottom of the world.
Exterior – Daytime shots of ships in the Chilean harbor	Tim – Then, some of my professors asked me if I wanted to join a research team there, and I jumped at the chance. So did three other graduate students.

Exterior – Closer shots of various ship flags and workers loading supplies	Tim – The starting point for our voyage is Punta Arenas, deep in southern Chile. Ships of many nations stop off here on the long trip around South America to take on fuel and supplies.
Exterior – The Maurice Ewing ship	Tim – During our seven-week voyage in Antarctic waters, we'll be working aboard the Research Vessel Maurice Ewing.
Interior – The scientists receive clothing for the trip from a cold-weather specialty shop	Tim – Though it is now summer in Antarctica, the weather can suddenly turn nasty. Everyone making the voyage is issued cold-weather gear.
Interior – Angle on Tim trying on the cold-weather clothing	Tim – I once did ice fishing in the Great Lakes, so I know every bit of this special clothing will come in handy where we're going.
Exterior – Crew members busily load the Maurice Ewing	Tim - It's taken 48 hours to load the Maurice Ewing and because the crew is now preparing for departure, there is no time to look after members of our scientific party.
Exterior – Tim and the other students (one male, two female) tote bulky gear up the gangway	Tim - So everybody, men and women alike, must pack aboard their personal gear and equipment.

Transcribing Footage

Once shooting is done, the next step after interviewing the subjects is transcribing their audio word for word. This once-ponderous chore is now simplified with computer software that can transcribe the audio in real time. These transcripts are then reviewed with an eye toward using the most dynamic quotes. Once these files are identified, a rough framework of the documentary starts to emerge.

If a narrator is brought in to supplement the first-person interviews, that narration is only written after everything else has been transcribed. There is a simple reason for this. Once an interview is recorded, the words said by the interviewees are locked in and cannot be changed. But the narration can be rewritten repeatedly to get the right tone, pacing, and verbiage.

Looking Forward

Documentary scripts are highly personalized to each producer, as there is no wrong or right way for an individual to determine their own workflow. Given the low cost of producing a documentary, it is only natural that more writers and producers will enter this field, bringing their own stories and points of view to a broader audience.

Similarly, the market for documentaries will continue to expand. Dedicated channels about documentaries, film festivals that welcome the genre, and easier distribution through platforms like YouTube will encourage filmmakers to try their hand within the documentary realm. After all, a documentary is simply a story that happens to be true.

Exercises

1. Outline a first-person documentary that you could produce about a subject that you are passionate about. You would serve as the host, appear on camera, and provide first-person narration. Describe what subject would you like to cover in your documentary and how you would fit into the narrative structure.
2. Outline an historical documentary that interests you from a topic more than 100 years ago. Approach this as a third-person project, thus it should not document your family history or any topic in which you might serve as a first-person narrator. How would you approach the narration for this project? How would you then script the project?
3. Imagine someone is producing a third-person documentary about your life. The subject can be your academic success, your athletic accomplishments, or an artistic exploit. Which famous celebrity (actor, musician, or athlete) would you like to have narrate the documentary about you and why?
4. FilmFreeway is an excellent repository of film festivals that can be entered by students and independent filmmakers. Check out the website filmfreeway.com and survey what film festivals could be suitable for a documentary you might produce. Make sure to browse for festivals based on what you could produce in categories such as student, festival focus, and geographic region.
5. You are assigned to write and produce a documentary on an environmental issue near campus. The video has stunning sequences and the audio interviews are strong. Would you approach this project concentrating on video or audio first?

Chapter Essentials

- The subject matter, the approach of the producer, and the budget determine a documentary's running time.
- Scripting a documentary can be done through a "video first" or "audio first" model.
- Documentaries may be told in the first-person or third-person point of view, which impacts how they may be scripted.
- A shooting ratio shows how much footage has been shot compared to how much will remain in the final edit.
- Touch and Go is a technique in which the writer references a shot of video and then delves into more narration.
- A sequence within a documentary is a series of video shots that are tied into a specific location or event.
- Parallel action is a technique that intercuts different scenes to imply they are happening at the same time.

Online Links

Documentary.net. This website from The Documentary Network casts a broad net to show documentaries from all around the world. The hosts are also active in social media and connecting documentary producers with one another.

IMDb.com. This holistic site spans all genres of film and television, but users can readily search for specific documentaries. IMDb provides information about each title including storylines, reviews, and technical specs.

Topdocumentaryfilms.com. This website allows free access to a number of compelling documentaries free of charge. Users can browse through the entire list or search through categories like Biography, Nature, and Performing Arts.

9 Television News

Key Words

Attribution
Descriptor
Inverted Pyramid
Lead
Market
News Hole
Package
Reader

Slug
Sound On Tape (SOT)
Stand Up
Toss
Total Running Time
Voiceover (VO)
VOSOT

Historical Overview

Television programming aired for more than a decade before attempts were made to create television newscasts. While TV stations and programming existed in the 1930s, World War II delayed consistent newscasts until the 1940s. Many of the first newscasts lasted only 15 minutes and were little more than announcers reading radio news stories in front of a camera. It wasn't until the early 1960s that 30-minute network newscasts became commonplace.

Local 30-minute newscasts similarly developed in various large cities across the country. Today, more than 200 television markets, or metropolitan areas, have their own news stations. As these stations signed on with newscasts, they competed for a share of the viewing audience. This competition spurred ongoing technical innovations; color images replaced black and white, microwave and satellite capabilities allowed reporters to deliver news live from the field, and the use of graphics redesigned the look of the evening newscasts.

Another major change occurred in 1980 with the debut of CNN as a news provider for cable subscribers. Other cable networks, notably Fox and MSNBC, joined as news stations in the following years. Regional news outlets, Spanish-language stations, and PEG (public, educational, and governmental) cable channels also began to offer their own news programs. Not only were the airwaves filled with a variety of newscasts, but broadcast journalists frequently moved from one station to another throughout their careers.

The end result of having so many channels with literally thousands of writers led to professional standards of how to deliver the news to a viewing audience. The style of broadcast news writing became codified regardless of network or channel affiliation.

Thus, television broadcast journalism organically developed as a unique style adhering to its own specifications and practices.

Technical Specifications

Several compelling forces dictate how television news should be written. The first concern is how it is consumed by the viewer. Many newscasts are watched by people eating dinner, cleaning the house, or performing other tasks at home. Television newscasts are also subject to a one-time viewing, meaning the information must be given conversationally and should be easily digestible on the first viewing. Detailed statistics, complex sentence structure, and intricate quotes should be simplified for the viewing audience. Unlike websites or newspapers, there is no opportunity to reread the information if it isn't understood the first time.

There are also severe time constraints that are not found in the digital or newspaper realms. A standard 30-minute local newscast contains only 22 minutes of actual news; commercials consume the remaining eight minutes of that half hour. When the news program is slotted into the evening's lineup, the commercials are the first elements inserted into that 30-minute block.

The remaining 22 minutes is known as the news hole. This is an echo from old-style newspaper formatting, in which news pages were printed and then laid out on large lighted boards. The newspaper ads were printed and typeset onto the blank pages first, leaving "holes" for the news editorial content.

Television news producers hold their journalists to strict standards regarding the news hole of any given newscast. This is done by enforcing the TRT, or total running time, of each story. Since commercials cannot be dropped from the newscast (those advertisers are paying for the privilege of being on the air), the producers must ensure that the TRT of the combined news stories does not exceed what's allowed in the news hole. The result is that clear, concise writing is highly valued in newsrooms.

Writing Fundamentals

The cornerstones of writing for television journalism can be broken down into the following areas: leads, descriptors, attribution, neutral words, numbers, times and places, and editing words out. Let's look at each of these concepts and what makes them so important.

Leads

Structurally, each story begins with a lead. This is an attention-grabbing sentence that hooks the viewer into the story. Most stories begin with hard leads, which immediately relay facts to the audience. For example, a reader that leads with "The City Manager will release a new budget proposal this Thursday" shows a hard lead that covers several elements (who, what, when). Other details, like why the budget is coming out, will be fleshed out in later sentences. This is like how newspapers originally told stories in an inverted pyramid style, in which the most important facts were placed in the first sentence. Less important details were dropped into the following sentences, so if a story couldn't fit into the paper's news hole, the paragraphs at the bottom of the story were simply cut.

Hard leads dominate most news stories because there is so little time for a story to wander before it gets to the point. But if the producer allows for a few extra seconds, a broadcast journalist can craft a memorable lead using one of the following proven techniques. We will use the hard lead example "The City Manager will release a new budget proposal this Thursday" as a jumping-off point. Other options for this story are:

- Soft lead – this allows a few words to introduce the hard lead, so the story would open with "A big week is up ahead at City Hall. The City Manager will release a new budget proposal this Thursday."
- Delayed lead – this is akin to the soft lead, but it buries the hard lead even further into the story. For example, "Politicians are no strangers to tough decisions. And local leaders are faced with challenges of either raising taxes or cutting city services. Local voters are keenly awaiting this Thursday when the City Manager will release a new budget proposal."
- Quote lead – used rarely, as it can disorient the viewer at the start of the story. But in this example (using the name Bob Forbes as the City Manager), one option would be "'Not everyone will like what they are going to see'. Those words today from City Manager Bob Forbes as he previews his new budget proposal. He will release it this Thursday."
- Shotgun lead – good for tying together multiple short stories, like football scores on a busy Friday night or giving a quick wrap of state headlines. For this example, it could read "Higher taxes, fewer services, and nervous voters are some of the possible options of the City Manager's new budget proposal. It will be released this Thursday."
- Negative lead – one of the few times when you will capitalize something in the teleprompter script to make sure the anchor emphasizes a negative word. In this case "The City Manager says he will NOT cut city services in his new budget proposal. Bob Forbes says he will release that document this Thursday."
- Trivia lead – used more frequently in features than hard news stories, it can still be employed strategically, such as "It will clock in at nearly 450 pages, weigh more than four pounds, and be double the size of what was debated just five years ago. It's the City Manager's budget proposal and it will be released this Thursday."
- Question lead – not used often, since reporters are in the business of answering questions for the viewer, not the other way around. However, one example would be "What will the City Manager release this Thursday that could impact your wallet? It's the annual city budget." Of course, if you use a question lead, the next sentence should immediately provide the answer.

Any of the above leads can be used to draw interest into the story. Broadcast journalism need not adhere strictly to the inverted pyramid style of news delivery as long as the facts are presented to the viewing audience in the time allotted.

Descriptors

Still, there are differences when writing broadcast journalism versus print journalism. One example is that descriptions of someone in the news should be written before the person's name. Newspapers and online media typically put this information after the name, which is fine for reading but not for listening to conversationally. The difference can be illustrated like this:

Newspaper style – Michelle Edison, 41, entered the contest.
Broadcast style – 41-year-old Michelle Edison entered the contest.

The description of the person in this situation is her age. It is conversational to place that before the person's name, even though that phrasing costs an extra second or two in total running time. Other examples include:

- Motorcycle owner Justin James is looking forward to the race this weekend.
- Bowling champion Eduardo Sanchez celebrated a perfect game at the local alley.
- Chef Charla Hartley let her family sample the southern cuisine before she decided to write a cookbook.

Formal titles are a form of a descriptor that always precede a person's name. These usually specify occupations, political offices, and military ranks:

Newspaper style – Elon Musk, the CEO of Tesla Motors, says the electric car is the vehicle of the future.
Broadcast style – Tesla Motors CEO Elon Musk says the electric car is the vehicle of the future.
Newspaper style – John Fretti, Mayor of Thomasville, said the new bus system would be a success.
Broadcast style – Thomasville Mayor John Fretti said the new bus system would be a success.

Attribution

Similar rules apply to attribution. Whenever a news source says something in a story, the reporter attributes the quote to that news source. In print style, the attribution follows the quote, such as:

"There will be no tax increase" says Mayor Lou Fallon.

This is called delayed attribution, since the quote takes place before the person who said it. But reading such a sentence out loud doesn't sound conversational. Since broadcast text is written for the ear and not the eye, the solution is to place the attribution first:

Mayor Lou Fallon says there will be no tax increase.

Other examples are readily available and sound conversational when heard out loud.

- The Secretary of Commerce says inflation should hold steady for the rest of the year.
- Coach Walter Timson says the new playoff system is rigged against nonconference teams.
- Actor Chris Evans says that his days portraying a Marvel superhero are behind him.

Neutral Words

You may have already noticed that the sample sentences in this chapter use the word "says" a lot. There is a reason for that. In an ideal television newscast, the viewer would not be able to guess the political affiliation for the person delivering the news. The journalist should be neutral enough to deliver the news in an objective fashion without swaying the audience to one position over another. Using neutral words is a simple technique to avoid bias. Compare the following examples:

- The President said he would work with the Senate Majority Leader over the weekend.
- The President screamed he would work with the Senate Majority Leader over the weekend.

"Screamed" is far too emotional of a word to describe the President's demeanor unless there is video of actual screaming happening. But the word is a trigger that can sway the viewer to an unfavorable impression of the President. If "said" is too dull or repetitious, other neutral words that could prove workable would be "stated", "confirmed", or even "promised". But "screamed", "hollered", or "cackled" are examples of words to be avoided.

Numbers

Numbers are problematic for broadcast journalists, as viewers do not want complicated math problems orally delivered to them. Instead, large numbers are always rounded off to make it easier for the viewer to comprehend (as well as for the anchor to read off the teleprompter).

Let's say the city of Fresno, California, has a deficit of $318,945,441.22 for the current fiscal year. Instead of taking that number to the last penny, the television reporter will round it to the nearest large number. In this case, the deficit should be phrased as "nearly 320-million dollars".

This example also shows large numbers are written. Putting the phrase "nearly 320,000,000 dollars" on the teleprompter is baffling to the anchor. The correct strategy is to write "320-million". This is legible to the anchor and easy to read. In fact, numbers like thousands, millions, billions, and trillions are all written in this way.

Spelling out smaller numbers is also standard. All numbers from zero through twelve are spelled out, then numbers are assigned from 13 to 999. Larger figures, like the 320-million, are written out as combinations of figures and words. Examples include:

The class of 550 students will celebrate graduation Friday night.
Clara owns seven dogs.
The governor vetoed all five bills.
The car repair bill exceeded 23-thousand dollars.
The toll booth collected nearly three million dollars last year.

As you can see from the last example, the correct spelling is "three million", not "3 million". This is because the number before the "million" is between zero and twelve.

Dealing with numbers leads to symbols like the dollar sign $. Any time a symbol like dollars, euros, or any currency is used, be sure to write it out. It is also good practice to avoid using symbols like %, &, or # in your script without notifying the anchor first.

% should be written out as "percent", & means "and", while # means either "hashtag" (for UK audiences) or "pound sign" (for American audiences and some social media applications). Spelling out these symbols is easier for whoever will read them off the teleprompter.

Times and Places

Two elements that can easily become overly complicated in a news script are when and where things happen. The easiest style rule to follow in these cases is to write whatever phrasing sounds the most conversational. Let's take a look at some basic leads with the time element written oddly:

> The football game will take place this Saturday, August 19th, 2023.
> The baker opens her shop every day at six a-m in the morning.
> The deadline for filing the taxes is at twelve p-m in the evening.

Each of these sentences is problematic due to the time element. In the first one, the day of the game should simply be "this Saturday". The date is irrelevant as long as the next Saturday on the calendar is the correct one. If the game is taking place with at least another Saturday before the event, then the date should be given. The year reference is the worst offender of all. If a story is delivered on the air, it is assumed that the event will happen this year. The only time a year should be referenced in a story is if it isn't the current one that we are in. When college football teams plan to switch conferences in a few years, an election is happening in two years, or someone is training for the Olympics that will take place years from now, the year reference is understandable.

The remaining two sentences suffer from redundancy. If the baker opens her shop at six a-m, your two options are to either write it as "six a-m" or as "six in the morning". You don't need both "a-m" and "in the morning", as they mean the same thing.

The final sentence has the same problem, but with a twist. Twelve p-m is the middle of the day, not the middle of the night. And like the previous example, you don't need both "p-m" and "in the evening" together in the same sentence. The easiest solution for this is to write "The deadline for filing taxes is at midnight."

Editing Words Out

Several techniques are employed to shave seconds from each story. The challenge is that the story must be accurate, clear, concise, and unbiased, so using the correct wording is paramount regardless of story length.

First, avoid "filler" words. These are often modifiers that add little impact to a sentence while taking up precious time. "Very" is an excellent example of a word that is often not needed in a sentence. Other casual words that creep into daily conversations aren't necessarily conversational; instead, they're just filler words such as "you know" and "like". Many adjectives and adverbs can also be dropped if the sentence is clear without them.

Next, write in the active voice, not the passive voice. Consider the following example:

> Active – The college students watched the eclipse.
> Passive – The eclipse was watched by the college students.

The active voice in the first sentence puts the subject first. This makes the wording smoother and tighter for the viewing audience. If you are unsure if a passive sentence has crept into your script, look for "by" and see if the sentence's components can be flipped. Here are some other examples:

Passive –

- The job was completed by the workers.
- The mayor was elected by the voters.
- The cat was chased by the dog.

Each of these sentences can be rewritten to flow more logically if they are structured in an active voice, such as:

Active –

- The workers completed the job.
- The voters elected the mayor.
- The dog chased the cat.

Another quick technique for dropping unneeded words is found in the "be . . . ing" structure. This example illustrates the problem, followed by the solution:

The firefighters will be hosting a fundraiser this Saturday.
The firefighters will host a fundraiser this Saturday.

Removing the "be . . . ing" does not change the tense or impact of the sentence. Instead, you are deleting the auxiliary verb (in this case, "be") and changing the primary verb from "hosting" to "host". Other examples include:

- The couple will be taking a limo to the prom.
- The koala will be eating a snack later today.
- The coach will be naming a starting quarterback this weekend.

Versus

- The couple will take a limo to the prom.
- The koala will eat a snack later today.
- The coach will name a starting quarterback this weekend.

Subtle changes like these are expected in broadcast journalism. Simply put, write the way someone would hear it if you were telling them the story with short, declarative sentences. Conversationally relating the events of the day is a skill that can be mastered with practice.

Types of News Stories

Every story starts the day with a title, known as a slug. This is usually two or three words, like "Heat Advisory" or "Mideast Peace Talks". While a story may be rewritten throughout the day, the slug remains the same. Also, each story is written in split-column format, in which the video (what the audience sees) is in the left column while the audio (what the audience hears) is in the right column. This split-column format is consistent with the four basic types of stories: readers, VOs, VOSOTs, and packages.

Readers are the simplest news stories. Their name derives from their delivery; the anchor sits at the news desk, addresses the camera, and reads the story. There is no video placed over the story, so the viewing audience only sees the anchor's face. Readers average only 20 seconds in length, so brevity is crucial when writing them. Let's assume our anchor Ashli Moon is on the set delivering the reader to a medium shot (MS) on Camera 2, or V2 on the switcher. The left column has her technical information while the right column contains a reader on a heat wave.

<<(Ashli/MS/V2)>>	A heat wave is hitting the southern states just before the start of the Labor Day weekend. A wide swath from Texas to North Carolina has experienced heat indexes of over 100 degrees over the past two days. Governors in Georgia and Alabama have already declared a state of emergency. The hot weather is expected to last at least another five days.

VO (pronounced vee-oh) is an abbreviation for voice over. Think of the delivery of a reader, in which the anchor reads the story to the camera. After a few seconds have passed to establish the story, the image cuts to video of the news event. However, the anchor's voice continues over the video, thus the viewer hears the anchor's voice over the field footage. Because the outside footage is more compelling than the anchor behind the desk, VOs receive extra time within the newscast with a bit more information. Let's "expand" the heat wave reader to a 30 second VO with some video to roll in on VTR 4.

<<(Ashli/MS/V2)>>	A heat wave is hitting the southern states just before the start of the Labor Day weekend. A wide swath from Texas to North Carolina has experienced heat indexes of over 100 degrees over the past two days.
<<(ROLL VTR 4 HEAT WAVE TRT :30)>>	Residents are urged to stay inside during the afternoon hours. Some clinics have reported seeing an increase in the number of people with heat stress. Governors in Georgia and Alabama have already declared a state of emergency. The hot weather is expected to last at least another five days.

If the field reporter interviews someone for the story, that interview may be inserted into the VO, transforming the story into a VOSOT. The SOT stands for sound on tape, meaning the field interview is providing a clip that will run at full audio. This clip is called

96 *Television News*

either a SOT or a bite. During the newscast, the anchor will speak over the video as before, but will then be quiet while the bite airs so the audience can hear the interviewee speaking. Incidentally, adding the SOT also changed the way the VO is pronounced, as it is pronounced vo-sot, not vee-oh-sot. Most bites last between 10 and 15 seconds, thus the TRT for a VOSOT is typically around 45 seconds. Adding a bite to our current example results in this:

<<(Ashli/MS/V2)>>   A heat wave is hitting the southern states just
                              before the start of the Labor Day weekend.
                              A wide swath from Texas to North Carolina
                              has experienced heat indexes of over 100
                              degrees over the past two days.

<<(ROLL VTR 4   Residents are urged to stay inside during the
HEAT WAVE TRT :30)>>   afternoon hours.
                              Some clinics have reported seeing an increase in
                              the number of people with heat stress.

<<(SOT Hugh Campbell)>>   "Most people are used to this sort of heat, but
                              we're concerned with children and the elderly.
                              And of course, anyone working outside should
                              take it easy until the evening hours."

<<(Ashli/MS/V2)>>   Governors in Georgia and Alabama have already
                              declared a state of emergency.
                              The hot weather is expected to last at least
                              another five days.

The final main category for news stories is the package. This is a self-contained story that is produced by a field crew. It contains video, sound bites, and narration from a field reporter. Because the story is in-depth and merits the attention of a reporter, a typical package lasts between 75 and 90 seconds. A package often contains a stand-up, which is a bite delivered from the field reporter directly to the camera.

Expanding on the previous example, let's say Ashli is the anchor who is introducing the package. The reporter who completed the field package is Eric Sommers.

<<(Ashli/MS/V2)>>   A heat wave is hitting the southern states just
                              before the start of the Labor Day weekend.
                              A wide swath from Texas to North Carolina
                              has experienced heat indexes of over 100
                              degrees over the past two days. News 12's
                              Eric Sommers has more.

<<(ROLL VTR 4 HEAT WAVE   To say it's brutal out there is an understatement.
TRT 1:30>>   Residents are urged to stay inside during the
                              afternoon hours.
                              Some clinics have reported seeing an increase in
                              the number of people with heat stress.

<<(SOT Hugh Campbell)>>	"Most people are used to this sort of heat, but we're concerned with children and the elderly. And of course, anyone working outside should take it easy until the evening hours." The problem is a stalled high-pressure system that is stuck over the southeastern United States. The hot weather is expected to last at least another five days.
<<(SOT Hugh Campbell)>>	"I don't see how some of our people are going to get through the next few days. It's gonna be tough. I mean, electric bills are really high. We're trying to get the older folks to the mall in the afternoon hours just so they can cool off."
<<SOT Eric Sommers Close>>	"Governors in Georgia and Alabama have already declared a state of emergency. Officials in Mississippi, Louisiana, and South Carolina say they are adopting a wait and see attitude, but similar declarations are expected soon. For News 12, I'm Eric Sommers."

Notice that the left-hand column's final SOT of Eric Sommers says "Close" after his name. That's because the stand up comes at the end of the package. Other stand ups can be at the start of a package (Open) or in the middle (Bridge). Regardless of where they are placed, the stand ups from the field reporter are still marked as SOTs so the technical crew can make sure the audio levels and graphics are ready.

Finally, stories in a television newscast do not have any special notations at their conclusion. Broadcast journalists do not write "The End" on a script, because they do not want the anchor to read those words if they appear on the teleprompter.

Unwritten Exceptions

Teleprompters are a crucial tool in news stations. They allow multiple writers to create stories from different workstations simultaneously. These stories feed into a centralized news script, which is then approved by the news producer before it is read on the air by the news anchor. This allows for all stories to be checked for clarity and accuracy.

There are a few exceptions to the structured script. These are the "tosses" between anchors when they change segments of the news program. One example is when the news anchor turns to the sports anchor and asks something like "What's going on in the world of sports tonight?". That simple sentence is called a toss. It is seldom actually written out on the teleprompter. Instead, the news anchor will see a sentence on the prompter that says "Toss to Sports". The anchor then pivots to the sports desk and causally asks what is going on.

These conversational tosses are simple with just minimal practice. Seasoned anchors typically talk to the sports desk during a commercial break or before the show to learn about the top sports story of the day. When the "Toss to Sports" cue comes up on the teleprompter, the news anchor then tosses with a more detailed question. Instead of just asking "What's happening in sports?" the anchor gives a stronger toss, asking "Can you tell us more about that big announcement about the new baseball player?".

The other unscripted exception happens when the newscast runs a few seconds short on time. This may be due to a story falling through (the video drive failed to play) or all of the stories added together being just ten or 15 seconds short. In these cases, the words "Adlib Weather" or "Adlib Sports" are quickly inserted into the bottom of the news script; remember, the script is a dynamic document that can be changed at any time from a number of different workstations. Once the producer sees the newscast is a bit short, she can type in the cue to adlib, then also tell the anchor through their earpiece to stretch for time. The sports or weather anchor receives the same cue, allowing them to adlib an unscripted reminder to watch out for the weather or to get ready for the big game.

Looking Forward

Telling a factual story that engages the viewing audience in a short time frame is the cornerstone of television news. Stories may be as short as 20 seconds, meaning the script writer must tell the important elements of the story while adhering to the standard practices of fairness and accuracy. This must be accomplished on multiple stories per newscast, all while knowing that the station may air newscasts in the morning, at noon, during the early evening, and then finally at night.

Adhering to the basics in TV news writing is expected in newsrooms. This means crafting compelling leads, using descriptors before the person that is referenced, avoiding delayed attribution, employing neutral words, writing numbers, times, and places correctly, and editing words out any unnecessary words. The final stories are then presented in a split column format with video on the left and audio on the right. When delivered correctly, the result is an interesting, factual, and concise program that relays the news of the day.

Exercises

1. Locate the first story on a newspaper's website. This can be a local newspaper or one with a more national perspective, such as *USA Today* or *The New York Times*. Look for the inverted pyramid style of writing to identify the who, what, where, when, why, and how of the story.
2. Using that same story, write the information to produce a reader that lasts no longer than 20 seconds. Convey only the important points while discarding the facts that aren't needed.
3. Write a story about an upcoming event on campus, such as graduation or a football game. What kind of leads would you consider for that story?
4. Again using a newspaper, identify three different stories that use delayed attribution after direct quotes. Recraft those sentences with the attribution preceding the quotes.
5. Ask a classmate their opinion about a campus issue, such as parking on campus or tuition costs. Write a VOSOT containing the student's SOT. Remember to write a descriptor for the student that the anchor can read right before the SOT runs. It should look something like "College junior Henry van Doren says he can't afford to pay more money for his tuition."
6. Write a package about a local news event. Interview two people to obtain SOTs, then write your own stand up close to wrap up the package.

7. Watch a television newscast and take notes of how many times the news team uses the word "says" or "said". Also count how frequently other words, like "stated" or "promised", are sprinkled into the newscast.
8. During that same newscast, watch how often the news team makes a time reference. Pay particular attention to how often they talk about events "coming up", "happening now", or "at this hour".

Chapter Essentials

- News producers determine the total running time (TRT) of each story and how it will fit into a newscast.
- Television news stories use the split-column format that shows video in the left column and audio in the right column.
- Unlike newspaper writing, broadcast journalism places attribution before quotes and descriptors before the person's name.
- Readers are the shortest news stories. They contain no video and are typically 20 to 30 seconds in length.
- Voiceovers, VOSOTS, and packages are longer and have additional elements, such as sound on tape (SOT), field video, narration, and stand ups.
- Writing should be conversational and easy to digest in one viewing.
- Rewriting time references, removing unnecessary words, and writing in the active voice are professional strategies in broadcast journalism.
- Teleprompters allow scripts to be updated on a continual basis, even during the actual newscasts.

Online Links

Apstylebook.com. This direct link to the Associated Press Stylebook is widely regarded as the standard of news writing for professionals.

Poynter.org. This valuable resource from the Poynter Institute offers news, training, fact-checking, media literacy, and job leads for journalists in all types of media.

Rtdna.org. The Radio Television Digital News Association's website offers training, resources, networking, and awards for broadcast and digital journalists.

10 Radio

Key Words

Advertisement
Cold Read
Headline
Music Bed
Outcue

Radio Play
Reader
Sound Bite
Total Running Time
Wraparound

Historical Overview

In the early 1900s, radio broadcasts were unlicensed and largely uncontrolled. Amateur hobbyists and engineers obtained components, wired together transmitters, and literally broadcast their own voices from their homes. The reach of these low-powered home stations was dismal, so audiences were small. Even worse, the limited radio spectrum meant broadcasters often overlapped one another with voices competing on the same frequency. If a broadcaster faced too much competition on their usual frequency (let's say 810AM), they would simply move to an open frequency, like 1050AM, and start talking. The Federal Radio Commission, which was the forerunner of the Federal Communications Commission, eventually stepped in and regulated who could broadcast on what frequency.

Pittsburgh's KDKA earns the distinction of being the first commercial radio station in the United States. On November 2nd, 1920, KDKA went on the air to broadcast the results of the Harding-Cox presidential election. KDKA also set other historical precedents. In 1921, the station broadcast commentary of a boxing match, thus becoming the first live sporting event to air on commercial radio. The station also aired the first regularly scheduled church service, the first broadcast of a presidential inaugural address, and the first broadcast from a theater. Clearly, the opportunities to experiment with different types of programs reach back to the earliest days of radio.

Radio plays also became a popular option, blossoming in the 1930s. Eager audiences tuned in for Groucho Marx, Abbott and Costello, Jack Benny, Bob Hope, and a long list of entertainers who were transitioning to the new electronic medium. The Golden Age of Radio transitioned vaudeville performers and Broadway veterans into household names nationwide. The genres spanned comedy, drama, and even alien invasion. On Halloween Eve in 1938, Orson Welles broadcast the infamous *The War of the Worlds*. Radio had become so powerful that this groundbreaking production convinced many listeners that aliens were invading Earth.

DOI: 10.4324/9781003274766-11

Television ownership increased after World War II, so more radio stations pivoted from scripted shows to playing music. Disc jockeys like Dick Clark, Wolfman Jack, Alan Freed and Casey Kasem became famous with their personalities rivaling those of the musicians that they played. News and talk stations gave wide audiences to hosts like Joe Pyne and John Nebel in the 1950s and 60s. These on-air personalities paved the way for later hosts like Rush Limbaugh, Howard Stern, and Sean Hannity.

More than 15,000 radio stations are currently broadcasting in the United States. About 2,000 of these are news or talk stations with the rest offering music in different genres, such as country, classic rock, hip hop, and adult contemporary. At first glance, it would seem the market for scripting radio to be limited, but this is not the case. News and talk radio stations obviously require a great amount of written scripts. But music stations still have commercials, disc jockey breaks, and the occasional updates in news, weather, traffic, and sports. Each of these types of on-air segments requires a script. Of course, some air talent can easily adlib a quick traffic or weather update, but there are countless voices on the radio that would be lost without a written script in front of them.

Technical Specifications

Radio presents a unique challenge in that it must convey information using only audio. Not only must the story be conveyed aurally, but the transmission must be accomplished while the listener is probably not giving the program their full attention. Radio stations have their highest listenership during drive time hours. This means that the largest audience is when people are driving to work in the morning and then back home in the evening. In no other medium is the receiving audience so engaged with another activity, especially considering that they are often driving cars that weigh thousands of pounds.

Producers are aware of these distractions but still do their best to put together dynamic programming. This is done through voices, music, and sound effects. By blending them correctly, a show producer can create an exciting show that listeners will pay attention to despite driving their cars at the same time.

There are four main types of audio productions on radio stations that use slightly different scripting formats. The primary types of radio productions are:

- News
- Disc Jockey Morning Show
- Advertisement
- Radio Play

The style for each format is straightforward, but the nuances among these four deserve closer examination.

News

Most radio stations have a music format, such as country, urban, or rock. Because of this heavy reliance on music, local news updates are delivered by an on-air host who is a disc jockey, not a trained broadcast journalist. This leads to "rip and read", where the DJ simply reads the news from a website without bothering to rewrite any of the copy. Incidentally, the phrase "rip and read" is a disparaging term used about early announcers who were too lazy to write their own copy before going on the air; they would literally rip the words off the station's news printer and read the words verbatim on the air.

Using printers now is an unnecessary step. The DJ sees an upcoming break that they need to fill for 60 seconds, they scan their favorite websites for a story, and they read directly off the computer screen when prompted. All radio station control booths are online with web access, so the DJ saves time and printing costs by just reading off the screen.

However, the demand for radio news writing still exists for several reasons.

- Stations with news or news/talk formats rely heavily on journalists to fill the airtime.
- Radio station consolidation means one company will own several stations in one city, so a small news team may provide the news to different stations.
- Breaking local news may not be available online or the details are just coming through social media posts and chatrooms.

News stories fall into the categories of readers and wraparounds; the primary differences between the two are the length of the story and if an external sound bite is inserted. A variation of a reader is the headline, which may be just one sentence. The readers and headlines differ only due to their length, but the mechanics of writing them is identical.

All on-air hosts should be able to write a basic reader or headline. This is necessary when relaying information about a local emergency, weather situation, or traffic update. Fortunately, writing these stories is pretty simple.

Readers

The reader is a short news story that the host reads on the air, hence the term "reader". Each story lasts about 20 seconds and contains the relevant information for the listener: who, what, where, when, why, and how. For example:

> Wheatland police are asking everyone to stay away from the Brookwood and Patterson intersection when driving home from work tonight. Utility crews are patching up a gas leak there until at least midnight. Authorities have shut off the gas and there is no danger, but traffic is backed up in all directions.

This typical reader illustrates how simple it is to pack the needed information into a short amount of time.

Who – Wheatland police
What – drivers should avoid an area
Where – the intersection of Brookwood and Patterson
When – tonight until midnight
Why – utility crews are working to fix a gas leak
How – the crews are blocking the road to complete their job

Another popular news item for any radio station is providing updates on the local sports team. This time, let's answer the basic questions, then use that information to write a simple reader about the local high school football team.

Who – Wheatland Mules football team
What – victory over Stoutland Tigers 21 to 7
Where – Stoutland
When – Friday night
Why – to advance in regional football action
How – Running back Joey Frazier ran for 120 yards

The Wheatland Mules are winners again! The Mules beat the Stoutland Tigers on the road 21 to 7 in regional football play Friday night. Running back Joey Frazier racked up 120 yards in rushing to lead the offense.

The reader is the cornerstone of a radio newscast. By answering the basic questions, the host delivers the basic information in less than 20 seconds. Not every reader will contain all these items, but most of the elements should be in there. If there isn't even enough time for a humble reader, then a briefer headline can be deployed.

Headlines

An even shorter version of a reader is a headline. This is a quick news blurb that is voiced by the on-air talent and conveys only the outline of a story. Let's take the two previous examples of readers and add a financial headline for a quick news roundup. It would sound something like this:

Avoid Brookwood and Patterson when driving home, there's a gas leak. In sports, the Wheatland Mules won 21 to 7. And in finance news, gold up, dollar down.

Headlines are deceptively tricky to write because you must concentrate on what information can be excluded instead of what should be kept in the story. Very few headlines contain the classic "who, what, where, when, why, and how" of a story. Instead, they offer only enough information to wrap up the most important elements of a story. They can literally be just a few short words, such as:

Russia invades Ukraine.
Royals clinch World Series.
Temperatures plunge below zero.

Since headlines are so short, they are usually bundled together in a news roundup that is wedged between songs. This allows the on-air talent to interject some quick information into the program without interrupting the programming flow. Of course, the different music formats means that the topic of each headline and news roundup will vary among the stations. A new Rammstein tour may be mentioned on a rock station, but that news would never appear on a country or hip-hop station. Traffic and breaking news events may span all formats, but genre-specific updates are best given to those listeners who are interested in that particular news item.

Sound Bites

The headline and the reader rely solely on the on-air talent talking directly into the microphone. Adding in audio clips from other people brings another dimension into the story; this also introduces a new scripting wrinkle.

Before we examine this format, a quick explanation of the terminology would be helpful. A sound bite is an audio clip of someone else (not the on-air talent) talking about a particular story. But this audio clip can be referred to by different names depending on which radio producer uses it. A sound bite may also be called a bite, a byte, a sound on tape, an SOT, an actuality, or the shortened form of actuality, which is an ack. These terms are interchangeable, yet it can be confusing when one person calls a bite a "SOT" and another refers to it as an "S-O-T" by voicing the individual letters out loud. For our scripting purposes, we will use "sound bite", although "SOT" is the other term that is used the most frequently.

The station's format, time constraints, and the importance of the story all influence the length of a sound bite. At a news station, sound bites tend to run longer to allow the interviewee to fully explain the story; 12 to 15 seconds is possible. Music stations that use shorter news segments will use shorter sound bites, usually between 5 and 10 seconds long. Shorter sound bites are possible if just a quick quip is needed. If the Wheatland Mules celebrate a huge football victory and the winning coach's sound bite is just an excited "We did it!", that may last less than two seconds but it conveys the emotion needed for the story.

Using sound bites brings immediacy to the newscast. Fortunately, inserting them into the program just requires the following steps:

1. Conduct an interview with the news maker and record it as an audio file.
2. Identify a sound bite from the interview and edit it into a standalone file on software like Adobe Audition.
3. Write the story with that sound bite in mind. The easiest technique is to create a wraparound, described below.

Wraparounds

Radio news stories that combine the reporter's voice with a sound bite are called wraparounds. The story begins with the reporter speaking, then a sound bite rolling, then the reporter speaking again to finish up the story. Literally, the reporter's voice wraps around the sound bite, giving this type of story its name. A wraparound may have more than one sound bite, with the reporter's voice interjecting throughout the story.

Let's use a local sports scenario as a typical example. The story is about the local high school football team, the Wheatland Mules, advancing to the state playoffs. The first item listed is the slug; that is a two-to-three-word title of the story, which is "Mules Playoffs" in this scenario. The reporter is listed next followed by TRT. This stands for Total Running Time, which is the length of the entire wraparound. The script would be presented like this:

Mules Playoffs – Wraparound
Reporter – Rondetta
TRT – 58 seconds

The Wheatland Mules are once again heading to the state playoffs. The team finished with a nine and two record in class 1-A football. Coach Sherman Evens says his team is looking forward to postseason play.

(sound bite) / 12 sec.
Outcue: ". . . bring the championship home."
The Mules will rely heavily on star running back Joey Frazier. Joey is averaging nearly one hundred yards on the ground in each game this season. The junior says he owes it all to his teammates.
(sound bite) / 10 sec.
Outcue: ". . . blocking is everything."
The Hermitage Hornets will visit the Mules in first round action this Friday at Harrison Stadium. Tickets are on sales at the school's website. With your sports update, I'm Tony Rondetta.

That wraparound illustrates several new concepts. First, the sound bites are formatted left justified with their TRT, or total running time. The first sound bite is 12 seconds long and the second one lasts 10 seconds. Next, the entire quote does not need to be transcribed as long as the final words are written down. These words are the outcue, meaning they are the last words spoken by that person. Seeing the written outcue alerts the announcer that once they hear these words, the quote will end. Finally, the wraparound ends with a standard outcue that contains a sign-off from reporter Tony Rondetta.

The most important writing trick is to always identify the speaker in the sentence directly before the sound bite. In the above example, the reporter said "Coach Sherman Evens says his team is looking forward to postseason play" right before the coach's bite. After a few more lines, the reporter said "The junior says he owes it all to his teammates" before the running back's bite is heard. This technique is important in radio because the audience has no visual cues for who is speaking. The reporter should identify the speaker of the upcoming sound bite, then that sound bite should immediately play. This allows the listener to keep up with who is speaking even though they cannot see them.

Beyond Sound Bites

Sound bites are not the only types of audio clips available for a wraparound. Music and sound effects may also be used with some success, provided they are a natural addition to the story. A quick wraparound of a local composer's music is written using the same formatting as for sound bites:

Harding Music – Wraparound
Reporter – Rondetta
TRT – 52 seconds

You may not know his name, but if this song sounds familiar, you should get to know this local composer.
(music swells up to full) / 10 sec.
(music fades under)
That song is "Winter Among the Marshy Fields". The governor just announced it as the song of the year for our state. And the composer, Carl Harding, lives right here in Wheatland. He says he's thrilled that his song will be featured across the Show-Me State for the next twelve months.

(sound bite) / 14 sec.
Outcue: ". . . in my wildest dreams."
The song of the year is traditionally won by composers in metroplexes like Kansas City and Saint Louis. Carl says his tune shows that even people in small towns can make it big.
(sound bite) / 11 sec.
Outcue: ". . . have great music too."
Carl will be honored at the Governor's Mansion in Jefferson City next month. The award also comes with several guest performances across the state and a cash prize of ten thousand dollars. With your news update, I'm Tony Rondetta.

The above example shows how a music clip can be embedded into a wraparound, but such instances are rare in traditional news reports. Music beds and sound effects are used much more frequently in radio plays, advertisements, and during disc jockey shows.

Disc Jockey Morning Show

Most radio stations play music with disc jockeys serving as on-air talent. Whether it is hip hop, classic rock, country, or any other music format, the difference in news delivery from a news-talk format is clear; the person reading the news is primarily an entertainer, not a journalist. The delivery will be more casual, less authoritative, and tailored directly to that specific audience.

The styles of scripting a live radio show vary wildly due to the talent and experience of the on-air hosts. Let's look at a scenario with the rock band Queensryche coming to town. The basic information is:

Who – Queensryche
What – Concert
Where – Riverside Coliseum
When – Friday night at 7pm

There are other details as well. John 5 is the opening act, tickets are still available at the Riverside Coliseum, and Queensryche is promoting their new album *Digital Noise Alliance*, which is their sixteenth studio release. Given this information, a DJ can adlib a basic reader that can be voiced between songs, such as:

"Queensryche hits Riverside Coliseum this Friday at seven to support their new album *Digital Noise Alliance*. John 5 is the opening act and tickets are still on sale."

Not bad, but the DJ's ability to adlib and their knowledge of the subject can make a stronger reader, like this:

"Metalheads, are you ready to rock out to Queensryche? The band has just released *Digital Noise Alliance* and will unleash fifty-thousand watts of rock and roll this Friday night at the Riverside Coliseum! It's their sixteenth studio album, John 5 is opening up the show, and you have zero, and I mean zero excuses to not be there! Get your tickets at the Riverside Coliseum while they last and I'll see you at the show!"

The information is the same, but the second DJ has more enthusiasm and salesmanship to promote the show. This is better for ticket sales and is more exciting for the listening audience. Since the DJ is cobbling together the reader spontaneously, he may also play some Queensryche music underneath his announcement. Using music as a background while talking over it is known as a music bed; the music plays as a secondary audio source at a lower volume while the primary audio source (the DJ) talks over it.

Aside from announcing what song is up next, the most frequent reader for a disc jockey is a weather update. These reports can occur several times an hour, especially if a storm is brewing or the weather will impact the morning or evening commute. These are unscripted and consist of the DJ looking at the information on the Weather Channel or weather.com. They then summarize the information while reading it off their phone or computer screen. Typical weather information would be:

- Current temperature 62, high tonight of 75, overnight low near 50.
- Sunny skies now, clouds moving in later tonight with a 30% chance of rain this evening.
- Winds from the west at 10 miles per hour.

The DJ then delivers a cold read, which is reading on the air without having a rehearsal beforehand. A veteran DJ can adlib the above weather data into a quick 5 second weather update or stretch the information into a 30 second forecast. Most DJs accomplish this while cueing up the next song or advertisement.

Advertisement

Radio ads tend to have a duration of 30 seconds each. They can be national spots that are fed to the station as audio files or they may be produced in-house by the station's advertising department. Disc jockeys make extra money for providing voices for these ads. Receiving a stipend of $100 for reading a short 30-second spot is the minimum, while DJs in larger markets command much more for essentially 30 seconds of work.

The spots are written in a simple format. Sound effects (abbreviated as SFX), music, and character names are in all-caps, left justified. The SFX, music cues, and the names of the voice actors, including a narrator, are written in all capital letters. The script that is read by the talent is simply written as standard narrative. For example:

SFX:	BUSY OFFICE.
PERSON:	Unbelievable! I forgot my lunch again and I have no idea who delivers.
NARRATOR:	Hungry for something new?
PERSON:	I'm hungry for something for lunch if that's what you mean.
NARRATOR:	Pedro's Pizza Pockets offers free delivery during lunch hours.
PERSON:	Hey, that's when I need lunch!
MUSIC:	HAPPY MUSIC BEGINS IN BACKGROUND.
NARRATOR:	Pedro's pizza pockets. Lunch for just six bucks. Add two dollars for a drink or salad, or ten bucks for the full meal.

PERSON:	I'm going online and ordering now!
NARRATOR:	Pedro's Pizza Pockets! Free delivery for lunch. Order online and we'll be on our way!
PERSON:	Thanks, Pedro's!
MUSIC:	HAPPY MUSIC UP TO FULL.

Radio ads are built one piece at a time. Once the client approves the script, a producer will recruit voice talent to record the narrator and actors' lines. The talent will record those lines and deliver the audio files to the producer. The remaining step is for an editor (usually the producer) to put the SFX, music, and voice files into an audio timeline in a postproduction platform like Adobe Audition. The ad is then timed to hit as close to 30 seconds as possible. If the ad is a few seconds too long or short, the software can easily adjust it to the desired length. If the ad is not close to the 30-second mark, then copy will be added or subtracted.

Radio Play

The radio play, once a mainstay of audio programming, started to diminish once television became popular in American households. One hundred years ago, audiences tuned in for shows like *Amos 'n' Andy, Fibber McGee and Molly,* and *Our Miss Brooks* that expertly blended different audio elements to paint visual pictures for the listeners. Many of these series were extremely popular; *Amos 'n' Andy* was the first syndicated radio program, and it aired in different radio formats from 1928 to 1960. Although these shows are no longer on the air, they can be easily downloaded from several websites.

These pioneering shows painted visual pictures for the listening audience. Radio plays rely on strong voice work with various accents and intonations from the voice talent, but those voices are just one of the three elements needed to make a successful radio play. Each successful play skillfully mixed the following:

- Voice actors including narrators
- Music
- Sound effects

One of the most compelling radio programs ever was *The War of the Worlds*. Orson Welles created the program about an alien invasion for The Mercury Theatre on the Air. It aired on October 30, 1938, and was so realistic that many listeners believed that aliens had actually landed in New Jersey. One short script excerpt shows how the different elements were blended:

PHILLIPS:	A humped shape is rising out of the pit. I can make out a small beam of light against a mirror. What's that? There's a jet of flame springing from the mirror, and it leaps right at the advancing men. It strikes them head on! Good Lord, they're turning into flame!
SFX:	SCREAMS AND UNEARTHLY SHRIEKS
PHILLIPS:	Now the whole field's caught fire.
SFX:	EXPLOSION

PHILLIPS: The woods . . . the barns . . . the gas tanks of automobiles . . . it's spreading everywhere. It's coming this way. About twenty yards to my right . . .
SFX: CRASH OF MICROPHONE . . . THEN DEAD SILENCE

Not only were radio listeners panicked by the production, but the 23-year-old Welles was rocketed to fame before going on to direct and star in his first film, *Citizen Kane*, in 1941.

While *The War of the Worlds* showcased dozens of voices and sound effects, not all elements are needed to make a successful production. The Abbott and Costello classic routine *Who's On First?* relied heavily on just the voices of the two comedians. When scripted, the interchange about the confusing baseball players' names was pretty straightforward. The script looked like this:

Abbott: I say, Who's on first, What's on second, and I Don't Know's on third.
Costello: Are you the manager?
Abbott: Yes.
Costello: You going to be the coach too?
Abbott: Yes.
Costello: And you don't know the fellow's name?
Abbott: Well, I should.
Costello: Well then who is on first?
Abbott: Yes.
Costello: I mean the fellow's name.
Abbott: Who.
Costello: The guy on first.
Abbott: Who.

Productions like this have survived generations of listeners despite the gradual demise of their genre. Radio plays declined over the years with The CBS Radio Mystery Theater being the last major production to shut down. Produced from 1974 to 1982, CBS RMT created 1,399 plays that averaged 45 minutes in length with scary and mysterious subjects. The opening featured E.G. Marshall speaking with a creaky door and ominous music in the background. The plays achieved a cult following and, although they are no longer on the air, are still readily accessible online.

Looking Forward

The number of people listening to radio stations has dropped in the past decades. News can be gathered from many online sources, weather updates are instantly available on your cellphone, and anyone can build their own music libraries with audio files on a number of platforms. The need for radio seems to have diminished.

Many radio stations have since consolidated and cut staff. This means the disc jockeys, announcers, and news anchors now work at different stations under the same roof. While there are fewer positions available, the need for competent radio employees who can generate professional scripts continues. The basic scripting formats are expected to remain the same even as radio finds a new niche in the media landscape.

Exercises

1. Listen to 15 minutes of a local radio station and make note of the things you hear that are not popular songs; you want to concentrate on the ads and spoken word breaks between the music. How many ads do you count in that 15-minute timeframe? How many times does the on-air talent speak in that time? Do the people speaking sound like they are reading a script or adlibbing?
2. What are the four main types of radio productions? Which of those do you think you could personally voice on the air without a script in front of you?
3. Listen to the original *The War of the Worlds* broadcast from Orson Welles and the Mercury Theatre; it lasts just under an hour and can be readily found on the Internet. What are your thoughts about the program? Can you explain how it could cause so many listeners to believe that aliens were really invading Earth?
4. Research how many radio stations are available in your listening area. The website radio-locator.com is an excellent starting point for your search. How many of these stations did you already know about? Which of these stations did you not know existed until you saw them on the list?
5. Use the following weather information to adlib three different weather reports. The information is a current temperature of 68 degrees, mostly sunny skies and light winds from the west. Today's high should be 70. Showers possible tonight with an overnight low near 45. Storms move in tomorrow morning and are expected all day with a high of 60 and a low again near 45. Rainfall tomorrow may be over an inch. The extended forecast has storms lingering for the next few days with total rainfall accumulation of possibly two inches with flooding in low lying areas. Using this information, adlib a ten-second weather report, a 20-second weather report, and a 30-second weather report. You will not use all the information in each weather update so concentrate on the most important elements in each one.

Chapter Essentials

- Radio scripting can be broken into four broad categories: News, Disc Jockey Morning Show, Advertisement, and Radio Play
- News stories are either readers or wraparounds. Headlines are a collection of very short readers. Adding a sound bite to a reader creates a wraparound.
- News reports are brief and can only convey basic information (who, what, where, when, why, and how) in a short amount of time.
- Disc jockey morning shows rely more on adlibbing and are generally unscripted; the DJ receives basic information from a website and paraphrases to their liking.
- Advertisements and radio plays use voices, music, and sound effects to convey their respective messages. The scripting is similar, with dialogue for the voice talent clearly spelled out and the other elements (music and sound effects) written into the script as well.

Online Links

Cbsrmt.com. The home of CBS Radio Mystery Theater provides access to all 1,399 episodes of radio shows that were produced from 1974 to 1982.

Radio-locator.com. A searchable database that allows you to enter your zip code and find all of the licensed AM and FM radio stations in your area. It lists the stations' call letters, frequency, format, and their city of origin.

Radio-online.com. A wealth of current radio news that covers radio stations, formatting, and personalities. It also contains ratings for radio stations in individual markets to reveal what formats are popular among listeners.

11 Interview Shows

Key Words

Active Listening
Closed-Ended
Follow Up
Hypothetical

Open-Ended
Outside-the-Box
Straw Man
Tough Questions

Historical Overview

Most people equate an interview as a necessary step to obtaining a job. Interviews in this sense will ask about your background, your qualifications, and other attributes to make sure you are the right fit for the advertised position. Otherwise, people tend to avoid taking part in formal interviews for most of their lives. Asking or answering direct questions can take on an adversarial tone that makes some people uncomfortable. For others, it is so rare to be part of an interview that it's somewhat surprising when it happens.

Talk shows have been a mainstay of television programming for decades. The first one debuted in 1951 in WJZ-TV in New York with host Joe Franklin. The show was so popular that it moved to WOR-TV in 1962 and ran successfully until 1993. The longest-running talk show, *The Tonight Show,* began in 1954 with Steve Allen serving as the host. Since then, duties have passed through hosts like Jack Paar and Johnny Carson before Jimmy Fallon assumed the reins. Other late night talk shows include *Jimmy Kimmel Live, Late Night with Seth Meyers*, and the *Late Late Show with James Corden.*

Afternoons are also prime hours for daytime talks shows. *The Oprah Winfrey Show* was the highest-rated daytime talk show in the history of American television, tallying more than 4,500 episodes over an award-winning 25-year run. Other daytime hosts like Phil Donahue, Sally Jessy Raphael, Ricki Lake, and Kelly Clarkson also found audiences craving celebrity interviews and "lighter" news, plus occasional musical guest performances.

Not all talk shows are the same. The late-night talk shows begin with the host delivering a comedy monologue and then concentrate on variety entertainment. Daytime talk shows feature longer celebrity interviews and may include some lifestyle or fashion segments. Sunday morning talk shows are hard-hitting programs that spotlight political interviews; *Meet the Press, Face the Nation,* and *Fox News Sunday* are three such programs.

DOI: 10.4324/9781003274766-12

Regardless of subgenre, talk shows share specific characteristics that define them in the media landscape. Most notably, talk shows:

- Involve a host who moderates the program and conducts interviews.
- Feature guests who may or may not agree with the host's point of view.
- Are produced at low cost with minimal post-production editing.
- Air outside of prime time viewing hours.

This chapter deals with scripting interview programs in which the interviewee will likely be a celebrity, politician, or some other public figure – literally, people who are accustomed to being in the spotlight and answering questions. A handful of these interviewees will demand a list of questions before appearing on camera while others are content to trust the host with any line of questioning. The most common scenario is between these two extremes; the host (or their producer) will provide the interviewee with the topics they will talk about before the cameras roll.

Technical Specifications

The situations addressed in this chapter are designed for an in-depth interview, not news interviews for television, radio, or newspaper news stories. Those scenarios often rely on quick moments when a newsmaker provides an update on a breaking story. As described in the television news chapter, the bulk of news stories focus on the 5 Ws and 1 H: who, what, where, when, why, and how. Interview programs go far beyond these cursory questions to find more in-depth responses.

There are four categories of interview questions: closed-ended, open-ended, hypothetical, and outside-the-box. Each of these types can be used throughout an interview and are worthy of further exploration.

Closed-Ended Interview Questions

A closed-ended interview question is formatted to elicit a simple response from the guest. These questions do not require an elaborate answer or detailed explanation. A yes/no question is typical, as it gives just two options for a succinct answer. Sample closed-ended questions would be:

- Are you going to press felony murder charges in this case?
- Are you looking forward to the game this weekend?
- Will there be a thunderstorm tonight?

Another option is when the question asks for an answer with an implied set of limited answers. This casts a wider net than the yes/no format, but there are still finite possibilities for an answer. Samples include:

- On what weekday will the road construction be finished? (The potential answers here are only Monday through Friday).
- What is your astrological sign? (There are only twelve signs in the Zodiac).
- What is your favorite color? (There are many colors in the spectrum, but this is closed-ended because the range of answers is still limited, plus the question can be answered with a single word, like "blue" or "orange").

A slightly broader variation of the closed-ended question asks for a response on a rating scale, such as the following questions:

- On a scale from one to five, how much did you like the movie?
- On a scale from one to ten, how hard was the test?
- On a scale from one to one hundred, how much did you hate the casserole?

A more formal standard, which is often used in statistical analysis, is the Likert Scale. This approach asks for an opinion but is phrased as a statement with possible options serving as the answers, like this:

- The website is easy to navigate.
- The Democrats have done a good job balancing the budget.
- It is a simple commute to my job during rush hour traffic.

The potential answers are then listed as:

Strongly Agree – Agree – Neither Agree nor Disagree – Disagree – Strongly Disagree

An important consideration when creating a Likert Scale is to offer an odd number of options. This allows a user to have a neutral opinion instead of having to choose a side when they don't have a strong feeling one way or the other. The Likert scale is generally not useful in an interview situation, as it comes across as stuffy and too formal; it's also ponderous to list all the answers in a verbal setting. However, an interviewer can offer an abbreviated version of a Likert Scale by just providing three choices, such as:

- Would you say the road trip was great, awful, or something between those extremes?
- Do you think Carl is a great friend, a terrible enemy, or neither of the above?
- For Thanksgiving, do you prefer to be with all your family members, by yourself, or somewhere in the middle?

Overall, closed-ended questions are useful in rapid-fire news scenarios where there is limited time to ask questions among a mob of reporters. The downside is that the answers do not allow the guest to convey emotion or additional information in their answers. If you have the luxury of conducting an interview one on one, a few closed-ended questions are fine to establish some basic facts, like:

- Will you promise to not raise taxes?
- Is this your final appearance in an *Avengers* movie?
- Did you travel to Germany to meet your girlfriend?

The benefits of closed-ended questions are that they can be answered quickly and simply, they can help to get rid of irrelevant answers, and they can be easily customized for each individual guest. The downsides are that they limit the ability to provide detailed information, too many of them in a row will feel like an interrogation, and a blunt question may be answered with a terse "no comment".

Once the initial facts are provided by the guest, it's time to move on to questions that will allow more elaboration and insight. These open-ended questions allow a deeper dive into the emotion and background of the person being interviewed.

Open-Ended Interview Questions

Most questions in media interviews are open-ended. These questions allow for the guest to give detailed answers and express their own point of view. The greatest advantage of these questions is that they can be used equally well in informative news interviews and emotional eyewitness interviews. There is literally no type of interview setting in which an open-ended question will not work. Samples of open-ended interview questions include:

- Can you describe what it was like to be back in the recording studio?
- What steps did you take to make sure you balanced the budget?
- What direction do you see your acting career taking in the next few years?

These questions solicit answers that provide unexpected new insights, give more background information, and allow the guest to express their opinion. The drawbacks are that they can lead to rambling, time-consuming answers, may contain irrelevant details, and may take the interview into an area that the host would rather avoid. However, the open-ended question is an excellent transition to the hypothetical question.

Hypothetical Interview Questions

A hypothetical question calls for speculation on the part of the guest because the answer is based on supposition, not facts. It can be used with great impact in a wide range of situations, ranging from serious political situations to freewheeling entertainment segments. Let's look at how a hypothetical question can be effective in serious interviews:

- What is your biggest concern if Democrats take control of the Senate?
- How do rising oil prices impact the average American family?
- What could happen if the European Union expands further into Eastern Europe?

Of course, a good hypothetical question is especially powerful when speaking with a creative person, such as an actor or a comedian. Hypothetical questions beg for unusual answers and can elevate an interview by providing outlandish scenarios to the interviewee. The randomness of a hypothetical question empowers them, so asking an unexpected question can lead to amusing results. Examples of hypothetical questions could be:

- If you had to be surrounded by just one aroma, and you and everyone around you would smell that for the rest of your life, what would that aroma be?
- You must eat lunch at the same restaurant every day for the next year. You can order whatever you like, but you must eat the entire meal every day. What restaurant would you choose?
- What is your best strategy for surviving a zombie apocalypse?

There are drawbacks to a hypothetical question. Once you ask a silly question to a comedian, the interview can quickly lose focus. In a serious setting with a politician, asking too many "what if" questions can lead to rampant speculation without any fact-checking. The hypothetical question should be planned well in advance, much like an outside-the-box question.

Outside-the-Box Interview Questions

An outside-the-box question gives the interviewee the chance to show their creativity and immediate problem-solving skills. These were first popularized in job interviews for salespeople. The hiring manager would show the job candidate a pen and say, "Sell me this pen". This simple exercise reveals how well the person responds under pressure to perform the job for which they have applied.

These questions are popular on late-night interview shows where the purpose is to entertain first and inform second. Asking a scandal ridden U.S. Senator about their favorite type of ice cream is insulting to the viewer and weakens your credibility as an interviewer. Instead, asking an unusual, outside-the-box question is used more effectively when trying to provoke thought from the interviewee. The questions may or may not be comedic (hypotheticals tend to be funnier), but they can elicit a range of answers from funny to serious, depending on the interviewee. Some examples are:

- What is the animal you identify with the most?
- What meal would you serve to picky elementary school children?
- What book would you recommend to everyone who wanted to know you better?

Ideally, hypothetical and outside-the-box questions should be reserved for the latter part of the interview. Once you open the door to speculative questions, it can be hard to pull the tone of the interview back to the simpler closed-ended and open-ended questions.

Mixing Questions

Interviews should contain a variety of the four types of questions. Most questions will be open-ended, but mixing in closed-ended, hypothetical, and outside-the-box queries will provide for a more well-rounded interview. Imagine an interview that contained only closed-ended questions. It would quickly come across as an interrogation that does not give the guest any chance to provide emotion or insight.

The same could be said for hypothetical questions. The first quirky question will pull in laughs. But repeatedly pitching bizarre scenarios to a guest will become stale, as no real information is passed along to the viewer. Only by mixing the types of questions can an interview be both informative and entertaining.

Professional interviews follow a consistent pattern. A host does not jump in with rapid-fire questions before the guest is introduced to the audience, nor does the interview end abruptly. The steps for an interview are:

- The host introduces themselves, the show, and the guest.
- The host personally welcomes the guest and thanks them for their time.
- The interview commences with a series of questions.
- The interview ends with a quick wrap-up and a preview of what is next.

A basic interview script follows this template by providing an introduction, the questions for the host, space for the guest to provide answers, and then a wrap-up. The format below is a simple template that can be used for one-on-one interviews in a studio setting.

The template features the title, centered and in bold with a larger font. The words "Fade In:" appear left-justified directly under the title. The single-spaced introductory paragraph briefly describes the set and identifies the host and the guest. If there is a studio audience or in-house musicians, they should also be mentioned here. The host and guest each have their names centered, in all capital letters, in bold type. The questions are centered and single-spaced with space left open for the guest's answers. The resulting script looks something like this:

"Frank Talk With Frank"

Fade In:
The studio is set with Frank Barnas in a director's chair to one side. Actor Brad Pitt sits in the other director's chair on the opposite side. A small bar-height table with soft drinks sits between them. The set has a fake window in the back to make it look like the Hollywood sign is in the background. An in-studio audience is off camera.

FRANK
Good evening, everyone, and welcome to Frank Talk With Frank. I'm Frank Barnas and my guest today is actor Brad Pitt.
(Crowd Cheers)

FRANK
Brad, thanks for joining us. Now, a lot of people know you're from Missouri, but not everyone knows your old high school was Kickapoo and the mascot was the Chiefs. What were your memories of some of the traditions there, like Pow-Wow Night and the Tomahawk Chop?

BRAD
(Brad Answers First Question)

FRANK
Some of the current students at Kickapoo say the mascot and the traditions are insulting to the Kickapoo tribe. What's your reaction?

BRAD
(Brad Answers Second Question)

FRANK
Regardless of which side of the debate people fall on, are you surprised that this issue has just recently come up with students?

BRAD
(Brad Answers Third Question)

FRANK
Brad, we appreciate you taking the time to stop by for a few minutes. And everybody, go check out his new movie, *Ocean's 14*. Up next, we'll catch up with rock star

Alice Cooper about his views on organized religion. That's right here after this commercial time out. Stay with us.

(Crowd Cheers)

Fade Out:

Starting a script for an interview show means you must prepare some basic information for the benefit of the viewing audience. A bit of research goes a long way, like in the previous example. A lot of fans may know that Brad Pitt is from Missouri, but just a few minutes of online sleuthing shows his high school mascot was a Kickapoo Chief. A bit more research reveals the controversy that can propel much of the interview.

Warming Up Interviewees

It is a common courtesy to treat interviewees with respect. This means meeting them before the interview and sharing some small talk to put them at ease. Most interviews are not adversarial but are an exchange of information that is designed to inform and entertain the audience. Having a relaxed banter with the guest is key to creating a natural conversation in front of the audience. This can only happen if the interviewee feels comfortable talking to you.

A producer may help with these warm-ups, but it is up to the host to take part as well. This only takes a few minutes and should be done as close to the interview as possible. Professional studios will have a green room for guests to relax in before appearing on the show; this is a perfect setting for the host to stop in, introduce themselves, and quickly run over the thrust of the interview (let's talk about your upcoming album, for example). This is not an in-depth meeting, but just a polite hello before the cameras roll.

Timing

Except for open-ended podcasts, interviews are subject to time and space limitations. Newspaper and magazine interviews have limits with how many column inches can be dedicated to a single source. Likewise, news and television interviews are under strict time constraints.

A typical late-night entertainment show lasts for 60 minutes. Subtracting 18 minutes of commercials leaves 42 minutes. The show will typically have an opening host monologue, a musical or stand-up comedy act, and a few interviews. Each interview will fill a different amount of time depending on how famous the guest is; actor Brad Pitt will receive a twelve-minute interview while a brand-new comedian will get just a fraction of that amount. It falls to the host and the producers to make sure that each interview segment is entertaining and fits the allotted time.

Let's take an example of a new movie debut with A-list actress Natalie Portman. Her agents and advance team will work with the producer to develop a list of questions for the show. After all, she is promoting a new movie and her appearance can spur ticket sales. Questions about the new film, its plot, and her character will serve as the basics. Then the producer and host will discuss how to talk about the film further. Is this movie a sequel to another blockbuster? Is it an action piece that required her to train for several months? Did she need to pick up a unique talent, like playing the mandolin or speaking Thai, to immerse herself in the character?

Once pre-set questions about the newest project are done, any remaining time will be filled with questions that are designed to put the guest in the best possible light. An actress like Natalie Portman is a veteran of hundreds of questions from countless interviewers, so this is an opportunity to ask her something memorable. This is the point of the interview to ask her a hypothetical or outside- the-box question. After all, who wouldn't want to know how Natalie Portman plans to survive a zombie apocalypse?

Active Listening

No amount of interview preproduction can prepare for an unexpected answer. While the host may generate a list of prepared questions, that same host must actively listen to the answers. This means engaging with the guest, making eye contact, and paying attention to the answers as they are being given. Zoning out during a conversation is not an option.

This is where the professionalism of the host comes into play. Not only is the host guiding the interview, but he is also receiving cues to keep the interview segment on time. Add to that the art of keeping composure in front of a studio audience and paying attention to the guest, often on live television, and the pressure on the host becomes immense. If Natalie Portman from the above example said she hated the director on her new film and she'd never work with him again, that is an unexpected answer that deserves a follow up question.

The Follow Up

Follow up questions are born from active listening and are often unscripted. The natural banter between the host and guest will allow for the interview to evolve like a casual conversation. Expanding on the above example, let's follow up with Natalie Portman:

Host:	And the director of your new film, how was he?
Portman:	Terrible. Literally, it was like amateur night at community theater.
Host:	That's awful. What happened?

If the host was following a predetermined list of questions, he could have simply glossed over her comment and moved on. Instead, listening actively opened a new line of dialogue that let her give a personal response for the viewing audience.

Asking Tough Questions

Most people avoid being confrontational and shy away from asking tough questions directly to someone. This is especially true when the subject matter may make the interviewee embarrassed, hurt, or even combative. There are techniques to handle such interviews and their approaches can vary greatly.

Jay Leno once had such an interview with actor Hugh Grant while hosting *The Tonight Show* in 1995. The exchange is so famous that it saved Grant's faltering career while also propelling Leno to his first-ever ratings win over David Letterman's *Late Show*. Grant had been arrested for lewd conduct with sex worker Divine Brown. As a British actor who traditionally played a reserved and proper character, this arrest made international headlines and threatened to sink his career. Leno booked Grant for the show and started the interview with "Let me start with question number one. What the hell were you thinking?". Directly asking the obvious question and allowing Grant to apologize for his actions was the right approach to handle this interview.

Other interviewers, particularly in politics, deflect the question to come from someone else's point of view. This is called a straw man approach in which the host is citing an unnamed person as the source of the question. An example would be "Some people claim that your diet pills are bad for teenagers. How do you respond to that?". The difficulty comes when the interviewee flips the question back at the host with "Who says that?". The better option is to cite an actual source, like "The FDA says that your diet pills are bad for teenagers. How do you respond to that?". This gives more credibility to the question and allows the host to frame it from a position of authenticity.

Wrapping Up the Interview

Once the time is up, you are ready to graciously wrap up the interview. This should be done in a three-step process that only takes a few seconds.

1. Thank the person for their time.
2. Promote what they are doing next.
3. Promote what you are doing next.

Assuming the interview is on live television, the easiest good-bye is thanking the guest for stopping by, then turning to the camera and issuing a call to action on behalf of the guest. If they have a new film coming out, a simple "check out her new movie in the theaters" will suffice. If it's an athlete, tell the audience to root for their team. A new ice cream shop? Tell the people to stop by to try out a delicious banana split.

The final step is to tell the audience what will be next on your show. This can be something vague like "Stick around, we'll be right back" or a more specific preview of the upcoming guest, like "When we come back, Aldo Nova will join us with a look back at his music catalog. Stay with us!".

Looking Forward

Compared to forms of television like news, episodic series, and even game shows, interview programs are cost-efficient for producers to create. Once a host and studio space are retained, the guests can be recruited for either free or a relatively small amount. Audiences find interviews with celebrities engaging, ratings are solid, and advertisers are happy to buy commercials on the shows. There is no reason to expect interview shows to falter in the coming years.

The basics of scripting for these programs shows no signs of immediate change, as the host is likely to follow their preferred format for years. Some hosts have detailed questions while others are more spontaneous. Either way, listening to the guest and creating a strong narrative flow throughout an interview is key to producing a successful show. In this program, the host largely determines the scripting format; once that is settled, a writer can expect that template to continue for the show's duration.

Exercises

1. List three people you would like to interview. They should consist of one musician, one politician, and one athlete. Which of the three would you like to interview the most? Why?

2. Of the three people in the previous question, jot down ten questions you would like to ask your favorite of that trio. Avoid basic questions that you can answer with an Internet search, like where they are from and if they are married. Instead, concentrate on their current projects. How do they feel their latest projects (a song, a legislative move, a game) turned out? What's next for them?
3. Imagine you have a time machine and can travel back to interview your ancestor from 200 years ago. Knowing that they do not have the references of technology, electricity, or any modern conveniences, what would be the focus of your interview?
4. Ask a classmate ten questions in a row but only use closed-ended questions. Does it feel like an interrogation, or does it feel like a natural exchange of information?
5. Come up with three hypothetical questions to ask your classmate; there are ample websites that offer examples. What kind of answers did you receive? Could you use these same questions to your family members or as conversation starters at a party?

> **Chapter Essentials**
> - Talk shows started in the 1950s and have appeared on the air ever since.
> - Interview shows can be broken into subgenres including late-night talk shows, daytime talk shows, and Sunday morning news programs.
> - Interview questions can be divided into four categories: closed-ended, open-ended, hypothetical, and outside-the-box.
> - The four parts of an interview are the introduction, thanking the guest for appearing, the questions, and the wrap-up.
> - Actively listening to the guest is the key to developing follow up questions.
> - Tough questions can be asked directly or by using a straw man approach.
> - The three elements to wrap up an interview are to thank the guest for their time, promote their newest product, and then tease what is coming up next in your show.

Online Links

conversationstartersworld.com. While not geared specifically for media interviews, this website provides lists of all philosophical questions, ice breakers, and other lines to start conversations in social settings. The list of 170 hypothetical questions is a must-read.

journalism.co.uk. This website features a great deal of information about the journalism field but typing "how to interview" into its search box will yield a stunning array of tips, articles, and ideas for every interviewing situation.

sportsandthemind.com. This site focuses on the mental side of sports, so it provides questions to obtain insight from athletes. The questions are broad enough to cover all sports and serve as a springboard for more in-depth queries.

12 Reality and Live Television

Key Words

Awards Show
Celebrity Show
Competition Show
Confessional
Live Event
Musical Concert

Personal Journeys
Relationship Show
Setlist
Shooting Ratio
Sports Event

Historical Overview

Television is awash with reality and live television programs. Reality TV is key to primetime television, with shows like *Hell's Kitchen, The Voice,* and *LEGO Masters* promising prizes to contestants in their unique competitions. Some cable channels base much of their programming around reality TV; the Food Network alone airs a buffet of reality series including *Chopped, Beat Bobby Flay, The Pioneer Woman, Guy's Grocery Games, Restaurant: Impossible, Cutthroat Kitchen,* and *Ace of Cakes.* Some shows are so popular that they have their own spinoffs, like *The Real Housewives* series on Bravo. It started in 2006 with *The Real Housewives of Orange County* but has since exploded to 11 American installments (*New York City, Potomac, Salt Lake City,* etc.), 20 international versions (*Melbourne, Amsterdam, Lagos,* etc.), and 26 spinoffs (like *Vanderpump Rules, Bethenny & Fredrik,* and even a show featuring the employees of a former housewife, *Vanderpump Rules: Jax and Brittany Take Kentucky*).

Live television is equally formidable. The Super Bowl averages 100 million viewers each year, making it the highest rated TV show in the US. Channels like ESPN and Fox Sports air live games in baseball, football, basketball, hockey, and a myriad of other sports to fill airtime. Not only do events like the *Scripps National Spelling Bee* and the *World Series of Poker* find a place on television, but even shows featuring contestants playing dominos and cornhole are readily available.

Live TV is not limited to just sports coverage. Awards shows like the Oscars and Emmys still command prime time slots and attract millions of viewers. Seasonal favorites such as Dick Clark's *New Year's Rockin' Eve* continue to draw audiences despite Dick Clark having passed away in 2012. MTV, Nickelodeon, ESPN, and an array of other cable channels have created their own annual awards shows to honor winners and pull in viewers. Even though live television requires a great deal of timing and coordination, audience demand to see things happen "live" is an ongoing phenomenon.

Reality and live television share one overriding characteristic regarding their scripting; they are outlined and guided, but not truly written as a final script. Unlike the other media in this textbook, these two genres do not have a script that is adhered to by a cast and production crew. Instead, a skeletal framework is established, and the program unfolds organically (like a baseball game) or is shaped more in postproduction (like a reality show). Although these approaches differ, the outcome for each is that the finished script contains many holes that are filled on the fly. We will step through each of these different yet surprisingly similar genres in this chapter.

The definition of reality television is open for debate. Broadly, it features people in real-life situations that do not have traditional scripts or story structure. The forerunner of modern reality TV was Allen Funt's *Candid Camera*, which debuted in 1948. The show featured unsuspecting people facing comedic situations while being filmed with hidden cameras. Other reality shows made it to TV, but the genre truly exploded in the early 1990s due to simple economics. Cable television channels were flourishing but they needed cheap round-the-clock programming. MTV unveiled *The Real World* in 1992, paying seven cast members a mere $2,600 each for appearing that season. The formula proved successful and modern reality TV was recognized as a viable programming option. Other shows, such as *Big Brother, Survivor,* and *The Amazing Race* soon followed, proving that even the traditional networks were happy to pay for lower-cost shows.

Traditional television series like dramatic one-hour crime series and half-hour sitcoms pay top dollar for the cast, crew, and studio sets. Reality television shows still need a crew, but it can be fewer people. Studio sets (like the office setting in *The Office*) don't exist in many reality shows that are set at cheaper locations. The biggest cost savings are with the cast; instead of paying the six stars of *Friends* a million dollars each per episode during that show's final season, a producer can cast someone in a reality television show for a few thousand dollars. While that reality show may not become the cultural phenomenon of a scripted series, there are plenty of reality shows that have generated ample money. *MasterChef, American Idol, 90-Day Fiancé, Teen Mom: Young and Pregnant,* and *Big Brother* are just a few examples of popular reality TV series.

The challenge with these reality TV programs is that, by definition, they are "real", thus no scripts are written for them. But there is no chance that a production company would simply aim cameras at ordinary people and hope for dramatic confrontations to ensue. Instead, the producers guide the story along by setting up conflicts, creating deadlines, pitting contestants against one another, offering rewards, and adding confessionals for the participants.

Live television operates under similar scripting parameters. There is no script for a football game, simply because no one knows the outcome until the game is over. Much of the excitement from a live event stems from the real dramatic tension over who will win an award or who will hit a home run. Yet a template (not a script) is created before the event so the production crew knows what shots need to be covered, when the mics should be turned on, and how long the commercial breaks will last. Like a reality TV show, a live TV producer will not simply arrive at the event and hope for the best. There must be a plan.

Technical Specifications

Reality television is based on narrative drama. Petty arguments, sibling rivalries, and budding relationships feed the dramatic narrative that moves the story along. Some categories are based on a "beat the competition" structure, with a ticking clock to help pace the episode. Other shows follow celebrities through their daily lives or focus on interpersonal relationships.

One common element of reality TV shows is the use of confessionals from the participants. These segments are when the person delivers their point of view directly to the camera. This storytelling technique does away with an omniscient narrator or graphics to move the plot along. Instead, the participant can talk about an event, describe their innermost thoughts, provide a recap of what has happened, and then tease a new upcoming event. These unscripted moments are guided along by the writer/producer, but no formal script is delivered. This keeps the delivery natural and believable.

Another factor that impacts reality TV is the shooting ratio. This is how much footage is shot for a program as opposed to how much is used in the final edit. For example, shooting 50 hours of footage for a one-hour show means working with a 50 to 1 ratio, shown as 50:1. A confessional with a sobbing teenager who was stood up on his date may have taken 45 minutes to shoot, but only a few clips lasting about 15 seconds each will make it to the final show. Clearly, a high shooting ratio gives the producer (and now the postproduction editing team) incredible latitude to shape the story. That sobbing teenager may have simply waved his hands in a "pushing" gesture, but when that is edited around the would-be girlfriend's image, it conveys that he is done with the relationship. Seeing the whole interview in context may have just shown he was frustrated with the questions being asked and his movement had nothing to do with the girlfriend.

Keeping the all-present confessionals and high shooting ratios in mind, reality television shows can be broken into four broad categories: competition programs, relationship programs, personal journeys, and celebrity programs. None of these has a locked script before production, but the guidelines used by each category are worth closer examination.

Competition Programs

Programs that feature competitions for a cash prize are a mainstay of reality television. These can be divided along a spectrum of whether the viewer could participate or merely observe. *The Amazing Race* features "regular" people who fit minimal criteria: the willingness to travel around the world, see exciting new countries, and participate in a wide range of challenges with your traveling partner. The team that comes in last each week is eliminated until only one remains at the end of the show. This winning pair receives one million dollars.

The middle of the spectrum are reality programs where the viewer may be good enough to win if they have some hidden ability. *American Idol* offers everyday people a chance at stardom if they can sing. *MasterChef* features regular cooks who may be brilliant, but theoretically anyone could compete. *Worst Cooks in America* takes the idea to the opposite extreme in which truly awful cooks are trained in a kitchen boot camp to improve their culinary skills.

The other option is competition shows featuring contestants that are already experts in their field. *Ink Master* displays seasoned tattoo artists, *Forged in Fire* brings together world-class bladesmiths, and *Blown Away* spotlights experts in creating glass blown sculptures. Each contestant competes to win a cash prize at the end of a show (*Forged in Fire* wins $10,000) or at the end of a season (*Ink Master* takes home $100,000 and a feature in *Inked* magazine).

Cooking competitions are another excellent example. The rules vary a bit, but the overall format is the contestants are given the same ingredients to create a flavorful dish in a set amount of time. The winner receives a cash prize and a title like *Chopped Champion* or *Star Baker*. The structure of these shows is aided by a ticking clock which shows a looming countdown.

Each of these is written slightly differently but the ticking clock and thinning of the competitive field provides a framework for the scripts. Let's assume a new show called *Sparky* which pits the best electricians against each other to win a $10,000 prize. It is set in a fully stocked electronics lab and hosted by Sherry Lee Cunningham. The outline looks like this:

FADE IN ON THE POWER SHOP
WS of the Power Shop, push into Sherry Lee behind a workbench. Judges Carlos Scunazzi, Bert Holmes, and Danielle Johnson sit to one side.

Sherry: Welcome to Sparky! I'm Sherry Lee Cunningham and this week, we'll feature three new contestants in the Power Shop. They will wire, perspire, and inspire their way to new electrical heights in their quest for $10,000! Let's meet them right now.

WS of contestants entering, cut to CUs when announced with DEKO graphics

Sherry VO: A former shop teacher from Sacramento, California, Leroy Jenkins!
An electrical engineer from Lansing, Michigan, Judith Lear!
A self-described tinkerer from Nampa, Idaho, Terry Palmer!
And an electrical lineman from Macon, Georgia, Conrad Elway!

MS of Sherry

Sherry: Thanks to all of you for being here. As you know, you'll face three electrical challenges today. Each round will eliminate one of you, but the last one standing will walk away with $10,000!

INSERT PRETAPED CONFESSIONAL

Terry: That's real money! I left my wife and kids to be here but that money will make it all worthwhile.

WS of Sherry with Judges

Sherry: Let's say hello to our panel again, Carlos, Bert, and Danielle. Bert, who stands out to you at first glance?

Bert: I'm keeping an eye on Conrad. Anyone who can work on electrical lines up on power poles in storms isn't going to back down from a challenge.

Danielle: That's true, but a former shop teacher is always a tough cookie. Leroy has seen a lot of different projects over the years.

Carlos: But then you have the two wild cards. An electrical engineer, plus a tinkerer out of Idaho? Both of them came here ready to do battle.

The rest of the show follows a simple pattern. Sherry introduces a challenge with a set time limit, the contestants work feverishly with frequent confessional cutaways, the judges evaluate the projects, and a contestant is eliminated (with a final confessional as they walk out the door). The opening introduction of the contestants is the only segment that is truly scripted. The welcoming banter with the judges can be written down or just adlibbed. There is a comparatively low shooting ratio, as there may be ten cameras covering the competition from all angles, resulting in a 10:1 shooting ratio. The ticking clock and the hope for a cash prize provide the dramatic tension.

Relationship Programs

Relationship shows are more fluid in their approach. If there is a ticking clock, it spans much longer than a 30-minute cooking show. One example is *90 Day Fiancé* that shows an American citizen dating someone from beyond the United States. Once that person arrives in the US, there are 90 days for that couple to marry to apply for a green card. Other relationship programs, like *The Bachelorette*, have contestants vie for a long-term relationship in an elimination program that spans weeks.

With the immediacy of an immediate ticking clock removed (they have months, not minutes), the writers still must craft some dramatic tension to engage the viewers. This is not scripted but outlined in broad strokes for the people on the show. A typical arc looks like this: a dilemma is presented to a contestant, they describe the situation in advance, the event happens, then they deliver a postmortem wrap-up that summarizes their feelings about the events. They then use this as a springboard to a new situation. For this scenario, we will have our main character Mark prepare for a first date with his girlfriend, Cate. The outline would look like this:

INT. MARK'S BEDROOM – DAY

Mark rifles through his closet.

MARK (VO)
My date with Cate needs to be perfect. I made the reservations for the seafood restaurant, even though she said she may be allergic.

CUT TO MARK'S CONFESSIONAL

MARK
But it could be a nut allergy, right? I've never heard of someone being allergic to everything that swims. She'll be fine.

EXT. CATE'S HOUSE

Mark rings the doorbell, Cate answers and steps onto the porch. Adlib comments to compliment each other, he promises the dinner will be great.

CUT TO CATE'S CONFESSIONAL

> CATE
> He looks so cute! And as long as it's not seafood, we're good.

EXT. SEAFOOD RESTAURANT

Mark and Cate pull up in his car. She sees the restaurant and reacts.

CUT TO CATE'S CONFESSIONAL

> CATE
> He had ONE job!

This genre blends scripting techniques and is loosely formatted like a film script. The main action is largely adlibbed with some guidance from the off-screen producers. They may prod the characters to cover a certain topic, like "How do you feel about him taking you to a seafood restaurant?". The confessionals are similar but there is more opportunity for retakes to get the right lines and emotions. The shooting ratio is higher with this genre, allowing producers to shape the narrative.

Personal Journeys

These programs follow someone as they undergo a dramatic change in their life. Not only do they take the longest time to produce, but they also have the highest shooting ratios of any form of reality television. The program *My 600-lb Life* documents morbidly obese individuals and their attempts to combine diet, exercise, and surgery to lose weight. The typical episode follows the individual for a full year. Similar shows that focus on a personal journey include MTV's *Teen Mom* or *16 & Pregnant*.

The extremely high shooting ratio leads to a very fluid scripting format. The linear flow is established by the sequence of events: the teenager realizes she is pregnant, there is conflict with her boyfriend and parents, doctor visits are planned, the pregnancy develops, and a baby is born. The scenes can be outlined as simply as PHARMACY VISIT, MONTH 5 and the sequence is developed. This will have her first confessional about going to the pharmacy (she's nervous), the brief interaction with the pharmacist filling the prescription, then her second confessional (she's relieved).

Celebrity Programs

There is no shortage of celebrities who are willing to invite viewers to see a "real" look at how they live. This can range from any Kardashian and *The Culpo Sisters* to previous shows like *The Osbournes* or *Gene Simmons Family Jewels*. Celebrity status is also granted to people in unusual situations, like multiple wives (*Sister Wives*), lots of kids (*Doubling Down with the Derricos*) or even living in frozen climates (*Life Below Zero*).

Each of these shows can be formatted the same way: producers meet with the celebrities before taping to discuss scenarios, the celebrities then perform once the cameras are rolling, then the producers edit the takes to create dramatic tension. Confessionals are used extensively and serve as bridges between scenes.

Let's create a show about two parents with eight kids. One of the kids, Murphy, is highlighted in each episode because he is incredibly cute – the show is called *Murphy's Big Family of Awesomeness*. This episode will focus on the hijinks of taking the kids to a petting zoo. The situation will be introduced, the event will happen, and then there will be a coda for the participants to recap their feelings. The structure is akin to this:

Scene One:	Mom and Dad prep breakfast for the eight kids in the kitchen.
Confessional:	Dad previews a surprise trip to the petting zoo.
Scene Two:	Mom and Dad tell the kids over breakfast. Lots of excitement!
Confessional:	Murphy (he's five years old and adorable) says he loves pigs.
Scene Three:	Chaos ensues as they all load into two minivans.
Confessional:	Mom explains the need for two vehicles.
Scene Four:	Fun at the petting zoo! Happy kids! But a pig knocks Murphy down!
Confessional:	Dad in panic mode. Is Murphy okay?
Scene Five:	The petting zoo owner helps Murphy to his feet. He's fine!
Confessional:	Mom admits she was scared.
Scene Six:	The family eats ice cream at the petting zoo café.
Confessional:	Murphy says he still likes pigs, but only baby piggies.
Scene Seven:	The family loads back into the minivans for the trip home.

The only scripting challenge for this genre is coming up with new events that allow the characters to interact each episode. Even a mundane event, like the *Real Housewives* having another dinner party or a huge family going to a ballet recital, can provide enough of a framework for a show.

Live Events

Live television encompasses a variety of multicamera productions, including music concerts, sports events, and awards ceremonies. Each of these presents unique challenges and are created somewhat differently, so we will examine each of these major types of live production for their nuances. There are other categories of live productions, like covering theatrical performances, but those are produced by following the same script that is given to the actors. *Saturday Night Live* is a great example of a weekly live production, but since it is formatted like an episodic television show, it can be learned by reading those scripts. Television newscasts are also live, however they are heavily scripted (and covered in depth in another chapter in this textbook), so we will omit them from this discussion.

Music Concerts

No live event is easy to cover, but music concerts present the least challenges to the production team for several reasons. Each concert takes place on a designated stage, with the performers facing toward the audience. The lighting and audio are set up in conjunction with the concert venue. Reaction shots of audience members are easily obtainable. With these production elements already handled, the scripting is based on one simple piece of paper.

That paper is the setlist. Musicians take care to perform the songs they think will best resonate with an audience; when a group is on tour, the set list may be the same for the tour's entire run that spans scores of concerts over several months. There are exceptions, such as Bruce Springsteen concerts that clock in at four hours in length and feature songs added at the singer's whim. Dream Theater used to offer its fans a singular experience every night, as they typically toured by playing a new set list during each concert on their tour. Still, they typed up a set list in advance of each show.

The set list is the de facto script for a concert. Assuming a concert is roughly two hours long, let's assume the list will have 20 songs. If you are the writer/producer in charge of covering the show, this list will guide you through the following steps:

- Confirm with the band that the set list will not change. Nothing is worse than expecting a ballad that is replaced by a new song during the actual show.
- Make copies of the set list for each crew member. This includes taping the list to the audio board and camera viewfinders.
- Note which cameras will cover which band members. A wide shot should cover the entire stage as a master shot in case a close-up or medium shot is missed, so the director can quickly bring up the wide shot if needed. Other cameras will focus on individual performers plus a crowd shot or two.
- Identify the solos (guitar, piano, drums, etc.) that will appear in the listed songs. When a drummer pounds out a monstrous solo, using the camera shot of the silent singer is a wasted opportunity.
- Attend rehearsal to practice the shot selection and pacing. Faster songs thrive on quick edits while a slow piano ballad begs for slow dissolves between shots.

Between songs, the producer/writer is careful to watch for unscripted moments that are adlibbed by the performers. When the lead singer belts out "How are you doing tonight, Santa Fe?", that needs to be covered by a camera. This is why having a master shot of the entire stage can be a lifesaver.

Sports Events

Sports events depend on the ebb and flow of the game, so much of the script is adlibbed. The opening introduction of the game and a few other minor items are written down in advance, but everything else is treated as "breaking news", so no actual words can be written in advance. Scripts for sports events vary based on the following:

- The skill and experience of the announcers. Veteran announcers can adlib with greater ease and are used to talking extemporaneously.
- The actual sport. Horse racing is a fast sport that requires ongoing updates, while baseball is more leisurely and needs less speaking.
- The producer. Some show producers like as much script as possible while others rely more on the fluidity of the announcers.

130 *Reality and Live Television*

Despite these variables, there are four types of announcements that are scripted in advance. These are read off the teleprompter (or from a printed script if the camera isn't on the announcers) and should be said verbatim given the precise information they contain. These are:

- Pre-Game Announcements. These kick off the show with a welcome, an introduction of the hosts, and setting the stage of the teams. Starting line-ups, team records, coaches' names, and what's at stake for the teams are all contained here.
- In-Game Announcements. Placed at certain times in the show, these announcements thank sponsors and promote upcoming segments, like if there is a singer appearing during the halftime show.
- Post-Game Announcements. At the end of the game, the announcers will wrap up with their thoughts of the game they just covered. They will say what is the next game for each team, repeat the final score, and say good-bye.
- Generic Announcements. This is filler material that can be dropped in whenever there is a slow point in the game. For a college basketball game, a quick announcement of the upcoming holiday food drive can be voiced during a timeout.

Aside from these notes for the announcers, there will be shooting diagrams and coverage charts for the production crew so everyone knows which camera has the wide shot, which one is covering the head coach, etc. But multicamera sports production is a grueling, fast-paced world that does not rely on written scripts for the entire show. The very nature of sports demands more attention to the actual game than the written word.

Awards Ceremonies

Of all the multicamera events that air live to an at-home audience, the awards show is the most reliant on an actual script. The primary concern is that the hosts have something to read on the teleprompter and the production crew has notes on who is entering and exiting the stage. Since multiple cameras are covering the same event from different angles, the director has the liberty to use a wide shot of the stage, medium shots of the presenters, reaction shots of the audience, or any other shot they deem pleasing.

Below is a sample script from an awards show. Note that several parts are still to be added, such as ANECDOTE TO COME or the names of the winners. These are both to make the show as topical as possible; the anecdote may be written just hours before the live program to give a "fresh" joke to the audience, while the names of the winners aren't known until revealed to the at-home audience.

The first line you see, the slug line, gives the title, the act, and the date. The act is the part of the program that is between commercial breaks.

<u>2023 CREATIVE ARTS AWARDS – ACT 10   4-26-23</u>

                       ANNOUNCER (V.O.)
        Ladies and gentlemen, please welcome one of the
        stars of "Alex Van Newsome's Family Road
        Trips", Mr. Alex Van Newsome, and one of its
        creators, Mr. Jason Van Newsome.

ALEX AND JASON ENTER.

JASON

Thank you. We're here to present the award for Non-Fiction Programming. These documentaries span the breath of human knowledge . . . History, the arts, science, nature, social issues . . .

ALEX

The kind of thoughtful, intelligent, high-quality shows I usually skip over on my way to watching a Chicago Cubs game.

JASON

ANECDOTE TO COME

ALEX

And so for Outstanding Directing for Non-Fiction Programming, the nominees are . . .

Let's introduce a new wrinkle to this awards show. Alex is about to read the nominees' names, but the nominees are sitting in the audience. This takes a bit of preproduction, as the director wants to show the nominees as Alex reads their names. This is accomplished by assigning seats to everyone in the venue. If you've ever watched the Academy Awards, you've seen the stars and award nominees located in the front rows. This is no accident. The director wants to get reaction shots of the celebrities near the front, plus it makes it easy for the winners to hop up to the stage to retrieve their awards.

Since the seats are assigned, we will rejoin Alex as he reads the nominees' names while showing how this looks on the script.

ALEX

And so for Outstanding Directing for Non-Fiction Programming, the nominees are Ron Burgundy for *This is San Diego*, Chazz Michael Michaels for *Ice Capades*, Lars Erickssong for *Songs of My Icelandic Family*, Brennan Huff for *My Brother Does Karate,* and Ricky Bobby for *Racing in Circles*.

JASON

I'm so excited! They're all so good!

ALEX

I know! And the winner is. . . .

TOGETHER

(ANNOUNCE WINNER)

132   *Reality and Live Television*

(SEAT 45)   RON BURGUNDY
             This is San Diego

(SEAT 12)   CHAZZ MICHAEL MICHAELS
             Ice Capades

(SEAT 77)   LARS ERICKSSONG
             Songs of My Icelandic Family

(SEAT 4)   BRENNAN HUFF
             My Brother Does Karate

(SEAT 101)   RICKY BOBBY
             Racing in Circles

(PRESENT AWARD)

DEKO: WIN MATTE
DEKO: WINNER INSTAGRAM HANDLE/HASHTAG

    (ACCEPTANCE SPEECH BY WINNER)

(EXIT)

DEKO: UP NEXT GRAPHIC

                  ANNOUNCER VO
Coming up: A special salute to the films of Clint Eastwood as he receives a lifetime achievement award in directing. Plus, the cast of the new film *Hangover 4* will present the award for Best Ensemble Cast.

(COMMERCIAL BREAK)

    This shows why the production crew must review the script before the live event. When Alex is reading the names of the nominees, the director wants to show them sitting in the audience. This means reading Alex's audio and the seat diagram simultaneously, but it is quite simple. Alex is essentially narrating the nominees out loud, so all the director needs to do is follow along with the visuals. As long as Alex sticks to the script and reads the names in order, the production should look seamless.

    Finally, there are new elements that are needed for the awards script. The winner's name cannot be written in advance (it's a surprise) and the winner's thanks for the award cannot be scripted (it's adlibbed or written on their own personal notecards). Other elements are added flush left in all caps, notably the word DEKO. This is a graphic package that shows names on the screen, so showing it on the script merely reminds the director to bring up a graphic. The other addition is the announcer's paragraph at the end. The announcer will read their words off-camera, meaning their voice will be over a camera shot of the audience. This voice over is noted as "VO" next to the announcer's name. The upcoming commercial break is then noted in ALL CAPS, in parentheses, on the left side. The Fade Out is implied and not in the script.

The essence of live television is that many memorable moments are unscripted. When Will Smith infamously slapped host Chris Rock during the Academy Awards, the producer/writer was following the action of the moment and not relying on a script. Live television demands vigilant attention from the production crew as the event unfolds in front of the viewing audience in real time. Unlike other forms of scripting, the nature of live events dictates that the production team must react instantly to what is happening before them. Live television reveals that even the best script must sometimes be set aside for the good of the program.

Looking Forward

Reality shows, be they in competition, relationship, or celebrity categories are not going anywhere. It is likely that the appetite for such programming will explode over the coming years as producers devise more angles to satisfy the public's appetite. A cupcake baking show is nice, but how about a cupcake baking show featuring country singers as the cooks? Plus, as an added twist, what if their cooking partner was an old flame they dumped back in high school? While there may not be any new ideas, there are certainly ways to recycle old ideas for the viewing audience. The scripts for these shows will still be guidelines for the characters, as much of the shows' structure is decided as the episode is edited.

Live television will also continue to thrive, particularly for high-profile events like professional sports and awards shows. Scripts for these shows are also guidelines as they juggle the talent, action, graphics, and whatever segments are developed in advance. Since live events create a cultural bond within a community, there will always be a demand for these productions. The best writer for these scripts knows to give broad latitude to these productions and let the events unfold organically.

Exercises

1. How many reality television programs do you watch on a frequent basis? Make a list of them and compare with your classmates. Which shows appear on more than one list?
2. Choose five people (family, friends, or a combination of both) to star in a reality show about your life. This program will focus on how you just won a ten million dollar lottery (congratulations!) and how you will deal with your new wealth. What story arcs do you foresee carrying the plot forward for the first season of fifteen episodes?
3. Find a concert setlist of your favorite band; the website setlist.fm is a great resource and provides lists for both current and previous concerts. Can you visualize how you would cover these songs? Are you aware of the instrument solos and know where the focus of the coverage should be at any given time?
4. Watch any live sports event on television. Can you count how many cameras were involved in the production? Are you able to anticipate what the next shot will be to follow the action?
5. Imagine you are pitching a new competition program to the Food Network; the link for that channel is provided below. What type of series could you produce that you think would get viewers to tune in? How is it different from the other reality shows that are currently on that channel?

Chapter Essentials

- Reality television shows exploded in the 1990s as new cable channels needed inexpensive programming.
- Reality shows can be divided into four broad categories: competition, relationship, personal journey, and celebrity shows.
- Shooting ratios compare the amount of raw footage shot versus the amount of edited footage used in the program.
- Confessionals are the segments of the reality show where a contestant addresses the camera and reveals their inner thoughts away from other people.
- Reality shows can be greatly altered by how the editing is done in postproduction.
- Musical concerts provide a skeletal scripting exercise, as the production team literally follows the set list of the songs that the artist will perform.
- Sports events are not scripted per se, but the coverage follows the ebb and flow of the game. Only a small fraction of the coverage, such as the opening statements from the announcers, are written down in advance.
- The four segments scripted for sports commentators are the pre-game, in-game, post-game, and generic announcements.
- Awards ceremonies are scripted with latitude so hosts may adlib and winners can deliver impromptu thanks to their supporters.

Online Links

Espn.com. As a leader in live sports coverage, ESPN provides comprehensive access to many types of collegiate and professional sports. This site offers video clips of games as well as listings of which events are about to air.

Foodnetwork.com. Although this cable channel offers recipes and information about chefs, the Shows tab links to an array of reality TV shows that are based on different types of cooking competitions. Programs featuring specific chefs (like Bobby Flay), themes (such as *Diners, Drive-Ins and Dives*) or dishes (like *Cupcake Championship*) are searchable here.

Oscars.org. This website for the Academy of Motion Picture Arts and Sciences shows clips of previous Oscar award ceremonies. Under the Awards tab, click Oscars, then locate the Ceremonies box. That link provides clips to Oscar award winners from nearly a century of ceremonies.

13 Episodic and Serialized Television

Key Words

Act	Rewrites
Arc	Scene
Episodic	Serialized
Plot Line	Soap Opera

Historical Overview

Three of the most popular formats to appear on television all fall under the broad category of episodic programming. Half hour sitcoms, one-hour dramas, and soap operas all tell their stories on an ongoing basis. Sitcom is an abbreviation of the phrase "situation comedy" in which characters encounter unique situations and resolve them in a comedic fashion in a neat 30-minute episode; *It's Always Sunny in Philadelphia, Young Sheldon,* and *Abbott Elementary* are all prime examples of this genre. The one-hour drama may be either a police procedural (like the *Law & Order* franchise) or a saga that explores relationships, such as *Yellowstone* or *The Good Doctor*. Soap operas, so named because their original daytime sponsors were detergent companies, are daily programs that revolve around the drama of an interrelated group of characters, like *Days of Our Lives* and *General Hospital*. Each of these fictional programs features characters that confront problems, struggle with relationships, and navigate extended story lines.

Episodic and serialized television programs differ by the content of their shows but not in how they are scripted. An episodic show is a stand-alone program in which the characters wrap up the entire plot within 30 or 60 minutes. Most crime procedurals are like this in that a crime happens, the detectives investigate and gather evidence, then the bad guy is caught in a dramatic car chase or shootout. You don't need to watch the preceding or following installment of *Law & Order* to know what is going on in a specific episode. There are longer story arcs that span the entire season, like if two of the detectives are dating each other, but the main narrative of each episode (solving a crime) is wrapped up by the episode's conclusion.

Serialized television episodes are more like chapters in a book that tell a much larger story. *Stranger Things. . ., House of the Dragon,* and *The Walking Dead* are essentially very long stories that span several seasons. They are perfect for binge-watching, since

DOI: 10.4324/9781003274766-14

the viewer can follow the story over a number of episodes. If you entered the *Game of Thrones* series in the middle of a season, much of the backstory and characterization wouldn't make sense. Serialized TV series are meant to be treated as one long tale to be watched from start to finish.

This difference reveals how arcs can impact the story telling in a series. An arc is how a narrative unfolds in a chronological story. In a sitcom, the entire story arc can be summarized as follows: the characters encounter a quirky situation, they sort through the problem together, and there is a happy resolution at the end of the half-hour episode. The story arcs of serialized programs, like *Better Call Saul* or *Mad Men*, were weaved over several seasons to deliver one epic story. However, the scripting formats for serialized and episodic shows share many of the same characteristics. One example is that they all begin with the same introductory pages.

Introductory Pages

The first pages of a television script contain standard information. There is always a title page, plus one or two pages before the actual script appears. The mandatory title page lists the name of the program, the episode title, and the writer's name. This information is centered on the page. The show title may be underlined, capitalized, in a larger font, or set in some dominant fashion, like this:

THE SECRET OF THE WHEELER FAMILY

"Pilot"
Written by
Andres Dominguez

Other information on the title page may include the episode's director, the date the draft was completed, and a copyright logo. This information is placed on the bottom of the page, either flush right or flush left, such as:

FINAL DRAFT
April 25, 2023

The next pages are optional but can be helpful once the script goes into development. One page may list the characters that appear in the script. This list is of the characters, not the actors who are playing those roles. It looks like this:

CAST LIST

SPECIAL AGENT BOBBY RULLENS
SPECIAL AGENT TINA ENGSTROM
DOCTOR TED GREENHALL
JUDITH WHEELER
THEODORE WHEELER
JOSEPH "DUKE" FAUX

VIDEO ONLY
PLANT NURSERY SHOPPERS

VOICE ONLY
RADIO NEWSCASTER

The other possible page is a list of the locations where the action takes place. These are broken into the categories of exterior and interior, then further divided into day and night locales. Split into two columns, the result readily shows what locations would be needed for the production crew:

<u>SET LIST</u>

EXTERIORS (DAY)	**INTERIORS** (DAY)
WHEELERS' NEIGHBORHOOD	WHEELERS' HOUSE
METRO PARK	BEDROOM
PLANT NURSERY	KITCHEN
PARKING GARAGE	LIVING ROOM
EXTERIORS (NIGHT)	**INTERIORS** (NIGHT)
WHEELERS' NEIGHBORHOOD	WHEELERS' HOUSE
METRO PARK	BEDROOM
POLICE STATION	POLICE STATION
	INTERROGATION ROOM
	CONFERENCE ROOM

Once the basic introduction is established, there will be some variables among the primary genres. We will look at the 30-minute comedies, one-hour dramas, and soap operas individually. Each of them evolved differently and contain their own unique backgrounds and formatting criteria.

Thirty-Minute Comedies

The honor of the first sitcom goes to the British Broadcasting Corporation. In 1946, the 30-minute show *Pinwright's Progress* appeared on the BBC as a live program. There was no way to record the broadcast, so none of the ten original episodes were saved. The next year, the first American sitcom debuted. *Mary Kay and Johnny* starred a real-life married couple, Johnny and Mark Kay Stearns. The 15-minute-long show was shot before a live studio audience and aired on the now-defunct DuMont Television Network. From 1948 until the show's end in 1950, the episodes were recorded onto kinescopes so they could be re-aired for West Coast audiences. These recordings were held until 1975, when DuMont's successor, Metromedia, dumped the archives into the East River in New York City. Only one episode is known to have survived.

Audiences demanded more sitcoms as televisions became commonplace in suburban homes. *I Love Lucy* debuted in 1951 and was the first sitcom to use a multi-camera format. Other shows like *The Honeymooners* (1955), *Gilligan's Island* (1964), *All in the Family* (1971), *Cheers* (1982), *Friends* (1994), and *How I Met Your Mother* (2005) each contributed to the genre and advanced story telling in their own way.

Technical Specifications

The half-hour comedy programs are broken into acts and scenes. The acts are the larger segments that are divided by commercial breaks. Within each act are smaller scenes, which are based on the location in which the action takes place. Act and scene headings are centered, in all caps, and underlined, as follows:

<u>ACT ONE</u>
<u>SCENE A</u>

This is followed by the scene headings and action lines. The scene headings contain the standard INT or EXT (meaning interior or exterior), the location, and the time element. If we have a scene with Charlotte watching TV in the evening with her friends Morgan and Tim, the scene heading would look like this:

<u>INT.   CHARLOTTE'S LIVING ROOM – EVENING</u>

Unlike other formats, the scene heading is underlined. Next are the action lines that describe the room, what's happening, and who's there. Since weekly comedies are shot repeatedly in the same rooms, there is no point describing Charlotte's living room again if the viewers are already familiar with the space. Instead, the characters for that scene are listed in parentheses, followed by a simple line of action. The action is in all caps, so the opening page looks like this:

<u>ACT ONE</u>
<u>SCENE A</u>

<u>INT.   CHARLOTTE'S LIVING ROOM – EVENING</u>
(Charlotte, Morgan, Tim)
THE TRIO WATCH TV, EATING POPCORN AND SHIELDING THEIR EYES.

The formatting also has subtle rules once the characters and dialogue begin. The character names are centered and in all caps. The dialogue is also centered but placing character reactions into the dialogue is acceptable. Dialogue that needs to be emphasized may be underlined.

CHARLOTTE
This is horrible! Why are we watching this?

MORGAN
It was Tim's idea!

TIM
Whoa, this was never my idea. I wanted to watch a comedy.

                              MORGAN
          I didn't pick this. (GLARES AT CHARLOTTE) And
          I certainly didn't hide the remote so we're stuck
          watching this.

                              TIM
          Wait, who? (NOW HE GETS IT) Ohhhhhh. . . .

                              CHARLOTTE
          I don't know what you're talking about.

                              MORGAN
          Where is the remote?

                              CHARLOTTE
          If I knew where it was, I'd tell you. (PULLS OUT THE
          REMOTE AND CLICKS OFF THE TV). But I don't
          know where it is, so you may as well stop asking.

                              MORGAN
          What's that in your hand?

Charlotte whips the remote under a couch cushion.

                              CHARLOTTE
          That was my phone. My mom just called and I don't
          want to talk to her.

                              TIM
          That makes sense.

The above scene also shows how action lines can be formatted in a comedy script. If the action happens within someone's dialogue, it is written in parentheses and ALL CAPS in the dialogue box. Should the action occur between two different characters' lines, the action is written as a regular sentence, left-justified.

Ending the comedy script is simple. The words FADE OUT appear, right-justified, followed by a period, like this:

                                                              FADE OUT.

One-Hour Dramas

The hour-long episodic is a mainstay of television programming. Shows like *CSI, The Good Doctor*, and *NCIS* bring in millions of viewers a week. The Western series *Gunsmoke* aired from 1955 to 1975, tallying 635 episodes. This mark stood as the highest total for an episodic series until it was eventually overtaken by *The Simpsons*. It should be noted that *Gunsmoke* was originally a radio program, plus more than two hundred of those television shows were only 30 minutes long. It is also one of the rare series to begin production during the black and white era before shifting to color television.

Today, it is more common for a successful series to not only last a number of seasons, but also to spawn several profitable spin-offs. *NCIS*, which birthed the spin-offs *NCIS: Los Angeles, NCIS: New Orleans* and *NCIS: Hawaii* was actually created as a spin-off from the series *JAG*. The *NCIS* universe boasts nearly 1,000 total episodes across all of its titles. This impressive number is topped by the *Law & Order* universe, where the various series and spin-offs (*Special Victims Unit, Organized Crime, Criminal Intent,* etc.) have churned out more than 1,200 episodes. Even more encompassing is the *Star Trek* franchise which, after the first TV series ended after just three seasons, spawned *The Next Generation, Deep Space Nine, Voyager, Enterprise, Discovery, Picard, Lower Decks, Prodigy,* and *Strange New Worlds*. This impressive list does not include an animated series, the upcoming *Section 31* spin-off, or the many movies that were inspired by the original show.

The scripts for these hour-long programs share many of the same attributes as those for a feature film; if you can write a feature film script, an hour-long episodic script is the most natural move to a television series. Let's step through a basic outdoor scene in which a young couple is planning a picnic in the park to illustrate the formatting.

Technical Specifications

The first element is the transition, which in film is usually shown with a FADE IN: before the action begins. In episodic television, FADE IN: can be replaced by the following:

FROM BLACK:

The scene heading follows immediately after this line. Like a narrative film script, there are three elements that make up the scene heading: an interior or exterior designation, the physical location, then a long dash followed by the time of day. For our example in an outdoor park in the daytime, a scene heading would look something like this:

FROM BLACK:

EXT. SUBURBAN PARK – DAY

There are several noteworthy items here. First, INT represents an interior scene and EXT depicts an exterior scene. The exception is when the scene is inside a vehicle that is traveling outside, so you'll type:

INT/EXT. CAR/CITY STREET – DAY

Back to our example in the park. Once you show it's an exterior location, then that setting is named with just a word or two. Do not overly describe the setting. If there are specific details that must be used to describe the location, they can go into the action line that follows. Finally, the time element is the last part of the scene heading. These can be broad (DAY, NIGHT, etc.), somewhat specific (DAWN, LATE AFTERNOON) or very specific if time is a concern (11:55AM).

Now that the scene heading establishes where the activity will unfold, some action lines are needed to guide the overall scene. These brief sentences will set the tone, introduce characters in ALL CAPS when we first see them, and reveal important props (also in ALL CAPS) that are relevant to the scene. Do not overly describe the scene, but brush in broad strokes:

FROM BLACK:

EXT. SUBURBAN PARK – DAY
A hot July afternoon as COLIN and JENNIFER, both 20s, tote in FOLDING CAMP CHAIRS. He also carries a small COOLER.

That simple sentence is all that is needed to establish the scene. We know that Colin and Jennifer are in their 20s and looking for a place to picnic. You do not need to give their height, weight, clothing choices, hair color, or any other details unless they are crucial to the story. If Colin is morbidly obese and is heaving under the effort, that may have an impact and should be noted. Otherwise, there will be a director, locations manager, set decorator, scene designer, and a host of crew members that will contribute to this scene. As long as there is a suburban park, do not over-direct from the script.

Next up are the characters and their dialogue. Notice that you should name the characters in the action lines. Do not simply say "a young couple in their 20s". Give them the names they will use throughout the script. You can be generic if there is a character identified by their appearance (like an ELDERLY MAN) or their profession (such as TEACHER or POLICE OFFICER).

Character names appear in ALL CAPS in the middle of the page with dialogue following directly beneath. There are several very good scripting platforms that will automatically format these elements so you do not need to constantly worry about setting tabs and margins. Final Draft is the industry leader, although options like youmescript.com are also available for free. Regardless of which platform you use, the script will read something like this:

FROM BLACK:

EXT. SUBURBAN PARK – DAY
A hot July afternoon as COLIN and JENNIFER, both 20s, tote in FOLDING CAMP CHAIRS. He also carries a small COOLER.

                    COLIN
          Can we please stop? We've been trudging all
          over for like an hour.

                    JENNIFER
          Seriously? It's been fifty feet.

Colin drops the cooler with a thud.

                    COLIN
          Here's fine.

                    JENNIFER
          There's no shade anywhere. Look, I
          see some trees right there.

                        COLIN
    Too far.

A LANDSCAPER walks past with a WHEELBARROW full of tools.

                        LANDSCAPER
    You don't want to stop here. We just put
    in grass seed.

                        JENNIFER
                        (shocked)
    Oh no! I hope we're not hurting the grass.

                        LANDSCAPER
    You ain't. But the chemicals in the seed will
    kill ya if you stay here too long.

Notice that the landscaper is introduced when he enters the scene, not in the early action lines at the scene heading. Also, there is a parenthetical added to one of Jennifer's lines. A parenthetical is used when a specific tone or reaction is needed from a character. These should be used sparingly since a director and the entire cast of characters will bring their own creative input to the script. The writer's job is to produce a screenplay, not to direct the program from their computer.

Ending the dramatic show is like the comedic series with one small addition. After the FADE OUT in the bottom right, END OF SHOW is centered and underlined, like this:

                                                                FADE OUT.

<u>**END OF SHOW**</u>

Soap Operas

Soap operas began as radio teledramas in the 1930s. These midday programs gained their unique name because their on-air sponsors were soap companies that were targeting housewives. When television became more popular in the 1950s, soap operas migrated to the TV format; by the 1960s, each soap opera had left radio in favor of television.

The running times also lengthened from 15 minutes to 30 minutes. While the actors and directors were happy to explore more involved story lines, the television stations merely saw this expansion as a way to double the number of commercials sold in each episode.

The 1970s brought the biggest change in soap operas, which is still reflected in scripts to this day. The advent of recordable media meant soap operas could be shot in advance, rather than live. Taping episodes in advance meant directors were able to reshoot scenes. This impacted the writing style, as notes for the director and actors were now written directly into the script. Soap operas again doubled in length to their standard hour-long format.

However, soap opera viewing has been on the decline. The loss of the traditional "housewife" audience, the explosion of viewing options on different channels, and the chance to produce cheaper daytime programs like talk shows all contributed to the demise of soap operas. As of this writing, only four remain in the US: *The Bold and the Beautiful, Days of Our Lives, General Hospital,* and *The Young and the Restless.*

Technical Specifications

While soap operas are episodic television, the scripts are written similarly to narrative film scripts. The character names are centered and in all capital letters and their dialogue is centered below the character names (with slightly wider margins). However, the scene headings and action lines reveal subtle differences.

First, the scene headings are sparse, such as:

BECKY'S BEDROOM

The rationale is simple. Since these programs have been on for decades, the stages have been set for years and Becky's bedroom has always essentially been Becky's bedroom. There is no need for a description like you would find in a film script, simply because the production team and the actors have been here before.

But there is a key difference with how action lines are delivered, as the script denotes many of the internal thoughts and emotions of the actors. Since soap operas are produced on a daily basis and convey a great deal of emotional content, the actors are accustomed to having their "inner" dialogue on full display on a recurring basis. These notes are directly written on the script for both the actors and the production crew. Let's run through a brief example with two actresses, Becky and Hannah, having a simple scene in Becky's bedroom. The script would be written as follows:

BECKY'S BEDROOM

(BECKY PERCHES ON HER BED, JABBING AT HER CELL PHONE. HANNAH RIFLES THROUGH THE CLOSET.)

                BECKY
     Still nothing from Marty. I'm getting nervous.

               HANNAH
     I'm sure he's fine. You'll still need an outfit
     for tonight.

                BECKY
     What if it's like last time?

(HANNAH SIGHS. IT'S LIKE PUERTO RICO ALL OVER AGAIN.)

               HANNAH
     He apologized, didn't he?

(BECKY CRUMPLES AT THE MEMORY.)

                                BECKY
              It's not enough.

                                HANNAH
              It never is. And it never will be.

(HANNAH SITS TO CONSOLE BECKY.)

                                BECKY
              Ever since his diagnosis, Marty had used it like
              a free golden ticket to get out of his responsibilities.
              It's the perfect excuse to get anything he wants and to
              get out of anything he wants. It's not fair.

                                HANNAH
              So I guess we don't need to pick out something for
              you to wear tonight?

                                BECKY
              I guess not . . .

(HOLD ON BECKY FOR THIS EXCHANGE.)

                                HANNAH
              You're not thinking about Tyler, are you?

                                BECKY
              Maybe that's the wakeup call that Marty needs.
              If I sacrifice one night with Tyler, it will prove
              that I shouldn't be taken lightly.

(TWO SHOT OF BOTH TO CATCH HANNAH'S REACTION.)

                                HANNAH
              But what if you push Marty too far?

                                BECKY
              That's exactly what I'm counting on. Find me
              something in that closet. It's time for Marty to
              see that Tyler is also interested in little Miss Becky.

<u>FADE TO: BLACK</u>
<u>COMMERCIALS</u>

The basics of the film style format are there, but the differences of the action lines in a soap opera script versus a feature film script are striking.

- The action lines are formatted in all caps and are bracketed in parentheticals.

- They are used to direct both the talents' inner emotions, such as in the line "It's like Puerto Rico all over again."
- The action lines are guides for the director and production crew for when to hold shots or cut to new camera angles.

The end of the script is also a slight tweak from other formats. The "FADE TO: BLACK" cue is in all caps, left justified and underlined. Finally, the closing line "COMMERCIALS" is similarly formatted and acknowledges that the scene is over and the television ads are about to roll. It looks like this:

<u>FADE TO: BLACK</u>
<u>COMMERCIALS</u>

Similarities Among the Genres' Scripts

Although there are formatting nuances among the different genres, there are striking similarities with how the stories are told. One basic theatrical concept is the three-act structure. This allows for a plot introduction in the first act, an escalation in the second act, and a resolution in the third act. The simplest analogy is the criminal procedural; the detectives discover a crime has been committed in act one, the sleuthing occurs in act two, and the criminal is brought to justice in act three. Even comedies adhere to this scenario where boy meets girl, they encounter obstacles, then the pair finally get together at the end.

Other elements share some similarities across the genres. These include the development of plots and subplots, using beats, establishing character arcs, and how to designate rewrites. We will look at each of these components in turn.

Plots and Subplots

A single plot line cannot sustain a 30- or 60-minute script. Even when commercial breaks are removed, the result is a 22- or 44-minute program that still requires more than one linear thread. The solution is to write a main storyline, called the A plot, supported by two or more lesser storylines, called the B and C plots. This means that the characters are dealing with a main plot while also encountering a subplot or two.

These plots can be easily found in online episode descriptions; when *TV Guide* and newspapers printed television schedules, the main plot was listed to entice viewers. Now, storylines can be quickly found online in websites like imdb.com. One example from the comedy series *Seinfeld* is an episode titled "The Alternate Side" in season three. The description is:

> Jerry's car is stolen. Elaine dates an older man. Kramer gets a small role in a Woody Allen movie filmed on his and Jerry's block. George must deal with the commotion of the movie filming as he gets a job parking cars on the block.

The main plot is the loss of Jerry's car. The secondary plots involve Elaine dating an older man, Kramer landing a movie role, and George dealing with that movie filming on his block. This synopsis reveals a valuable trick in writing subplots, as two of them are clearly linked to one another. Good stories are well written, but great stories interweave the plots together to create more dramatic tension.

Beats

At its essence, a beat occurs in a fictional script when something happens, changes, or is introduced that shifts the story dramatically. They are also called "moments" because they are so quick, yet they carry a significant impact on the story. A beat can be as simple as a character walking into a room or having a change of heart. Let's use a scene in a bank vault as an example:

INT.   BANK VAULT – DAY

JAKE yanks open the safety deposit box. Empty. HARRY laughs behind him.

> HARRY
> Did you think I was that stupid?

The beat is the realization that Harry has set up Jake. Writers used to type in the word BEAT to communicate this shift in tone, but these moments are often discovered by the actors during the shooting. However, beats are still used in episodic scripts when the act is ending and the show is cutting to a commercial break. A miniature cliffhanger is written into the script to make sure the audience sits through the next few minutes of ads.

The placement of the beat becomes critical to end the act, as the TV network must make sure the commercials air on time. In a half-hour comedy, there will be a beat at the end of act one before the commercial hits; Ross accidentally hangs up on Rachel, for example. An hour-long cop show will have a beat that reveals a smudged fingerprint at the crime scene, then the commercial rolls. For soap operas, the beats can range from former lovers joining cults to the hospitalized fiancé waking up from a coma. A beat is a vital moment that moves the story forward and is integral to all forms of episodic TV writing.

Arcs

An arc is made up of a series of events that signify change in a character. This is usually positive, like when Meredith Grey starts as a surgical intern and evolves into a leader on *Grey's Anatomy*. This arc sustained hundreds of episodes and included many intermediary steps, like completing a successful surgery or landing a competitive grant. Other arcs may last just a season, such as when a character decides to try out a new job for several episodes.

Not all arcs span multiple episodes. A character arc can be delivered in a single program if the writing is focused and contained along a major plot line. If someone is hit with devasting news of an estranged family member's death, they could start the episode by still hating the person but then come to love them at the end of the episode. However, most powerful story arcs need more time to mature and are spread over several shows.

Rewrites

Regardless of genre, all television scripts are subject to multiple rewrites. These occur when a showrunner (the person tasked with overseeing the show) takes notes from actors, the director, producers, and other series writers. These notes are then given to that episode's writer, who revises the script on an ongoing basis. That revision is then distributed, new notes are given, and the writer revamps the script once again. No script is immune from a rewrite and script writers must accept that their work will be pecked at from all sides. While writing is a singular chore, rewriting quickly becomes a community effort.

The challenge is to make sure that all members of the cast and crew have an up-to-date script so everyone can hit their marks and speak the correct lines. To accomplish this, script revisions are distributed on different colors of paper, noted like this on the cover page:

> Shooting script: 4/22/23
> Blue (FULL):   4/25/23
> Pink (FULL):   4/28/23
> Yellow (FULL):   5/01/23

The reason for the color-coding is simple. If everyone on the set is holding a yellow script, it will be obvious if one person is reading from a pink copy. Getting everyone an up-to-date color is a necessary job. The old copies are discarded to prevent confusion once shooting begins.

Looking Forward

Networks are a business, so executives are always searching for shows that will pull in high ratings without costing too much to produce. Reality TV can be produced for less money than episodic TV, but episodic television has incredible longevity and an impressive track record. Rewatching an old series like *The Office* is a comforting pastime for millions of viewers, plus those syndicated airings continue to earn money for the studios. You may rewatch an episode of *Friends* despite knowing the outcome but revisiting an old episode of *Survivor* doesn't have the same emotional payoff. After all, you already know who won that game.

The demand for quality stories continues in episodic television, thus the need for professional scripts will remain. Whether a show is told as a serial drama or as a new derivative of the *Star Trek* franchise, writing an engaging story takes incredible skill and dedication. Knowing how to format the scripts to an industry standard is expected among all television writers.

Exercises

1. Watch any episode of a soap opera currently on daytime television, noting the pacing, settings, dialogue, and "inner" dialogue that is conveyed through the use of camera angles. Discuss how you imagine the script was written for the characters.
2. Take a scene from an hour-long dramatic television script and rewrite it as a soap opera script. Specifically, you need to scale down much of the scene description and insert the production notes and character prompts as desired.
3. Write a five-page soap opera scene using the following prompts: it must take place in a law office, a lawyer must be talking to two clients in person, and the lawyer must hand one of the clients a typed letter that contains shocking news. You must decide how much of the news is shared with the audience (and even the other client in the room).

4. Act out the above script with several of your classmates. During this walk-through, make notes of how the camera shots should convey the emotional impact of the scene. Then rewrite the script to add the director's notes. Make sure to properly format these notes as shown in this chapter's sample script.

Chapter Essentials

- Episodic television scripts all have similar formats, yet there are subtle differences among the three.
- One-hour episodic scripts, like those used in crime dramas, most closely follow film-style formats.
- Half-hour comedies and hour-long soap opera scripts follow similar patterns in their action lines since they often contain directions for both the talent and the production crew.
- Serialized television refers to a series in which each episode adds to the overall story; the episodes should be watched in sequence so the longer story arc makes sense to the viewer.

Online Links

epguides.com. For a deep dive into specific episodes of more than 10,000 television shows, this website provides an extensive catalog of television series and their individual episodes. It does not provide scripts, but it offers a wealth of information about television programs.

imdb.com. The Internet Movie Database is not just for movies. Television shows can be researched by episodes, actors, ratings, and a host of other filters. Other options include ranking the top TV shows, browsing television shows by genre, and even what celebrities are born today.

scriptreaderpro.com/best-tv-scripts/. This website says you can "learn how to write TV scripts by studying the best TV pilots and applying their techniques to your own". It provides pilots of 50 of the best TV series for screenwriters to review. The scripts are divided into action/adventure, comedy, drama, horror, and thriller genres.

wgfoundation.org. The Writers Guild Foundation is an excellent resource for researching all facets of writing for episodic and serialized series. The site also connects veteran screenwriters with screenwriting students through outreaches such as the Visiting Writers Program.

14 Feature Film

Key Words

Action
Character
Dialogue
Parenthetical
Page Count

Plot Point
Scene Heading
Shooting Script
Spec Script
Transition

Historical Overview

The first films by the Maysles brothers in France, Edison's crew in New Jersey, and other film pioneers dealt with documentary subjects. *The Sneeze*, a ten- second film of a man sneezing, is regarded as the first film made. Other groundbreaking films followed people as they walked on boulevards, boarded ships, and went about their daily lives. Any script was simply a sentence or two of what general action would be captured by the camera.

This basic style was followed in 1902 when George Méliès wrote the first narrative film script for *A Trip to the Moon*. At the time, there were no standards for dialogue lines, action lines, or scene descriptions; his script merely described 30 basic actions and locations for his silent movie. For example, the first scene in his script was "The Scientific Congress at the Astronomic Club". There was no dialogue, the action was a series of individual lines, and the description of the club was limited to "a large hall embellished with instruments". Since this occurred long before computer software, early film scripts were written on typewriters, using tab functions to align different elements of the script.

Even the Academy Awards had difficulty with the concept of honoring early screenplays. During the first Academy Award ceremony in 1927, Ben Hecht's *Underworld* won Best Story. At the time, the submissions most resembled film treatments, which are narratives that describe the character and the plot but do not contain dialogue. Once the story was written, a screenwriter would then add in dialogue, thus changing the story into a screenplay. There was also a category for Best Adapted Screenplay, which honored scripts based on pre-existing plays or novels.

The First Academy Award for Best Original Screenplay didn't appear until Preston Sturges won for *The Great McGinty* in 1940. The category for Best Story was finally eliminated in 1956, thus leaving the categories of Best Original Screenplay and Best Adapted Screenplay to continue on.

Word processing programs standardized the script format over the years, allowing writers to focus more on the creative story than the technical problems of tabbing, spacing, and centering. Final Draft is regarded as the most popular program and is widely used in the film industry. Youmescript.com, writerduet.com and celtx.com all provide similar formatting although the keyboard macros differ. If you can use one of these programs, you can easily adapt to the others.

Technical Specifications

Narrative film scripts adhere to certain guidelines. For example, the running time of a standard motion picture is between 90 minutes and 120 minutes. Comedies and horror films tend to be on the shorter side, while action films and dramas are closer to the two-hour mark.

These running times impact the length of the script, or page count. One page of script equals approximately one minute of screen time in a film. This may not happen for each individual page, but over the duration of a complete film, a 90-page script will yield a movie approximately 90 minutes long. This rule of thumb is vital to film producers when evaluating incoming scripts. It is such an accepted rule that most screenwriting competitions set page limits of between 90 and 120 pages per submission. Anything longer or shorter is not regarded as "industry standard" and is not eligible for the competition.

Other industry standard requirements deal with the elements that appear on each page of the script. These are Scene Heading, Action, Character, Dialogue, Parenthetical, and Transition. There are other minor elements (General, Shot, and Cast List) that are available to help organize the script.

A script starts with a transition, which is in ALL CAPS, right justified, and ends with a colon. The typical instruction to fade in to start the movie appears like this:

FADE IN:

Other transitions, such as CUT TO, DISSOLVE TO, FADE OUT, START MONTAGE, or INTERCUT AS NEEDED are only used when needed. If you have a scene ending in a kitchen and then your next scene is in the living room, you do not need CUT TO as a transition between the scenes. Such an edit is implied by the change in scene headings. However, if there is a time passage or a flashback, DISSOLVE TO is acceptable before the next scene heading appears.

The scene heading consists of three parts written in all capital letters. The first is interior or exterior, written as INT. or EXT. There are a few exceptions which we'll cover soon, but INT. and EXT. will handle the majority of your scenes.

The second part of the scene heading is the location, such as KITCHEN or LIVING ROOM. This must be focused so the producer, director, and other crew members can execute the scene properly. Do not use broad physical descriptions, such as HOUSE. If you shoot inside of a house, the kitchen, bedroom, bathroom, and all other rooms within the house are different arenas for the production crew.

The third part of the scene heading is a time element. This is at the end of the heading and is set apart by a "–". Time elements like DAY and NIGHT are standard. You can also use times that are more specific, such as SUNRISE or AFTERNOON.

Combining interior or exterior, the location, and the time element results in a scene heading. A sample heading for a breakfast scene would be:

INT. KITCHEN – MORNING

The scene headings are not descriptive. If you want it to be a messy kitchen, you'll add those details in the action lines.

You will sometimes come across I/E. This means Interior/Exterior and is only used where the scene takes place inside a location which is outside of another. Vehicle scenes are the most frequent uses and look like this:

I/E. TAXI/DOWNTOWN STREET – NIGHT

By using the I/E. in the scene heading, you establish the action is taking place inside of the vehicle while simultaneously showing the location outside. In the above case, the producer knows that the taxi must be on a downtown street, so the location that is seen through the taxi windows will be appropriate.

Returning to our sample kitchen scene, our opening script page looks like this:

FADE IN:

INT. KITCHEN – MORNING

The next element to add are action lines. These briefly describe who is in the scene and what is happening. Action lines should be in blocks of four sentences or less. For characters, they should be in ALL CAPS the first time we meet them. For example:

Flour coats a countertop. BETH, 40, kneads a mound of dough. It collapses. DYLAN, 20, ducks in and grabs a soda from the fridge.

Less is more here. The kitchen isn't over-described; unless this is a period piece, we can assume a stove, counterspace, refrigerator, and other basic elements are there. Do not mention specific items unless they are relevant to the story. For example, if we point out a row of knives or a thick cleaver is present, we would assume those items would be used as props. All that is necessary for this sample scene is the dough. Everything else in the scene will be provided by the set designer.

The characters are similarly a blank canvas. Unless there is a specific physical attribute, like race, height, physical impairment, or hair length, don't mention it. If Beth needs to be seven feet tall or if Dylan limps when he walks, put it in. If there is no specific need to point something out, paint only in broad strokes. The producer wants to see a lot of white space on the page, so blocky action paragraphs of more than four lines should be avoided.

Our sample script page now looks like this:

FADE IN:

INT. KITCHEN – MORNING

Flour coats a countertop. BETH, 40, kneads a mound of dough. It collapses. DYLAN, 20, ducks in and grabs a soda from the fridge.

So far, we've introduced Beth and Dylan thus far in the action lines. Note that we don't say "A WOMAN" kneads dough and "A YOUNG MAN" grabs a soda. Use their names, like BETH and DYLAN, on first reference.

The final main script elements are characters and dialogue. We've already given the characters their names. To have them speak, type their names in the center of the page in ALL CAPS. Their dialogue will be added directly under their name in blocks that are heavily indented from both the right and left margins. Your scripting program will have margins already preset for you, but if you are using basic word processing software, the dialogue should be indented 2.5 inches from the page's left-hand side. It will look like this:

>DYLAN
>Is it supposed to do that?

>BETH
>I think I have the measurements wrong. Her recipe
>said to add water to the mix.

>DYLAN
>It didn't say how much?

Beth tosses more flour onto the dough and resumes kneading.

>BETH
>It just said water. I put in too much.

>DYLAN
>You'll get it.

The final element is the parenthetical. The difficulty in using a parenthetical is that using one can easily lead you to using them frequently. Add them sparingly, if at all. An example from the above scene would be:

>DYLAN
>Is it supposed to do that?

>BETH
>(sadly)
>I think I have the measurements wrong. Her recipe
>said to add water to the mix.

>DYLAN
>It didn't say how much?

That may be acceptable, but you cannot lapse into a parenthetical fever where you insert emotions into every line. One poor example would be:

>DYLAN
>(mockingly)
>Is it supposed to do that?

>BETH
>(defiantly)
>I think I have the measurements wrong. Her recipe
>said to add water to the mix.

>DYLAN
>(condescendingly)
>It didn't say how much?

Beth tosses more flour onto the dough and resumes kneading.

                    BETH
                  (proudly)
        It just said water. I put in too much.

                    DYLAN
                  (contritely)
        You'll get it.

The overuse of parentheticals defeats the purpose of bringing in actors or a director. In essence, you've assumed their roles by weaving emotion into each line. Use parentheticals rarely and only if needed. Otherwise, let the script (and characters) speak for themselves.

This can be best illustrated by using dialogue to move the story forward. Consider the following short scene as an example of minimal description while relying on the characters' words to tell the narrative.

INT. MEDICAL WAITING ROOM – AFTERNOON

BEN, 21, perches on a seat in the nearly empty room. He taps idly on his cell phone, then pockets it. JERRY, also college-aged, slumps in a nearby chair.

                    JERRY
        Chill. You'll find out when you find out.

                    BEN
        Results shouldn't take this long.

                    JERRY
        Yeah. You're probably gonna die.

                    BEN
        Dude!

                    JERRY
        And I'm gonna be stuck telling everybody
        what happened to you. It's embarrassing,
        really. Just very, very uncool.

                    BEN
        Will you stop it?

Jerry sits up in feigned terror.

                    JERRY
        Your mom! Oh, man, I forgot about her!
        Did you tell her yet?

                    BEN
        No! No way!

>   JERRY
>   You oughta give me your phone. You've
>   got her number in there, right?

Relying on dialogue makes several things apparent. First, Ben has a medical condition and is awaiting the results. Jerry is clearly his friend because he knows about the medical condition and jokes about Ben's mother. Also, whatever is wrong with Ben can't be overly serious, as Jerry is kidding about the seriousness of it while also acting horrified. Odds are the medical condition is simply embarrassing.

Good dialogue also does not state the obvious to the viewing audience. A poor version of the above script would look like this:

INT. MEDICAL WAITING ROOM – AFTERNOON

BEN, 21, perches on a seat in the nearly empty room. He taps idly on his cell phone, then pockets it. JERRY, also college-aged, slumps in a nearby chair.

>   JERRY
>   Ben, you are my friend and I am happy
>   to be with you here at the medical clinic.
>
>   BEN
>   Thank you, Jerry. But this is taking a long
>   time.
>
>   JERRY
>   I know, Ben. Let us wait here until the
>   test results come in.
>
>   BEN
>   Okay, Jerry.

There are several stark differences between the script samples. The second version has dialogue that is neither conversational nor particularly interesting. Instead, it comes across as stilted words that sound wooden when they are said out loud. The other rookie mistake is the constant name-dropping when the characters speak to one another. Think of the last conversations you had with your friends. Did you repeatedly refer to each other by your first names in the conversation? Most dialogue reveals that first names are seldom used at all. Instead, people will resort to using nicknames like "dude", "babe", "bro", or "man". Above all else, the dialogue must match the tone of the characters so they speak in the manner that is expected of them.

Other scenes rely more on action lines to move the story forward. For our next example, let's run through a brief scene with little dialogue. This scene also introduces the phrases ANGLE ON or CLOSE ON. These words are left-justified when the writer must convey something of importance. Also, there is a parenthetical used when the voice of the Odessa Control Tower operator comes through the radio. You will also notice that some sounds and props are capitalized. This is meant to draw attention to them due to their importance in the scene.

I/E: SMALL PLANE COCKPIT – DUSK

CARL (45) pilots the Cessna solo, bouncing in the captain's chair. Nasty clouds surround the windows. It's getting dark fast. Sweat on his brow. The control yoke shimmies in his left hand. He grabs the MIC with the other and speaks shakily.

> CARL
> Odessa Tower, Odessa Tower, this is
> November One-Six-Two-Juliet-Charlie. Heading
> four-five inbound for final approach.

> ODESSA TOWER
> (over radio)
> November One-Six-Two-Juliet-Charlie,
> This is Odessa . . .

A BLAST OF STATIC cuts off the transmission. Carl stares at the mic blankly. The plane rolls.

> CARL
> No!

He drops the mic, grabs the yoke with both hands, struggles to right the plane.

ANGLE ON THE MIC. It flops in the passenger side footwell, out of reach.

A FLASH OF LIGHTNING floods the cockpit. Carl SCREAMS. THUNDER BOOMS. The plane vibrates wildly.

CLOSE ON THE ALTIMETER. The needle spins counterclockwise.

> CARL
> Odessa!

In this case, you are in a confined space with only one person on the screen. The other voice is relayed through a radio speaker. To keep the action moving forward, you should guide the reader with specific close ups that convey the dramatic tension. This holds true in other action-driven scenes as well. If there is a battle in a superhero movie, aim a few of the sentences to a close up of a laser or a fallen villain.

Another seemingly difficult scene to script is any time two people have a phone conversation. This introduces the new time element "CONTINUOUS" to our scene headings, which we will use in the scene below. If friends Natalie and Jessica are in two separate physical spaces but are talking on the phone to each other, it is far too cumbersome to list their respective film locations between each line of dialogue. You would end up with something unreadable like this:

INT.   JESSICA'S BEDROOM – EVENING

College-aged JESSICA lounges in her well-kept bedroom, talking into her cell phone.

                        JESSICA
                  Hey, Nat, what's up?

INT.   NATALIE'S BEDROOM – CONTINUOUS

NATALIE (22) talks into her phone. Her bedroom is messy with clothes strewn on the futon.

                        NATALIE
                Same ol', what's with you?

INT.   JESSICA'S BEDROOM – CONTINUOUS

                        JESSICA
              About to head out to Peter's,
             he's got that party in an hour.

INT.   NATALIE'S BEDROOM – CONTINUOUS

                        NATALIE
                  Oh, that's tonight?

INT.   JESSICA'S BEDROOM – CONTINUOUS

                        JESSICA
              Yeah. You want to come with?

INT.   NATALIE'S BEDROOM – CONTINUOUS

                        NATALIE
              Don't know. You driving?

INT.   JESSICA'S BEDROOM – CONTINUOUS

                        JESSICA
            Me? Nah, you gotta drive.

   Phone conversations can be easily solved by following two rules. First, establish who is on each end of the phone. Once done, left justify the phrase INTERCUT AS NEEDED. This allows the director, talent, and editor the liberty to hold longer on reaction shots and let the shots "breathe" instead of supposing edits after each line of dialogue. The better result looks like this:

INT.   JESSICA'S BEDROOM – EVENING

College-aged JESSICA lounges in her well-kept bedroom, talking into her cell phone.

JESSICA
Hey, Nat, what's up?

INT.   NATALIE'S BEDROOM – CONTINUOUS

NATALIE (22) talks into her phone. Her bedroom is messy with clothes strewn on the futon.

NATALIE
Same ol', what's with you?

INTERCUT AS NEEDED

JESSICA
About to head out to Peter's,
he's got that party in an hour.

NATALIE
Oh, that's tonight?

JESSICA
Yeah. You want to come with?

NATALIE
Don't know. You driving?

JESSICA
Me? Nah, you gotta drive.

This simple tool allows a more natural flow to the writing, providing a cleaner and more legible script. At the end of the conversation, simply write BACK TO SCENE with whichever character continues the scene or cut to a new scene.

The Film Script

Knowing the specifications allows you to format a screenplay correctly, but there is still the matter of fleshing out an entire story that will engage an audience for more than 90 minutes. The protagonist, which is your main character, is introduced in the opening pages. The film's setting, tone, and other major characters are also introduced.

Compare the opening pages of the two following scripts. Our first example, *The Aging*, is a horror story about four elderly residents of a decrepit nursing home that faces foreclosure.

FADE IN:

INT. NURSING HOME MAIN ROOM - DAY

Light dust and a thin layer of sweat hang over sagging furniture and dated wallpaper. A sign on the wall reads CARRABELLE PINES – A HOME WITH YOUR FRIENDS.

FOUR RESIDENTS, all well into their 80s, fidget in the room. BEV busies herself at a counter, reshuffling a half dozen stray KEYS. The SERGEANT pushes open the window curtain as dust motes scatter.

> BEV
> They'll be here soon enough.

> SERGEANT
> Those keys aren't any good now.

> BEV
> If they want to see them, I have them here.

> SERGEANT
> Won't matter. This is decided.

Spinsters LINDA and HELEN perch stiffly on a love seat. Their clothes were appropriate for a Sunday service long ago. Linda plucks stray bits from her worn sleeve.

> HELEN
> It's fine.

> LINDA
> It's not fine. I can see it.

> HELEN
> I can't. Well, not too much.

> SERGEANT
> Are you hens ready? They're almost here.

EXT. NURSING HOME – CONTINUOUS

Mangrove swamps, ferns, and thicket surround the aged, U-shaped home. Set back in the dense Florida wilderness, vines and weeds have encroached on its former grandeur.

A SWIMMING POOL shimmers in the heat. A handful of walking trails disappear into the brush. TWO LARGE SUVs crawl down the long, decrepit driveway.

That brief introductory scene reveals several key elements to the overall story. First, the main characters are seen interacting with one another and their environment. Second, the setting of an old nursing home along the Florida coast is introduced. Finally, the tone of the writing is clear from the descriptive words in the action lines. Sagging furniture and dated wallpaper are described, but the individual pieces of furniture are left to the set designer; it is enough to convey the overall feeling of the setting with just a few examples instead of getting bogged down in extraordinary details. The tone of the writing is also evident using words like aged, decrepit, and former grandeur.

Contrast that to the tone of a comedy script. The second example, *Taggers,* follows a quartet of Martians who secretly monitor Earthlings.

FADE IN:

EXT. PHOBOS MOONSCAPE – DAWN

A dark, creepy, forbidding rocky terrain, bereft of life. MARS and Phobos' sister moon, DEIMOS, hang in the sky.

A small SATELLITE DISH is hidden among the rocks. Next to it is a rough CAMP. A Martian, CAPTAIN DELPOCK, sleeps on a pad next to the dish. He has two bug eyes, green skin, and four fingers on each hand. Typical alien.

A SUNBEAM hails the dawn, as the sun peeks over the horizon. The light creeps over Delpock's face. He swats at it, grunts and wakes up. He sees the satellite dish. And SCREAMS.

Lurches to his feet. Sees Mars overhead. SCREAMS again. Sees his sleeping pad. SCREAMS some more.

He drops abruptly, as if smacked in the face. He wheels, gets to his feet, frantic. And SCREAMS. The invisible force smacks him to the ground again.

INT. UFO DELPOCK'S QUARTERS – NIGHT

Delpock is asleep in his bunk, being slapped by another alien, MOOTOP. Delpock's still SCREAMING in his nightmare.

> MOOTOP
> Captain! Wake up!

He smacks Delpock again. Delpock comes to, panicked.

> DELPOCK
> You slapped me!

> MOOTOP
> Five or six times, sir. I lost count.
> You were screaming again.

> DELPOCK
> Sorry. Bad dream.

> MOOTOP
> Not another nightmare about being
> stationed on Deimos.

> DELPOCK
> Phobos this time. It looked like Phobos.

> MOOTOP
> Ah, the crappier of the Martian moons.
> You all right?

> DELPOCK
> No.

> MOOTOP
> How many fingers am I holding up?

He splays out all four fingers on a hand and waggles them.
> DELPOCK
> All four.

> MOOTOP
> You're good.

Again, major characters are introduced quickly. In this script, Captain Delpock is the leader of the Martian team. We've established that he is on a spaceship, his working relationship with his subordinate Mootop is flexible since Mootop slaps him awake, and he is terrified of being marooned on the Martian planet Phobos. The tone is more relaxed than *The Aging*; Delpock screams at a satellite dish, Mootop waggles four fingers at him, and his brief introductory physical description ends with the words "Typical alien".

The first few pages are just the launching of the story with basic elements outlined. Within the first 15 or 20 pages, a major event presents a challenge to the main character. Whether they lose their job, win the lottery, or witness a crime, this event must spur the action forward as the main story arc. Syd Field called this plot point one and noted for it to occur around page 19. This event serves as a major catalyst that demands action from the script's protagonist. There are exceptions to this rule, with directors like Quentin Tarantino and Christopher Nolan gleefully delivering nonlinear films. The vast majority of films, however, still adhere to a simple three-act structure.

In *The Aging*, the elderly nursing home residents learn that their home will be destroyed to make way for a golf course (the SUVs creeping up their driveway in the first scene contain the bankers with the repossession papers). In *Taggers*, the Martian quartet finds out that budget cuts back on Mars will force them to stop operations, endangering their jobs.

The second act of the script begins after plot point one. This is where subplots, like family difficulties or love interests, are developed as secondary storylines. These plot threads increase in tension and complexity until the midpoint. The midpoint happens literally near the middle of the script between pages 45 and 60 (depending on the overall script length). It is similar to plot point one in that it marks another major development in the story.

Act two continues past the midpoint as stakes are raised and the odds are lengthened against the protagonist. In a romantic piece, the lovers may learn that their future is even more imperiled than first thought. In a bank robbery movie, the police surrounding the thieves in the bank may discover they cannot possibly cover all of the exits. The same dramatic tension exists with our previous examples. In *The Aging*, the elderly quartet violently confronts the bankers. *Taggers* has a similarly physical (albeit comedic) battle, in which the Martians launch an attack against an Air Force base in hopes of preserving their jobs. The end of act two escalates with the situation becoming increasingly hopeless for the protagonist.

This marks the arrival of plot point two as the turning point between acts two and three. Heading into the last 15 pages into the script, the protagonist summons inner courage, unleashes a bold plan, or discovers a daring solution. This is the climax of the movie in which the hero saves the day, the subplots come together, and there is a final showdown between the protagonist and the opposing forces. Of course, not all scripts end with a happy resolution or a tidy ending. Some endings are shocking (the nursing home burns down at the end of *The Aging*), others have twists (the renegade Martians assimilate with the Earthlings in *Taggers*), and many franchise films serve as springboards to sequels. Whenever beginning to write a script, have an idea of your ending before you commit time, effort, and your creativity to the project. It's acceptable to have a general idea that you will hone as you approach the final act. However, it is poor planning to write 100 pages of a feature script and not have the final scenes in mind.

This brings two notes of caution about the importance of proper formatting and the ability to create a quality story. Feature film screenwriting is a notoriously difficult field to enter. To make sure that fledgling writers have the proper skillset, film producers and agents will not waste their time evaluating your talent unless you demonstrate the correct script formatting. This is done by writing a spec script, which is short for speculative script. This is an original story, written by you, that shows potential job leads that you understand the professional norms of screenwriting. A film spec script lasts between 90 and 120 pages (again, industry standard for a feature length film) with proper formatting, tone, scene descriptions, characterizations, dialogue, and all of the nuances that create an interesting screenplay.

Your spec script must be an original idea, so writing the next *Mission Impossible* or *Fast and Furious* movie is pointless. Producers want to see that your talent can be properly formatted and delivered as a readable project. Your spec script will probably never be produced, yet it is an important step in the development of your screenwriting career. It is not uncommon for beginning screenwriters to have two or three spec scripts completed before looking for industry representation through an agent or manager.

If your spec script is picked up by a producer and moves into the production phrase, it will then evolve into a shooting script. This is a much more detailed version of your spec script. While it contains the same dialogue, scenes, and characters as before, it also includes camera moves and numbered scenes. This is the version of the script that will be used by the crew to make a movie.

The final formatting note is for the last words on the script. Once the script is completed, the words FADE OUT or FADE TO BLACK are right justified after the last lines are delivered. It is also customary to write THE END at the conclusion of the script, so your final lines will look like this:

FADE OUT
THE END

Looking Forward

Feature film production felt a major financial hit when Covid forced movie theaters to either limit the number of attendees or to just close altogether. The film industry has since rebounded by looking at new delivery options away from the traditional theater. Netflix, Hulu, Amazon Prime, and other streaming services are eagerly bankrolling movies to show on their own platforms. The number of films may have slowed temporarily, but it has roared back on household TV screens at an astonishing pace.

Since filmmaking is such a collaborative effort, having a standard script template is essential so the writers, producers, director, talent, and crew members all have a central touchstone for the film. The locations manager can read the script to see that an old restaurant is needed as an interior location while the casting director can note how many scenes will need to have extras milling around in the background. The standard script provides everyone on set with the information they need to produce the feature film.

Exercises

1. Write a one-page scene of two diners at a restaurant. Their dialogue must reflect the financial situation that one has much more money than the other. The relationship between the two diners is entirely up to you. They can be siblings, old friends, or two coworkers who cannot stand each other but found themselves at the same restaurant.
2. Pitch a 48-hour film festival script using the following elements: a character who is a baseball player, a prop that is a ham sandwich, and the line of dialogue "Whenever Sebastian says something like that, I never believe him." The finished script should span four to seven pages in length.
3. Imagine a character who refuses to take selfies and put their image online. Discuss different methods to reveal that character's trait through dialogue, then describe how to accomplish the same attribute through action only.
4. Write a four- to seven-page script that takes place exclusively in a kitchen. Would you be able to write a funny or scary script in that location with that limited page count? Make sure to use movie terminology like ANGLE ON or CLOSE ON if you need to draw specific attention to individual items in the scene.
5. Discuss a movie that has made an impact on you. Was it because of a strong plot, a memorable setting, a fascinating character, or some other factor? There are no "right" or "wrong" answers to what movie impacted you, but you should be able to explain why it is important to you.
6. Check out an online movie script database (these are readily available online). Locate one of your favorite films. Then, watch the film again while having the script available to you. Pay attention to how the writer constructed the dialogue while the actors and director expanded upon the characters.
7. Research screenplay contests that are open for student writers. Check their submission guidelines for desired script length, genre, and other requirements. If you have a spec script and would like to be noticed by an agent, entering (and winning) a screenplay contest is one of the most proven paths to success.

Chapter Essentials

- Page count and the length of a narrative film are directly related. Each script page averages one minute of running time in a finished movie.
- Locations are not overly described. They stand as a framework for the director and set designer without too much detail.
- Action lines are short, punchy sentences without excess words.
- Dialogue drives the story forward without the use of parentheticals unless absolutely necessary.
- Plot point one, midpoint, and plot point two serve as guideposts for the overall development of the script.

Online Links

Scriptmag.com. Scriptwriting articles, competitions, adaptations, tools and tricks for both novice and seasoned writers alike are available on *Script Magazine*'s website.

Studiobinder.com. Providing an excellent look at some of the best screenwriting contests that are open for students, the Studio Binder website is motivation for students to finish their screenplays.

Wga.org. The website for the Writers Guild of America West offers resources including information about contracts, lists of exemplary screenplays, and links to film and television industry guilds and unions.

15 Social Media and Podcasts

Key Words

Informational
Interview
Message
Narrative

Podcast
Post
Social Media

Historical Overview

Of the many forms of media that require scripting, one of the most diverse topics is also one of the newest. Social media is essentially all forms of media that lets users create and share content. These posts run the gamut of self-promotion, beauty tips, religious notes, political commentary, and pictures of what someone is about to eat for lunch.

LinkedIn was one of the first social media platforms to allow profiles and messaging among its users. Launched in 2002, it was geared toward white collar professionals looking to network and potentially land new clients or jobs. Other platforms quickly joined the fray, including MySpace in 2003, which was the first social network to reach a global audience. Facebook launched in 2004, followed by the messaging platforms Twitter in 2006 and WhatsApp in 2009. In the next few years, Instagram (2010), Snapchat (2011) and TikTok (2016) each carved out their own niche in social media messaging.

Billions of users subscribe to one or more of these services, making them the fastest growing media platform in history. Early newspapers were hampered by printing costs and literacy rates. Radio and television needed technology to create, air, and then receive the signals. But social media rocketed into media dominance in less than two decades.

Reporters monitor the platforms for breaking news, politicians send tweets to their constituents, celebrities post about their latest project, and everyday people have taken to social media as a fast, inexpensive, and portable source of information.

The same ease of market access that spurred social media simultaneously created the podcast. In 2004, Adam Curry was a former MTV video jockey and Dave Winer was a software developer. Together, they saw a way to build a bridge between content developers and users. The market exploded with podcasts covering a massive array of topics; more than 30,000 active podcast creators are currently producing audio and video content. To simplify this medium, podcasts can be broken down into three broad categories: Interview, Informational, and Narrative.

DOI: 10.4324/9781003274766-16

Social media platforms and podcasts are joined because they are platforms where anyone can be a creator and user simultaneously. The barrier for entry into these platforms is incredibly low; most social media networks simply require an app to be downloaded onto a cell phone while podcasts can be created with minimal technical gear. The accessibility makes these messaging systems similar. However, each platform has its own specific requirements regarding content and style.

Technical Specifications

What can be posted on social media has limits. Content restrictions against profanity, vulgarity, and nudity are universal. But ongoing debates about access, hate speech, and free speech reveal the fluid nature of social media as users test the limits of what is acceptable to post online. To maintain some community standards and to set themselves apart in the market, each social media giant has its own specific set of technical rules.

The following list provides a brief overview of just a handful of the social media platforms that are currently available. Other platforms, like Reddit, Pinterest, Tumblr, and Flickr are also popular with hundreds of millions of users. Internationally based platforms, like WeChat, QQ, Sina Weibo, and Line show that social media is popular in all corners of the globe. The common thread that links these platforms is that they all provide access to everyday people.

Facebook

The dominant social media service in the world, Facebook claims three billion users on its platform that is accessible via the Internet or on its app. Users build a profile with their personal information and post updates as often as they wish. Facebook recommends no more than five posts a day, although users claim the limit is really 25 daily posts.

In addition to linking audio and video files, the limits of a Facebook text post are exceptionally long in social media; the upper limit is 63,206 characters, which allows users to tell detailed stories or offer in-depth explanations. Most posts are far shorter and average less than 50 characters each. The Facebook Marketplace allows users to buy and sell items to each other.

Instagram

Instagram allows sharing photos and videos on its networking service. These can be edited with filters and organized by hashtags or geographical tagging. The upper limit for captions is 2,200 characters, but most posts are far shorter than that.

Instagram also allows users to add up to 30 hashtags per post, but fewer hashtags (less than ten) are more effective at reaching an audience. These hashtags have inspired trends within Instagram, like #SelfieSunday where users post pictures of their faces. The site is also known for its use of photographic filters that improve the look of the images.

LinkedIn

This service is designed for professional networking among workers and their employers. Each user is assigned a profile page which can be populated with employment history, awards, publications, and other business-related honors. LinkedIn also allows job seekers to post their resumes in hopes that potential employers will contact them directly.

As a social network, LinkedIn maintains a focus on business and does not deal with trivial or personal content; a video clip of a grandchild's dance recital is not meant for this platform. However, it has more than 400 million members in more than 200 countries.

Snapchat

Snapchat creators communicate with one another through Snaps, which are photos or short videos that can include text and drawings. These Snaps can be messaged privately to one person, made semi-private via a "Story" option, or sent publicly via "Our Story". What makes Snapchat unusual is the time limit for the Snaps. Snapchat servers delete Snaps once all recipients have viewed them.

If a Snap is sent one-on-one and the receiver does not view it, the Snap disappears after 31 days. A seven-day auto-delete function happens to Snaps that are unopened on Group Chats. Snapchat has about 350 million users.

TikTok

TikTok is an international version of the Chinese app Douyin, focusing on short videos that are often stunts, pranks, jokes, and short performances. The videos last between 15 seconds to ten minutes in duration. The app recommends videos to users on a "For You" page based on the user's previous views.

Some of the features are a "react" button that lets users film their reaction to specific content, a privacy setting so creators can limit who sees their posts, and direct messaging with videos, emojis, or texts.

Twitter

Twitter is a social media platform that allows users to act as a broadcaster, a receiver or both. All comments are limited to 280 characters. These comments, called tweets, are microblogs that allow users to quickly scroll through. People can post text plus photos, videos, and links to other websites. The 280-character limit prompted users to create several space-saving shortcuts, such as:

> @name – This is used to tag someone else on Twitter. By using the ampersand "@" sign with the other person's Twitter username, that person will receive a notification in the "Mentions" section of their account. This simple ampersand is the key to starting communications on Twitter.
>
> # – This symbol is Twitter is called a hashtag, but it is still called a pound sign on a telephone; the original name of the symbol is the octothorp, which was used when touch-tone dialing began in the 1960s.

WhatsApp

This messaging app is owned by Facebook and boasts more than two billion active users every month. In addition to standard text messages, users can also have voice calls and send photos, videos, voice messages, and documents.

The maximum text limit is 700 characters, while other media like photos, videos, or voice messages are capped at 16MB. This will range from 90 seconds to three minutes of video content depending on the quality of the user's cell phone camera.

Social Media Campaigns

Getting the word out on social media is inexpensive, fast, and allows the creator to connect directly to the user without an intermediary. The difficulty is that the different social media platforms have various acceptable lengths for text posts, photos, and videos. There is no universal standard.

The benefits of a social media campaign are obvious. Spreading the word with such a campaign is incredibly cheap, fast, and connects the sender to the receiver directly. Unlike newspaper or radio, there is no intermediary standing in the way. The drawbacks are the technical limitations, since a file that will work on one platform may not work on another. The key is to build a user profile on as many platforms as practical, then tailor the basic message to each platform as needed. If a user sees the same message coming through their Twitter and Facebook feeds, that will send a powerful message. This technique has been shown to be highly effective to launch new products, promote the debut of new feature films, and to motivate people to vote in elections.

Podcasting

A podcast is an audio program that provides a series of spoken word episodes that are related to a particular theme. Nearly 2.5 million podcasts exist today, offering more than 66 million episodes. The main reason why there are so many podcasts is because the barrier to entry is very low. With a computer and a microphone, literally anyone can start a podcast by recording their voice into an audio file. This file is then uploaded to a podcast service, which charges a small monthly fee to host, promote, and track the podcast – Libsyn, BuzzSprout, and Podbean are three of the most popular options. This host then connects the podcast to platforms like Spotify, Apple Podcasts, Google Podcasts, and Stitcher. This workflow allows the podcaster to produce an episode and distribute it to a global audience with minimal technical effort.

Very few podcasts make money, so creating them is a labor of love for most creators. Most podcasts create ten or fewer episodes over their lifetime, while the average number of episodes is 30. Still, the demand for podcasts is forecast to grow more in the coming decade. More than 100 million Americans currently tune in and more than 400 million listen to podcasts worldwide.

Podcasts can be produced daily, weekly, or whenever the podcaster simply feels like adding another episode. Because podcasting is so individual, there is no template for the "right" type of script. Some shows are done with just a handful of written notes, then the creator edits out the weak parts of the show before posting the podcast. The other extreme of podcasts mimics old-time radio shows, complete with sound effects, musical cues, and multiple voices. To best determine the type of script that may be appropriate, let's examine the three basic types of podcasts: Interview, Informational, and Narrative.

Interview

The Interview Style is based on the host establishing a rapport with the guest, usually over a phone line. One variation is the panel program, when a host (or co-hosts) brings together several guests to include a variety of voices. For simplicity, we will focus on a one-on-one interview format for this chapter.

The Chad Whittle Show is an example of an interview podcast. Host Chad Whittle (who also serves as producer) tracks down an interviewee a few days prior to the interview. After establishing initial contact, Whittle emails a series of questions to the interviewee for approval. Whittle then arranges a time to call the interviewee and records the interview for the podcast. Once the interview wraps, he uploads the podcast for distribution. Below is the script for an episode in which Whittle interviewed Atlanta radio personality Jeff Dauler. The script begins with an introduction of the guest, then Whittle steps through the list of questions. When completed, Whittle thanks the guest and reads a standard outro to wrap up the episode. The shows vary in length but tend to last about 40 minutes each.

Jeff Dauler – "The Upside" podcast host and former Atlanta radio personality

Introduction:

My guest is a former radio personality in Atlanta with 25 years of experience in the radio industry. In 2019, he started a podcast with his wife Callie, the Upside, which reached the top ten on the Apple Podcasts chart at its launch. Jeff, it's nice to have a chance to speak with you.

1. Tell me a little about your background. What made you interested in a career in radio?
2. The Upside podcast has been successful. How did you and your wife, Callie, decide to produce a podcast as opposed to you trying to find a new job in radio?
3. Jeff, I started in radio when I was 17, and I have seen a lot of changes during that time. You have seen even more changes than me since you've had a longer career. In your opinion, what is the current state of the radio industry?
4. What do you miss most about working in radio?
5. What do you like about podcasting compared to radio?
6. What has been the biggest surprise with The Upside?
7. Do you produce/edit all the episodes yourself, or do you outsource the production work?
8. Do you feel as pressured producing a podcast as you did in radio? Of course, you have to worry about download numbers, and you want to continue to expand your audience, but with radio, you always have to worry about the ratings.
9. Do you plan your podcast like a radio show, or do you produce it differently?
10. Why do you think your podcast connects with your audience?
11. If you were an independent podcaster just getting started with no following, do you think you could've succeeded?
12. The Upside is all about gratitude. What are you most grateful for in your life?

OUTRO:

Jeff, good to speak with you today. You can listen and subscribe to the Upside on Apple Podcasts, Spotify, and wherever you listen to podcasts.

Informational

An Informational Style podcast centers on the hosts discussing factual topics. Below is a script from *Voca Vacay*, a travel podcast hosted by the authors of this text. The show begins with a cold open, which occurs when the host begins speaking without benefit of a pre-taped introduction.

Much of the program is adlibbed and the script is only a skeleton for the program. All items listed in bold text indicate special segments or cues for the show; the "new countries" prompt, for example, notes where the hosts acknowledge countries that now have listeners of the podcast. Equally important is that the script is broken into small segments which are indicated by separate paragraphs. The hosts talk about a segment, such as "French Quarter is not ADA friendly" as a conversation, not just as a recitation of that sentence. Once finished, they move on to the next paragraph. Each episode's duration is between 60 and 90 minutes.

Voca Vacay – "N'awlins Part Deux"

Cold Open – Named this because we know people who say "N'awlins" when they've never been there. It's like Shy-town!
Spokesguy Taped Open
   New Countries – Slovakia, Turkey, Mali
   French Quarter is not ADA friendly.
   Walked through the movie set on Royal Street. The PA guys lied and said it was a U-Haul Commercial, but it was an Anne Rice vampire show.
   Royal Street is highly underrated, one block off Bourbon Street. Lots of museums, street art. Bourbon Street is more focused on nightlife.
   Start at Brennan's with Bananas Foster. Local guy a bit crazy in line. No reservation, sit at the bar. I got Eggs Hussarde, Brennan's original with homemade English muffin, coffee-cured Canadian bacon, hollandaise, marchand de vin sauce. Marie got Duck Confit flannel hash, smoked duck confit, over easy duck egg, tomato jam, horseradish hollandaise sauce. Couple next to us only got BF, we did, then the other side did, then next to them did. It's awesome!
   Went to Pete the Cat museum and shop. Picked up Street Art on the way back. Rested at room for big evening, then to local bar Rusty Nail. KC Chiefs lost to the Bengals, sat an at outdoor table.
   Acme Oysters! Incredible! Short line at door, then sat at the bar. A dozen fresh oysters, split a Fried Peace Maker po'boy, fried oysters and shrimp with tobasco infused mayo. Guys shucked oysters right in front of us.
   Next morning, Café du Monde for beignets. Been serving them since Civil War era. They come in a three pack, street band outside. We each had a beignet, then gave our third to a local guy on a bench.
   Walked through Jackson square. Andrew Jackson, 7th US President and hero of the Battle of New Orleans, statue on horseback in center. In 1803, this is where Louisiana joined the US as a territory because of the Louisiana Purchase, was signed at the old city hall just north of square. Next to that is the St. Louis Cathedral, designated a minor basilica by Pope Paul VI.

Cooking class! New Orleans School of Cooking. First option is the demonstration class, $35 or $40 depending on time of day, you watch them cook, then eat. OR, hands-on cooking class, $145 each, 3 hours long, to prepare chicken and andouille gumbo, BBQ shrimp and grits, bananas foster crepes. Turns out the exhibition class was cancelled due to low enrollment, so we're good! Open Bloody Mary bar, mimosas, beer, wine, tea, water. Chef Rene, small class of 15.

Last night, Louis Armstrong Park. Saw base camp for the Vampire production!

Got a local pizza (bicycle delivery) and ate in the room.

After such a great trip, you'd think we'd never fight again. Wrongo! Ever disagree with your travel partner? Ever bicker on a vacay? Well, let's hash this out right now!

Spokesguy Taped Monica and Joey Intro
Monica and Joey Argument

Does it count to go to New Orleans when it isn't Mardi Gras?

You need to know this travel nugget!

Spokesguy Taped Travel Nugget Intro

Do what locals do! If you drink, find a local speciality. If you like a certain local food, find the best restaurant. Avoid chains at all costs. Even our local pizza was great!

Spokesguy Taped Guacamole Open
What the Holy Guacamole!?!

Be a king or queen for the next ten years! Applications are invited to secure a ten-year lease for The Ship Inn, on Piel Island, sitting half a mile off the Furness coast in Barrow-in-Furness. As well as running The Ship Inn, the successful applicant will manage other parts of the island, including its small camp site.

The scenic Island, which is 50 acres in size, hosts an array of wildlife and is home to the ruins of Historic England-run Piel Castle, a now derelict structure built in the 14th Century. They'll also be crowned "king" or "queen." According to the council's website, the tradition is a nod to the 15th century. This is when a claimant to the English throne landed on the island, before being defeated 10 days later. The monarch of Piel will be crowned by having a beer poured over their head while sitting on a throne.

Visitors can also stay overnight at the island's campsite or by booking accommodation at The Ship Inn. The island is reachable via a short ferry crossing from April to September while planned guided walks across the sands also take place during days of finer weather.

Candidates must be comfortable with unpredictable weather and work long hours.

Thanks for checking out Voca Vacay, and remember to keep up with us on Facebook, YouTube, Twitter, and Instagram! We'll see you in a fortnight!

Spokesguy Taped Close

Narrative

A Narrative Style podcast is the most labor-intensive format, as each sound effect, dialogue line, and musical sting is laid out in advance. Narrative podcasts are also the slowest to produce due to the amount of preproduction. The creator of a narrative podcast does not have the luxury of simply sitting in front of a microphone; a great deal of scripting must take place beforehand.

The following example, *Santa Maybe A Criminal*, was a 12-part series created by Jason Usry. It features a cover page for the script, a list of voice talent, music cues, and the script itself.

Jason Usry – "Santa Maybe A Criminal"
Introduction:

THE FIRST DAY OF CHRISTMAS
A PARTRIDGE IN A PINE TREE
CHARACTERS:
AUTOMATED VOICE
SANTA
RICHIE BUCK
RODNEY DALE MURPHY
SHERIFF BRADLEY DEWBERRY
DISPATCH

DISCLAIMER:

This program contains talk about criminal activity and may paint a not so flattering picture of one of your childhood heroes. It even includes a few cuss words and may not be appropriate for your young'ns, so you might wanna earmuff 'em or send 'em outside to play. Thanks for listenin'.

BETTER ELF SPONSOR

This podcast is brought to you by Better Elf.

[BETTER ELF AD]

AUTOMATED VOICE MESSAGE

The following is a collect call from a person presumed nice until proven naughty . . .
    [SANTA CLAUS]. . .
    . . . an inmate at the Ware County Correctional Facility . . .

RICHIE VO:

Yep, you heard that right. **Santa. Claus.**
    Name's Richie Buck. I'm a pest control technician, a carpenter, sometimes tenor in my church choir, and as unbelievable as it might sound, I'm here to save Christmas.

MUSIC AND OPEN UP.

RICHIE VO:

This is *Santa Maybe a Criminal* . . . a 12-part yuletide investigation . . .
    This is . . . *The First Day of Christmas – A Partridge in a Pine Tree.*

MUSIC END.

RICHIE VO:

It all started almost a year ago on Christmas Day . . . when a story fell into my lap . . . *hard* . . . like a fat kid on a mall Santa.

ATMOSPHERE UP.

You see my cousin, had a life-changing experience *on* Christmas Eve.

RODNEY:

It was that *damn* bird.

RICHIE VO:

That's Rodney Dale Murphy. He's my momma's brother's son. Rodney and his wife Linda live on a 12-acre plot of land . . .

ATMOSPHERE

Some would say it's in the middle of nowhere or "B.F.E.". . . 'round here we just say it's *"in the county"*.

RODNEY:

He'd been outside our bedroom window since Thanksgiving . . . just a-chirpin' and a-chirpin' . . . and here it was Christmas Eve . . .

Anyhow, I wanted to get to sleep so Santa would come on and bring me the camo waders I'd asked for. I'd been real good so far, too, no arrests or anything . . . the whole year!

RICHIE VO:

It was no secret in our family . . . Rodney was a troublemaker . . . and he'd had his run-ins with the law . . . you almost expected a call at two o'clock on a Saturday mornin' to go up to the jail to bail him out. But he was right, this year, he'd been good.

SOUND FX: CIGARETTE LIGHTING UP

RICHIE VO:

Rodney lights a cigarette. It makes me miss the days I used to smoke . . .

RODNEY COUGHS.

RODNEY:

Anyhow . . . we'd had a little shindig that evenin', Linda'd tucked the kids in and realized we didn't have no milk. I was like, "Well . . . what do we do now?" I mean we had the cookies . . . but you ever try to eat one of Linda's peanut butter cookies without no milk . . . ?

RICHIE:

Why didn't you go to the store?

RICHIE VO:

I wish I could describe the look Rodney gave me after this question. It was sorta a cross between, "you're kidding me, and what planet are you on . . .", then –

RODNEY:

You know Gators' is closed after eight on Christmas Eve . . . 'sides, neither of us shoulda been drivin' anyway.

RICHIE VO:

Gators was a legendary store in the county. They had the best fried tomaters you ever ate . . . And they'd burned down four times, only to rebuild with more fryer space than before . . .

RODNEY:

But that's when I had *the idea*.

Looking Forward

No scripting templates for podcasts and social media existed 25 years ago, simply because those forms of media had not yet been created. These new communication platforms show that interactive ways of people sharing ideas with one another will always evolve with the newest technology. Just the idea of portable phones was a fantasy to your grandparents; when you wanted to talk to someone in the middle of the previous century, you called their home, not their person. Now, calling, texting, tweeting, messaging, and emailing are simply a handful of forms of social communication between individuals.

Forecasting what is next in social media scripting comes down largely to what technology can deliver in the coming years. Speed, convenience, and mobility have driven social media and the various scripts that we use to deliver messages. As new forms of social media and podcasts enter the markets, the scripts needed to communicate will evolve as well.

Exercises

1. Survey your friends to see how many of them have accounts on the social media platforms discussed in this chapter. Which platform is the most popular? How many friends/followers do they have? Finally, on which social media platforms do you have an account and how many friends/followers do you have?
2. Picture a scenario in which you need to send a message to your best friend that you are meeting tonight at 8pm. You may use any type of media, including using your cell phone and computer, to relay this message. How many different ways can you deliver this message to your friend?
3. Of the social media platforms discussed in this chapter, which of them (if any) have you not used? Why not?
4. Design a podcast with the topic of your choosing. Which type of script would you use and why?
5. Research podcasts on a provider like Spotify or Apple Podcasts. Which of those podcasts interest you? Which ones do not intrigue you at all?

Chapter Essentials

- Social media accounts and podcasts both have low thresholds that creators need to meet in order to share messages.
- Social media platforms are barely two decades old, with LinkedIn, Facebook, Twitter, and others all joining the market after the year 2000.
- Some restrictions against nudity and profanity are the same across several media platforms.
- Each social media platform has their own unique requirements and limitations for content creators.
- A social media campaign is when one creator puts the same message out on multiple platforms to reach the broadest audience possible.
- Podcasts fall into three categories: interview, informational and narrative.
- Podcasts are unique in the media landscape in that they are open-ended; the duration of an episode is entirely at the whim of the creator.

Online Links

Influencermarketinghub.com. Influencers on social media platforms can find tools, links, and strategies for promoting their brands on this all-encompassing website. It also discusses the 133+ social media websites that are available beyond the typical Twitter and LinkedIn options.

Podcastinsights.com. An excellent resource on the Podcasting Insights website is the detailed, step by step guidance it offers on how to start a podcast, podcast hosting, and podcast gear guide.

Searchenginejournal.com. This website offers information on a variety of media, but the contents of its social media categories are especially valuable. Social media news, strategy, advertising, and specific links to platforms like Facebook and TikTok are all covered in-depth.

16 Virtual Reality

Key Words

Augmented Reality
Avatar
Extended Reality
Field of View
Fully Immersive

Genesis Point
Non-Immersive
Point of View
Semi-Immersive
Virtual Reality

Historical Overview

The term virtual reality is in itself an oxymoron, meaning that the definition contradicts itself. Virtual is often perceived as "fake" while reality refers to something that is real, so a false reality presents an interesting dilemma. One exceptional definition comes courtesy of NASA, which uses virtual reality in some of its training programs. That definition is "virtual reality is the use of computer technology to create the effect of an interactive three-dimensional world in which the objects have a sense of spatial presence".

Of all the types of media that are covered in this textbook, virtual reality (VR) may be assumed to be the newest. But early efforts in creating VR stretch back into the 1960s. In 1962, Morton Heilig created Sensorama, which was a small machine that allowed a single person to sit inside and face a stereoscopic, 3-D color display. He called this "Experience Theater" because it simulated riding a bicycle through New York City. Heilig added fan-generated wind, noises of traffic in hidden speakers, and even smells of pizza stands and bus exhaust fumes. Heilig could not find funding for wide distribution and the Sensorama was ultimately shelved. However, the seeds were sown for future VR attempts.

Harvard University's Ivan Sutherland teamed with several students in 1968 to create the first head-mounted display that could shift the perspective of the image as the wearer moved their head. Their invention, *The Sword of Damocles*, was a mechanical tracking system that pioneered a virtual reality system in a first-person environment. In the 1980s, computer scientist Jaron Lanier coined the phrase "virtual reality" when he founded VPL Research; this was the first company to sell VR goggles and wired gloves.

Other VR applications joined the technological surge at a rapid clip. Sega launched a VR motion simulator in its arcades in 1994. Google unveiled Street View in 2007, providing 360-degree looks at streets everywhere. The design for the first prototype of the Oculus Rift headset was revealed in 2010.

DOI: 10.4324/9781003274766-17

Titans of the gaming industry quickly realized the potential for VR and spent millions of dollars on research and development. Sony launched Project Morpheus, which was a VR headset for the PS4 system, in 2014. The next year, Apple won a patent for a head-mounted display system, Google unveiled Cardboard (a head mount to turn a smart phone into a portable VR system), and Samsung debuted the Gear VR headset.

Some forecasts predict that VR will be a 28-billion-dollar market by 2030; by comparison, film critics describe a Hollywood film as a "blockbuster" if it sells just 100 million in tickets. That means there would need to be 280 Hollywood blockbuster movies just to equal the revenue generated by virtual reality.

It is worth noting that virtual reality is hardly an all-or-nothing paradigm. There are actually three levels of virtual reality, some of which you probably already use on a daily basis. There are non-immersive, semi-immersive, and fully immersive levels of VR, which are best illustrated as follows:

- **Non-immersive.** These platforms are often overlooked because they are already integrated into our lives. When you bring up Google Maps, your interactions with that environment are an example of a virtual reality that you are looking at while controlling your actions as shown by an avatar (usually just a moving blue dot on a map). Video games are similar technology, allowing you to interact with a computer-generated environment while still living in a physical environment. As an example, if you're playing a video game in your living room, you're controlling the action on the virtual screen while resting comfortably on your couch.
- **Semi-immersive.** Using 3D graphics and a greater sense of being in the virtual environment, a semi-immersive experience takes the user one step further from their physical surroundings. Flight simulators are perfect examples. The user assumes the role of pilot of a Cessna 152 and "flies" the plane using a yoke and aviation control panel. Racing simulators allow the users to "drive" a Formula One race car while a trucking simulator lets the user feel like they are behind the wheel of a big rig. The user is aware that they are in a simulator but the realistic controls and displays create a more immersive experience.
- **Fully immersive.** This is the final frontier of virtual reality and the focus of this chapter. Here, the user puts on a head mount display (HMD) that provides a stereoscopic 3D experience, allowing the person to see in all directions as if they are in the virtual world. This type of VR is primarily used in video games, although other applications are being developed on a continual basis. Exciting developments in VR fields like aviation and medicine allow the user to simulate a real-life scenario in stunning detail.

Immersion is not the only element that impacts the VR experience. This field of creating new realities has spawned different categories to better describe what is on the horizon. For example, the phrase "virtual reality" refers to a 3D environment that a user may enter as a completely artificial world. Entering this realm means the person must wear specialized equipment, like a helmet or special goggles that are filled with motion-activated sensors. This experience was once limited to an individual in a studio setting, but the availability of consumer-level headsets means users can now enter an immersive experience from their own living room.

Augmented reality (AR) is slightly different, as it resembles a lens placed over the user's actual reality. Think of wearing a pair of sunglasses with deep red lenses; you are still seeing your reality, but the perception is altered by adding the red color over the landscape.

The user interacts with the AR environment as they would their "real" environment with only the "look" of their reality changed. Many apps on your cell phone will morph, distort, or otherwise alter the view that you can see. This is the basic concept of augmented reality. VR will immerse you into an alien world with evil droids firing phasers in your direction, but AR will superimpose the image of an alien into your front yard when you look through your cell phone's display.

The next term to describe all these advances is XR, or extended reality. XR blends both VR and AR capabilities and then allows the user to view them in more organic fashion. The best way to picture this is VR will put you on Mars to fight aliens. AR will make the aliens appear in your front yard. XR will merge these technologies so you are now fighting the aliens in your front yard. This reality-bending environment will also need scripts, as well as people to write them for the end user.

The level of immersion impacts the script, as more specific language must be scripted for the other creative team members who will further develop the VR product. Like feature film or episodic television, the script for virtual reality will pass through an intermediary before it reaches the end user. A newspaper article connects the writer directly to the reader. A radio script pairs the announcer's voice to the listener. But a VR script tells a story that will pass through a team of animators, graphic designers, voice actors, and a host of other creative professionals before the it reaches the consumer. This is why there are specific cues to the technical team that are woven into the script.

As the technology leaps forward, the need for content will grow rapidly. Scripts for virtual reality will be most popular among immersive games, but training platforms and educational uses will also make use of the virtual environments. The challenge is that these VR script formats are still evolving, so there is no "right" or "wrong" industry standard yet. Happily, there are some standard practices as the professional templates evolve.

Technical Specifications

There are unique considerations for scripts in virtual reality. The first is one of perspective. Unlike watching movies or listening to the radio, VR demands active, not passive, participation. VR offers two options, depending on the program's design. The first option is third-person interaction in which the user watches events unfold before them. This happens in a virtual setting, but the user is essentially still just observing events. It's akin to watching a movie while being immersed in the settings.

But VR can offer much more of an interactive experience, especially in a first-person platform. This powerful option allows the user to physically interact with the virtual surroundings, move through the settings, and communicate with the characters inside of the virtual world. This movement is done through an avatar, which is a virtual representation of the user in the artificial world. If the user is fighting in the Middle Ages, the avatar could resemble a knight. Of course, since this virtual reality allows limitless potential, the avatar could be an ant in an insect world, a great white shark in an ocean, or an alien droid flying through the Horsehead Nebula. The avatar may be revealed through a mirror's reflection or similar trick to show the user how they are perceived.

Genesis Point

Each scene begins with what we will call a genesis point. This is like the curtain rising on a theatrical production or a screen fading from black to the first scene in a movie. The story starts here. More importantly, the entire paradigm of the production is unveiled at this opening point. The mood, the setting, the lighting, the sound effects, and the user's point of view are all revealed in the first few seconds. The user's avatar is also revealed if there is a reflective surface.

Within this opening scene, the user will see that the spatial dynamic of virtual reality is unlike any form of previous media, but it is exactly like real life. The selling point of VR is to make it as close to reality as possible, thus you can immerse yourself in a 360-degree landscape, interact with objects, and move with impunity. This presence makes other media seem flat by comparison. You can watch television, read a magazine, or listen to the radio, but interacting with the imaginary environment in a VR setting makes it unique among all media. The scripting for virtual reality is also unlike anything used anywhere else. The challenge is to address all directions in the encompassing environment simultaneously.

The range of vision available to the user is called the Field of View (FOV). This is the potential areas that the avatar can see, so all 360 degrees encompass the FOV; the writer must be aware of this. However, the perspective, or what the avatar sees in the virtual environment, is the Point of View (POV).

This POV directly impacts how the script is written. A first-person POV means that the player sees the world through the eyes of the avatar; if the character looks to the right, then the screen's point of view shifts to the right. A third-person POV is an omniscient, disembodied viewpoint that looks down from the top of the FOV, so the user is basically looking down at the avatar from an overhead vantage point. If the avatar looks to the right, the POV sees the avatar turning toward the right but that is just one part of the FOV. The overhead viewpoint sees all.

For this example, we will establish the genesis point in a dimly lit living room and assume a first-person POV. Like a narrative film script, the scene will start with two elements: the FADE IN: at the top of the script justified to the left margin, and the scene heading. Like the scene headings in a film script, the heading is in ALL CAPS and divided into three parts. The first part indicates whether the scene in interior (INT.) or exterior (EXT.). The second part is the location and the final part indicates the time of day. Our scene will begin with:

FADE IN:

INT. LIVING ROOM – NIGHT

Once the scene heading is established, the script will continue to have elements of the narrative film script within. The difference comes from accommodating the avatar's spatial view. This means that all directions that are possible from the player's FOV must be depicted whether the player chooses to look in a certain direction or not. This is done by limiting the FOVs into six different simultaneous areas, which are UP, DOWN, FORWARD, REVERSE, LEFT, and RIGHT.

The nature of virtual reality technology is that these different areas are seamlessly stitched together. When your avatar spins around, the environment should appear as one integrated world with no hiccups between the six areas. The visuals should blend and overlap without distortion or interruption. This is a technological issue and not a concern for the script. This is pointed out so the writer understands that the six FOVs will overlap and switch places as the avatar moves; when the avatar turns 180 degrees, the FORWARD area is now REVERSE, the LEFT area is now RIGHT, and so forth. It is a simple concept in real life (that's how you move around constantly with a shift in your perspective) but scripting it requires identifying direction within the spatial environment.

The easiest analogy is points on a compass. FORWARD is North, RIGHT is East, REVERSE is South, and LEFT is West. No matter which direction that you (or your avatar) are facing, those cardinal directions still exist in the holistic environment. It is worth pointing out that many games have a compass reset button. Pressing this button resets the virtual environment so the game continues but the avatar is once again facing North in their world.

The standard for virtual reality scripting is to concentrate on the six FOVs. You can give as much or as little detail as needed for the game designer when describing these areas. Let's use our dimly lit living room as an example for our six FOVs. The first FOV is FORWARD. For this example, we will start with FORWARD and then move in a clockwise rotation. Some prefer FORWARD, REVERSE, RIGHT, and LEFT as a North, South, East and West pattern. Either option is fine, but once established, that order should be maintained for the duration of the script.

FADE IN:

INT. LIVING ROOM – NIGHT

FORWARD FOV – EMERSON – male, 85, in a threadbare suit – stands in front of a roaring fireplace. It is the primary light source for the room. He reads a weathered book. Above the fire, two muskets are mounted to the wall. Large bookshelves flank the fireplace with hundreds of dusty books filling the shelves.

RIGHT FOV – two empty sitting chairs with a small table between them. A key ring with a single golden key is on the table.

REVERSE FOV – a closed door with a sturdy lock on the knob.

LEFT FOV – JUDITH – female, 80, in a frayed ballgown – admires a record spinning on an aging Victrola.

UP FOV – The ceiling is high with thick wooden beams across it.

DOWN FOV – A wooden floor.

Now that you have established the six FOVs, you will enter the action lines, characters, dialogue, and atmospheric audio. The action lines are written in short, punchy sentences, justified to the left margin. The dialogue is formatted like a film script (tabbed under a centered character name). Any atmospheric audio is preceded by the sound effects abbreviation SFX: written in bold, left justified, like this:

SFX:

Below that, the audio element is written in italics and is opened and closed with the brackets "< and >" at the start and end of the audio description. If the audio source is visually referenced, you should indicate where that sound will enter the player's world, like this:

<*A tinny song, old and romantic, thinly plays from the LEFT POV (the music plays from the left headphone speaker)*>

<The fireplace crackles with occasional small pops from the FORWARD POV (the sound will fill the speakers equally)>

JUDITH sways silently near the record player.
EMERSON thumbs through his book. He grumbles, snaps it shut, and shuffles to the right-hand bookshelf. He slides it back, retrieves another, and peers at it.

>   EMERSON
> It was here all along.

>   JUDITH
> Will you put that silly thing down already?

>   EMERSON
> This book shows how to get out. The map is
> right here.

JUDITH crosses to him and admires the book.

>   JUDITH
> Is that the only map?

>   EMERSON
> It is.

They grin evilly at each other, then directly at the avatar. EMERSON throws the book into the fire. It burns with a blue flame. JUDITH points at the avatar.

>   JUDITH
> Will your poor soul escape?

EMERSON and JUDITH's faces morph into demons and charge the avatar.

If the avatar does nothing, Emerson and Judith will quickly attack the player and pin the avatar to the ground. That scene is simple to write, like this:

EMERSON and JUDITH tackle the avatar. Their hands are now demonic claws, their faces twisted. The POV pivots UP to the ceiling.

SFX:

<Sounds of a struggle and JUDITH cackling (these sounds will come from all speakers equally)>

FADE TO BLACK.

In the above scenario, the avatar did nothing and the creatures attacked. The options are to now end the game (which would prompt the player to restart the adventure and take a different action) or to dissolve into another scene, like a hospital room. This hospital room becomes the next genesis point as the writer must establish the new virtual environment with its props and characters.

Let's say the player did something, like pivoted to the REVERSE FOV and ran for the locked door. The avatar's actions need to be noted with a new mark, as you are essentially telling the computer programmer to insert an IF/THEN action; IF the player makes a move in the physical world (like pushing the control buttons to make the avatar run a certain direction), THEN the avatar and the script react. For this example, we will use braces "{ and }" to encompass those directions. The scene of running for the door would unfold like this:

{Avatar pivots to REVERSE and runs to locked door}
REVERSE FOV – The door looms nearer. The avatar hands tug the knob. Locked.

> EMERSON
> (off-screen)
> Leaving so soon?

SFX:

<*Sounds of a struggle (these sounds will come from all speakers equally)*>

FADE TO BLACK.

A good effort but the door is locked. However, the above scene shows how the avatar's action can be depicted, plus it adds a spatial voice direction for the character. When Emerson says "Leaving so soon?", those words are off-screen. We don't see Emerson say the line, but his voice comes through the speakers.

For our final option, we will let our avatar escape. This will blend avatar action lines (shown in braces) interacting with another element in the virtual world. It will look like this:

{Avatar pivots to RIGHT FOV and grabs the key from the table}
{Avatar runs to REVERSE FOV, shoves key into door and yanks it open}

> EMERSON
> (off-screen)
> We will meet again!

FADE TO BLACK.

Success! The avatar has escaped the living room and has entered a new room, which we will make the hallway. This new genesis point requires six new FOV indicators, complete with props and characters as desired, like this:

INT. HALLWAY – NIGHT

FORWARD FOV – TANYA – female, 25, in a bright red cloak – stands at the end of the long hallway.

RIGHT FOV – a row of four windows shows the moonlit darkness outside.

REVERSE FOV – a closed door with a sturdy lock on the knob.

LEFT FOV – a long line of painted portraits.

UP FOV – the ceiling is high with a series of three chandeliers. They provide the illumination for the hallway.

DOWN FOV – A wooden floor.

Now that the new environment is established, the writer is free to move the narrative forward. Adding in new characters, dialogue, and action lines will largely mirror those templates already established in feature film narrative scripts. VR and narrative films share some underlying story-telling principles, so it is only natural that screenwriters from the film industry will migrate into VR scripting, bringing their film templates with them. These will be tweaked along the way to accommodate 360-degree settings, but some of the basic formatting styles will carry over to VR scripts.

The final example is how the VR script ends (much like a film script). Once the story is done, the VR script concludes with the words FADE TO BLACK in all caps, bold, right justified and followed with a period. One line below that, the words THE END will appear, centered, underlined, and in bold. The conclusion will look like this:

FADE TO BLACK.

<u>**THE END**</u>

Looking Forward

Virtual reality will expand greatly in the coming years in new fields, all of which will demand new writers to create their scripts. Leading museums are developing virtual visits, the travel industry allows users to see different places, and even the military uses VR to simulate combat environments. This is in addition to the educational applications, gaming, and corporate uses. Not only will VR expand across various industries, it will also become more commonplace in non-immersive and semi-immersive applications.

The need for a standardized scripting template is clear. As more writers dip into the VR arena, there will be expanded opportunities for those writers to move from one project to the next. Having a common template will allow them to easily transition from a medical VR platform into an industrial training setting. While that professional template is still evolving, the basics of starting with a genesis point, defining what is in the six fields of view, providing characters and dialogue, and then delineating how the avatar moves through the virtual world are all elements that need to be in the final script.

Exercises

1. Think of the types of virtual reality you already use on a frequent basis. This can include navigation tools on your phone, food delivery services like GrubHub, or video

game consoles. Which of these VR platforms would you be willing to give up and which ones would you like to keep?
2. Identify the gaming consoles and individual games that you have played that immerse you in a virtual world. This can range from soldiers in battle in the *Call of Duty* games to Mario and Luigi driving cars through the Mushroom Kingdom. How many of these games are the same as those of your classmates?
3. Virtual reality environments are unlimited in their potential. Describe an environment for a VR game that you would like to design. The realm can be at any time in the past, present, or future, plus it can be set anywhere (space, under water, or in a fictional land). What would you like to create?
4. Think of a classroom exercise that can be replicated through VR training in the medical field. Would you like to participate in such training? Why or why not?
5. VR environments allow the users to assume avatars as any sort of creature. If you could choose what kind of animal you would like to have as your avatar, what would you like to be in a VR game?

Chapter Essentials

- The earliest attempts at forms of virtual reality date back to the 1960s with Sensorama and *The Sword of Damocles*.
- Virtual reality platforms can be broken down into non-immersive, semi-immersive, and fully immersive experiences.
- XR (extended reality) is the blending of VR (virtual reality) and AR (augmented reality).
- The genesis point is the opening moment in which the VR experience starts, setting up the tone, perspective, and setting of the virtual environment.
- The point of view (POV) indicates whether the environment is experienced from the first person or third person viewpoint.
- The fields of view (FOV) show what is happening in the six prime fields around the character in the forward, right, reverse, left, up, and down directions.
- The four lateral fields of view (forward, right, reverse, and left) correspond with the cardinal directions of North, East, South, and West.
- Scene headings, action lines, characters, parentheticals, and dialogue are formatted largely like feature film scripts.
- The writer should note if audio should be placed in a certain area of the environment so it is heard through the appropriate speakers.
- The avatar's movements suggest an IF/THEN relationship for the computer programmer so that the virtual movements will correspond with the user's actions in the real world.
- Avatar movements are illustrated by the braces { } symbols.

Online Links

socreate.it. The home page of SoCreate screenwriting software, this platform actively explores the VR scripting realm (as well as other media formats).

viar360.com. This site provides a deeper dive into VR scripting possibilities, including creating individual training scenarios and guides for brainstorming 360-degree videos.

vrscout.com. This website provides a wealth of knowledge about virtual reality development, games, and industry news. Articles about new items and VR uses give a holistic view of this expanding media industry.

References

The following websites and organizations were referenced in the writing of this textbook.

99designs
Academy of Motion Picture Arts and Sciences
Advertising Age
Adweek
American Advertising Federation
American Society of Magazine Editors
Associated Press Stylebook
Blurb.com
Braun Film
Broadway.com
Cary Playwrights Forum
CBS Radio Mystery Theater
Columnists.com
Comicbook.com
Comichron
Conversation Starters World
Dark Horse Comics
DC Comics
Demand Sage
Dictionary
Documentary Network
Dramatics
Dramatists Guild
Epguides.com
Epiphan Video
ESPN
Final Draft
Food Network
Fred Van Lente
Grammarly
Heizenrader
IMDb.com
Influencer Marketing Hub
Jericho Writers
Journalism.co.uk
Kwantlen Polytechnic University
Marvel Comics
Meltwater
NASA
Newspapers.com
Playbill
Podcasting Insights
Poynter Institute
PR Newswire
Public Relations Society of America
Public Relations Student Society of America
Radio Television Digital News Association
Radio-locator.com
Radio-online.com
Refseek
Script Magazine
Script Reader Pro
The Script Savant
Search Engine Journal
SoCreate
Sports and the Mind
Sportsannouncing.com
Stacker
Studio Binder
Topdocumentaryfilms.com
Viar360
VRScout
Writers Guild of America
Writers Guild Foundation
Writopia Lab

Index

Academy Awards 149
Academy of Motion Picture Arts and Sciences (AMPAS) 77
action verbs 49
active structure 11
active versus passive voice: editing words out 93–94; sentence structure 11–12; television news 94
acts: Act/Scene Names 18, 19; five-act plays 16; one-act plays 16; two-act plays 16, 17, 18
adjectives 6, 7, 10, 31; compound 5
adverbs 6, 7–8, 10, 31, 93
advertising 46–55; alliteration 12; amount of page covered by 28; banner ads 52; character names 50; client needs, identifying 48; closings 53; copy 47, 49, 53, 54; crafting of commercials 48; digital ads 53; digital media 52–53; evolution of ads 46; formatting 49–53; full-page ads in newspapers and magazines 28; future developments 53–54; historical overview 46–47; legal disclaimers 53; logos 53; newspapers/magazines 28, 29; online links 54–55; placing of ad 28; popup ads 52; print ads 46–50; radio 46, 50–51, 107–108; researching of product 48; revenue 28; role of advertisers 46; settings 51; sidebar ads 52; signatures 53; slogans 53; Slurp Cola example 48, 49–50, 51; small ads 49; solutions, offering 49; sound effects (SFX) 47, 50, 51; targeting the audience 48; technical specifications 47–49; writing tips 49
Aeschylus 15
The Aging (horror film) 157, 160, 161
AIDA (Attention, Interest, Desire, and Action) 48–49
Airbnb.org 65
Albee, Edward 16
alliteration 12
The Amazing Race (competition program) 124

ampersand (&) 13
anchors 59, 90, 92, 95–98; seasonal 97; sports 97, 98; tosses between 97, 98; weather 98
apostrophe 5
arcs 37, 136, 145, 146
Aristotle 56; *Poetics* 24
articles 9
Associated Press Stylebook 99
At Rise 20; *see also* Setting/At Rise, theatrical plays
Atlanta Journal-Constitution 33
attribution: delayed 29–31, 91, 98; newspapers/magazines 29–31; television news 91
audiences: defining, for video 75; targeting 48; theatrical plays 25
augmented reality (AR) 176–177
awards ceremonies 130–133

The Bachelorette 126
back-and-forth dialogue, graphic novels 41–42
banner ads 52
Batman 37
beats 146
Bernays, Edward 56
Best Original Screenplay 149
blackout, theatrical plays 22
blocking, and stage directions 23
braces 6
brackets 6
brands 47
British Broadcasting Corporation (BBC) 137

cable networks/networks 88, 123
call to action (CTA) 47, 49, 53, 120
campaigns: multimedia 65; public relations 64–65; social media 167
Camtasia (professional software platform) 75
Candid Camera 123
captions 32, 50, 165; graphic novels 38, 39, 41
Cast of Characters Page, theatrical plays 16, 18

celebrities 51, 80, 133; endorsement 50; interviews 112; programs 124, 127–128; status 127
center stage 23
The Chad Whittle Show (podcast) 168
character names: advertising 50; arcs 146; episodic/serialized television 138, 143, 145, 146; graphic novels 40, 41, 43; radio 107; theatrical plays 18, 20, 21; virtual reality (VR) 179
characters: audience interaction 25; background 20; Cast of Characters Page, theatrical plays 18; dialogue 41, 42; episodic/serialized television 141, 142; feature films 77, 151, 157, 160, 162; graphic novels 39, 41, 42; names *see* character names; parentheticals 20; pauses 42; reactions 138; theatrical plays 15, 18, 22, 24, 25; timing 118; virtual reality (VR) 178, 181
closings 53
CNN 88
cold read, radio 107
colon 5, 39
column inches 28–30, 34, 49, 118
comic books/strips 36, 37–38, 43; *see also* graphic novels
comma 4
commercial breaks 123, 130, 138, 145
communications: crisis 57, 58, 63–64, 66; internal 58, 65; strategic 57
community relations 56, 57
competition programs 124–126
complex sentences 11
compound adjectives 5
compound sentences 10–11
confessionals 123, 124, 127, 128
conjunctions 8–9
conversational language 49
cookery programs 124, 125
coordinating conjunctions 8–9
copy: advertising 47, 49, 53, 54; defining 28; episodic/serialized television 147; newspapers/magazines 13, 28, 30, 34; pink 147; public relations 58; radio 101, 108
corporate settings 75
corporate videos 68–69
Courier font (12-point) 16
Covid pandemic 68, 69, 75
crime series 123
crisis communications 57, 58, 63–64, 66
CTA *see* call to action (CTA)
cuneiform script 3
curtain, theatrical plays 22
cut 65, 81, 89, 125, 145, 157; final 79
cutlines, newspapers/magazines 32–33

dash 5–6; double dashes 42; long dash 42
daytime talks shows 112
Del Guardo, Lenny 65
delayed attribution 29, 30, 31, 91, 98
delayed leads 90
demographics 33–34, 47, 53
demonstratives 9
descriptors: newspapers/magazines 31; television news 90–91
determiners 9–10
dialogue: back-and-forth, in graphic novels 41–42; characters 41, 42; double dashes 42; episodic/serialized television 138, 139, 141, 143; feature films 13, 149, 151, 152, 153–156, 161; graphic novels 38–43; "inner" 143; interjections 9; interview shows 119; parentheticals 20; Shakespearean 11; theatrical plays 16, 20–23, 25; writing in scripts 6
digital ads 53
digital media: advertising on 52–53; platforms 57; *see also* podcasts; social media
disc jockey morning radio show 106–107
documentaries 77–87; compared with feature films 77; contemporary versus historical 78–79; feature-length 77, 78; future developments 85–86; historical overview 77–78; linear and nonlinear 78, 79, 80, 84; market for 85–86; mini documentaries 77; online links 87; point of view 77, 78, 79–82; quote 83; real-life events, capturing 78; running time 77; scripts 85; sequences 79–84; shooting ratios 80; sound effects (SFX) 77; stringouts 84; symphonic nature of 77; technical specifications 82–85; Touch and Go principle 80–81; transcribing footage 85
double column format 38, 43, 74
double dashes 42
downstage 23, 24
drama: growing of playwriting 16; one-hour dramas 139–140; plots and sub-plots 145; radio plays 100, 106, 108–109; soap operas 142–143; theatrical plays 15–26; *see also* episodic/serialized television
Dramatis Personae page, theatrical plays 16, 18
dramaturgy, theatrical plays 23
Dream Theater 129

editing, television news 93–94
educational videos 75
ellipsis 6, 42
end designations, theatrical plays 22–23

188 *Index*

English language 3–4
episodic/serialized television 135–148; arcs 145, 146; beats 146; cast list 136–137; character names 138; characters 141, 142; copy 147; dialogue 138, 139, 141, 143; episodic shows 135; future developments 147; historical overview 135–136; introductory pages of a script 136–137; one-hour dramas 139–140; online links 148; parentheticals 142; plots and sub-plots 145; rewrites 146–147; serialized episodes 135–136; similarities among scripts 145; soap operas 142–143; technical specifications 138–145; thirty-minute comedies 137
Euripides 16
exclamation mark 4
external format 22

Facebook 164, 165, 166
FADE IN 117, 140, 178
FADE OUT 118, 142, 161
FADE TO BLACK 144–145, 161, 180–182
feature films 149–163; Best Original Screenplay 149; "blockbusters" 176; characters 77, 151, 157, 160, 162; compared with documentaries 77; dialogue 13, 149, 151–156, 161; endings 161; future developments 161–162; historical overview 149–150; off-screen 40; online links 163; parentheticals 150, 152, 154; screenwriting 161; scripts 157–161; technical specifications 150–157; voice-over 39
Federal Radio Commission 100
Field of View (FOV) 178
filler words 93
films *see* feature films
Final Draft program 150
first-person: documentaries 79; interview shows 77, 85; narrators 71, 80; platforms 177; point of view 178; political and social commentary 78
Flickr 165
Ford Motor Company 47
formats: in advertising *see* formatting, in advertising; dialogue 42; double column 38, 43, 74; external 22; feature films 161; graphic novels 37, 38; internal 21–22; scripting, for periodicals 34; serialized episodes 136; single column 38; specialized 13; split-column 51, 71, 95, 98; theatrical plays 16
formatting, in advertising: for digital media 52–53; for print 49–50; for radio 50–51; for television 51

Fox cable network 88
Franklin, Ben 27

Game of Thrones 136
genesis points, virtual reality 177–182
Google 175
graphic novels 36–45; back-and-forth dialogue 41–42; captions 38, 39, 41; character names 40, 41, 43; characters 39, 41, 42; dialogue 38–43; double column format 38, 43; ellipsis 42; fiction 36; final page count 43; formatting 37; future developments 43–44; historical overview 36–37; interjections 9, 13; nonfiction 36; off-panel 40; online links 45; panels 38, 40–41; pauses 42; rivers 38; scenes 40, 43; settings 38; single column format 38; sound effects (SFX) 41; speech balloons 38, 39, 41; SquirrelJenny example 40–42; SteveRabbit example 38–42; superheroes 36, 37, 42, 43; technical specifications 37–43; thought bubbles 38, 39; *see also* comic books/strips
group settings 74
gutters, graphic novels 36

hard leads 29, 89, 90
hashtags 165
headlines: financial 103; interview shows 119; newspapers/magazines 32–33, 34; radio 103; short 103; state 90
Heilig, Morton 175
hyphen 6

in-house production studios 69
Instagram 164, 165
interjections 9, 13
internal communications 58, 65
internal format 21–22
Internal Revenue Service (IRS) 29, 30
interview shows: active listening 119; closed-ended questions 113–114, 116, 121; follow-up questions 119; future developments 120; historical overview 112–113; hypothetical questions 115; mixing questions 116–118; online links 121; open-ended questions 113–115, 116, 118; outside-the-box questions 116; technical specifications 113–116; timing 118–119; tough questions, asking 119–120; warming up interviewees 118; wrapping up the interview 120
inverted pyramid writing style 27–28, 89, 90, 98

jagged speech balloon 39
Japanese language 4

KDKA, Pittsburgh 100

language: conversational 49; families 3; foreign language newspapers/magazines 28; foundations of 3–14; future developments 13; historical overview 3–4; level of difficulty for non-native speaker to learn 3–4; online links 14; punctuation marks 4–6, 13; sentence types 10–11; technical specifications 4–6; types of words 6–10
Lanier, Jaron 175
leads: delayed 90; hard 29, 89, 90; negative 90; newspapers/magazines 29–30; question 29, 90; quote 90; shotgun 90; soft 29, 90; strong 30; television news 89–90; trivia 30, 90
Lee, Ivy 56
Likert scale 114
linear and nonlinear structures, documentaries 78, 79, 80, 84
LinkedIn 164, 165–166
live events 78, 123, 128, 132, 133
live television 122–123

Mad Men 136
Marvel Studios 36
MasterChef 124
media relations 57–58
medium shot (MS) 95
Méliès, George 149
messaging platforms 164
moments 146
monologues 112
movies *see* feature films
MSNBC (cable network) 88
multimedia PR campaigns 65
music beds 47, 50, 106, 107
music concerts 128–129
MySpace 164

narrative flow 12
negative leads 90
The New Yorker 37
news: radio 101–106; readers 102–103; *see also* newspapers/magazines; television news
news hole 29, 34, 89
news writing 98
newscasts 88, 89
newspapers/magazines 27–35; active versus passive voice 30; advancing stories 33; advertising 28, 29; attribution 30–31; comic strips 36; conversational broadcast style 31; copy 13, 28, 30, 34; cutlines 32–33; descriptors 31; editorial page 32; foreign language 28; future developments 34; headlines 32–33; historical overview 27–28; impact of radio, television and digital media on readership 28; leads 29–30; news hole 29, 34; newspapers versus magazines 33–34; objectivity versus subjectivity 31–32; one-sentence paragraphs 13; online links 35; partially blank sheets 29; quotation marks 13; quote 30, 31; style 29–32; technical specifications 28–33
Nike Shoes 47
nonlinear structures *see* linear and nonlinear
Nouget, Janine 50, 51
nouns 6–9, 13
novels *see* graphic novels

objectivity, presentation of newspaper stories 31
on-air talent, radio 103, 104, 106
outcue 105, 106

packages, television news 95, 96, 97
Page Numbers, theatrical plays 18
page numbers, theatrical plays 18–19
panels, graphic novels 38, 40–41; panel strip 37
paragraphs 12–13
parentheses 6
parentheticals: characters 20; dialogue 20; episodic/serialized television 142; feature films 150, 152, 154; theatrical plays 20–21, 25
passive structure 11–12, 30, 94
Pennsylvania Railroad 56
Penny Press 27
Pepsi Cola 47
period 4
personal journeys 124, 127
phrases, alliterative 12
Pinterest 165
Plato 56
plays: five-act plays 16; one-act plays 16; radio 108–109; theatrical 15–26; two-act plays 16, 17, 18
plots and sub-plots 145; linear 79; plot lines 146
podcasts 164, 167–173; future developments 173; Informational Style 167, 169–170; Interview Style 167–168; Narrative Style 167, 170–173; online links 174; open-ended 118; *see also* social media
Point of View (POV): documentaries 77, 78, 79–82; first-person 178; neutral 31
popup ads 52
Portman, Natalie 118, 119
possessive determiners 9
possessives 9

190 *Index*

POV *see* point of view (POV)
PR *see* public relations
prepositions 8
press *see* newspapers/magazines
press releases 56, 58–63; anonymous 60; basic 58; duality 59; standard 60, 64, 65; written 59–63, 65
print media: advertising 46, 49–50; press releases 56, 58–63; *see also* newspapers/magazines
Project Morpheus (Sony) 176
pronouns 8
psychographics 33, 34, 47, 53
public relations 56–67; alliteration 12; copy 58; crisis communications 57, 58, 63–64, 66; future developments 65–66; historical overview 56–57; internal communications 58, 65; media relations 57–58; multimedia campaigns 65; online links 66–67; PR campaigns 64–65; press releases 56, 58–63; technical specifications 57–58; written press releases 59–63
Publick Occurrences (first US newspaper) 27
punctuation marks 4–6, 13, 39, 42

quantifiers 9–10
question leads 29, 90
question marks 4
quotation marks 5, 13
quote: attribution 30; direct 6; documentaries 83; nested (within a quote) 5; newspapers/magazines 30, 31; placing 31; radio 105; television news 91
quote leads 90

radio 100–111; advertising on 46, 50–51, 107–108; on-air segments 101; on-air talent 103, 104, 106; character names 107; copy 101, 108; disc jockey morning show 106–107; future developments 109; going beyond sound bites 105–106; headlines 103; historical overview 100–101; news 101–106; online links 111; quote 105; readers 102–103, 107; "rip and read" 101–102; sound bites 96, 102, 103–104; sound effects (SFX) 101, 105–107, 109; Sound on Tape (SOT) 95–97, 104; stations 101; technical specifications 101–109; wraparounds 102, 104–105, 106
radio plays 100, 106, 108–109; teledramas 142
readers: radio news 102–103, 107; television news 89, 95

reality television 122–134; awards ceremonies 130–133; celebrity programs 127–128; competition programs 124–126; future developments 133; historical overview 122–123; live events 128; music concerts 128–129; online links 134; personal journeys 127; relationship programs 126–127; scripts 123; sports events 51, 128, 129–130; technical specifications 124
Reddit 165
relationship programs 126–127
Republic of China 68
rewrites 146–147
rivers, graphic novels 38
Rockefeller, John D. 56

Saturday Night Live 128
scenes: action-driven 155; beats 146; crime 24, 79, 146; designation 19; documentaries 78, 79, 81, 83, 84; episodic/serialized television 138, 139–142, 145, 146; exterior 140, 178; feature films 149–151, 154, 161; final/endings 22, 150, 161; graphic novels 40, 43; headings 138, 140, 142, 143, 178; interior 140, 178; lines 22; numbered 161; opening/initial 79; outdoor 140; reality television 128; reliance on action lines 154; tone 21; vehicle 151; virtual reality (VR) 178, 180, 181
screenwriting 161
scripts: documentary 85; feature films 13, 157–161; film spec 161; introductory pages 136–137; live television 123; parameters 123; periodicals 34; playscripts 16; reality television 123; similarities among genres 145; soap operas 143; standardized template 182
Sega, VR motion simulator 175
semicolon 5, 42
Sensorama (VR machine) 175
sentences: complex structure 11; compound structure 10–11; narrative flow 12; one-sentence paragraphs 13; organization of words into 4; simple structure 10; structure 10–11, 31; supporting 12; tone 12; topic 12; types 10–11
sequences: action 38; back-and-forth dialogue, graphic novels 41; documentaries 79–84
setlist 129
Setting/At Rise, theatrical plays 18, 19–20
settings: advertising 51; corporate 75; feature films 157, 158, 162; graphic novels 38; group 74; interview 115; naming 140;

office 123; professional or amateur 25; social 121; studio 116, 176; theatrical plays 19–20, 23, 25; 360-degree 182; verbal 114; virtual reality (VR) 177, 178, 182
Shakespeare, William 11
shooting ratios 124, 126, 127; documentaries 80
shotgun leads 90
sidebar ads 52
simple sentences 10
sitcoms 123, 135, 137
slug (title of news story) 94–95, 104, 130
Slumber Party (Gerard Key Hutcheson) 17, 18, 19
Snapchat 164, 166
social media 164–174; campaigns 167; Facebook 164, 165, 166; future developments 173; historical overview 164–165; Instagram 165; LinkedIn 165–166; MySpace 164; online links 174; platforms 164, 165; Snapchat 164, 166; sound effects (SFX) 167, 170; technical specifications 165–167; TikTok 164, 166; Twitter 164, 166; WhatsApp 164, 166–167; *see also* podcasts
soft leads 29, 90
Sony 176
Sophocles 15–16
SOT *see* Sound on Tape (SOT)
sound bites, radio 96, 102, 103–104; going beyond 105–106
sound effects (SFX): advertising 47, 50, 51; documentaries 77; graphic novels 41; radio 101, 105–107, 109; social media 167, 170; virtual reality (VR) 178, 179
Sound on Tape (SOT) 95–97, 104
specialized formats 13
speech balloons 38, 39, 41
split-column format 51, 71, 95, 98
sports events 51, 128, 129–130
square speech balloon 39
stage directions, theatrical plays 21–22
Standard Oil company 56
stand-up, television news 96, 97
strategic communications 57
streaming services 161
Street View 175
stringouts 84
subjectivity, presentation of newspaper stories 31
subordinating conjunctions 8, 9
Super Bowl 122
Superman 37
Sutherland, Ivan 175

Taggers (comedy script) 158, 160, 161
taglines 48, 50, 53
Tamil 3
teleprompters 97
television: advertising on 51; episodic/serialized 135–148; news 88–99; reality/live 122–134
television news: attribution 91; descriptors 90–91; editing words out 93–94; future developments 98; historical overview 88–89; leads 89–90; neutral words 92; numbers 92–93; online links 99; packages 95, 96, 97; quote 91; readers 89, 95; stand-up 96, 97; technical specifications 89; times and places 93; tosses between anchors 97, 98; total running time (TRT) 89, 91, 104, 105; types of stories 94–97; unwritten exceptions 97–98; writing fundamentals 89–94
The Hill of Witches (documentary) 82–85
theatrical plays 15–26; act/scene names 19; audience interaction 25; blackout 22; Cast of Characters Page 16, 18; center stage 23; character names 18, 21; characters 15, 18, 22, 24, 25; Characters/character names 18, 20; curtain 22; dialogue 16, 20–23, 25; downstage 23, 24; dramaturgy 23; Early Greek 15–16, 23; end designations 22–23; future developments 25; historical overview 15–16; online links 26; page numbers 18–19; parentheticals 20–21, 25; Setting/At Rise 18, 19–20; stage directions 21–22; Stage Left 19, 24; Stage Right 19, 23, 24; technical specifications 16–23; three-act structure 16, 23, 24, 37, 145, 160; Title Page 16, 17, 18
Thespis 15
third-person 77–79, 177, 178
thought bubbles 38, 39
TikTok 164, 166
Title Page, theatrical plays 16, 17, 18
tone 12
tosses between anchors 97, 98
total running time (TRT) 89, 91, 104, 105
training videos 72–73
trivia leads 30, 90
TRT *see* total running time (TRT)
Tumblr 165
Twitter 164, 166

Ukraine Campaign, Airbnb.org 65
United States: Civil War 27; *Publick Occurrences* (first newspaper) 27

verbs 6, 13, 31; action verbs 49; auxiliary 7
videos 68–76; brief 70–74; corporate 68–69; defining the audience 75; educational 75; future developments 75; historical overview 68–69; in-house 68; online links 76; safety and training 72–73; technical specifications 69; viewer environments 74–75
virtual reality (VR) 175–184; characters 178, 181; fully immersive level 176; future developments 182; genesis points 177–182; historical overview 175–177; non-immersive level 176; online links 183–184; semi-immersive level 176; sound effects (SFX) 178, 179; technical specifications 177
Voca Vacay (travel podcast) 169
voice-over (VO) 39, 95, 96, 133

VOSOT (voice-over sound on tape) 95–96
VR *see* virtual reality (VR)

Wade, Janet 30
The War of the Worlds (radio program) 108
Welles, Orson 100, 108
WhatsApp 164, 166–167
Who's Afraid of Virginia Woolf? (theater play) 19
word processing programs 150
words: boldface type 40; editing out 93–94; filler 93; graphic novels 38; moving the plot along 38; neutral 92; organization into sentences 4; types of 6–10, 13; underlining 40; *see also* captions; speech balloons; thought bubbles
wraparounds, radio 102, 104–105, 106